GETTING THE MOST OUT OF WASHINGTON

Also by William S. Cohen

OF SONS AND SEASONS
ROLL CALL

Also by Kenneth Lasson

THE WORKERS: PORTRAITS OF NINE AMERICAN JOBHOLDERS
PROUDLY WE HAIL: PROFILES OF PUBLIC CITIZENS IN ACTION
PRIVATE LIVES OF PUBLIC SERVANTS
YOUR RIGHTS AND THE DRAFT
YOUR RIGHTS AS A VET

GETTING THE MOST OUT OF WASHINGTON

by
Senator William Cohen
and
Kenneth Lasson

Facts On File Publications
460 Park Avenue South
New York, N.Y. 10016

GETTING THE MOST OUT OF WASHINGTON
Using Congress to Move the Federal Bureaucracy

Copyright © 1982 William S. Cohen and Kenneth Lasson

Library of Congress Cataloging in Publication Data

Cohen, William S.
  How to get the most out of Washington.

  Includes index.
  1. Administrative agencies—United States—Handbooks, manuals, etc. 2. United States. Congress—Handbooks, manuals, etc. I. Title.
JK464 1982.C63   353'.000202   81-12573
ISBN 0-87196-537-2   AACR

10 9 8 7 6 5 4 3 2 1

Printed in the United States of America

*to all dedicated congressional caseworkers,
both on Capitol Hill and back home*

CONTENTS

ACKNOWLEDGMENTS

We are grateful to all those who helped in the preparation of this book, and especially to the following: Senators John Chafee, Gary Hart, Carl Levin, Sam Nunn, William Roth, Warren Rudman, Paul Sarbanes, Alan Simpson and John Tower; Howard Cohn, Lee Eidelberg, Andy Felser and Chuck Michaels (research assistants); Ella Agambar and Amy Rubin (typists); Tom Daffron and Ed Knappman (editorial consultants); and to Margaret Carroll, Joyce Chesnut, Susan Collins, Jim Dykstra, Jack Girard, Tom Heyerdahl, Bill Holen, Patricia Kelley, Pearl Lipner, Sally Lounsbury, Jim McKenna, Jackie Parker, Molly Pryor, Phil Rivers, Dolores Rottman, Bob Umphrey and Doris Underwood (congressional aides).

INTRODUCTION
Battling the Bureaucracy

My reading of history is that most bad government has grown out of too much government.

—JOHN SHARP WILLIAMS, *Thomas Jefferson*

A big, bungling, boondoggling bureaucracy. That's the image that many Americans have of the federal government, and—at times—it may not be far from accurate.

When forced to deal with the massive machinery of their government, citizens frequently come away feeling confused, frustrated and inadequate. There are three million individual federal employees, but their human side is effectively camouflaged by a system overwhelmed with regulations and buried in an avalanche of required paperwork. Public employees are often perceived as little more than pencil-pushing automatons, caught in a colossal entanglement of red tape. It is not fair, but the image tends to overwhelm the reality: many bureaucrats are concerned and sympathetic human beings who are also frustrated by the size and complexity of our governmental process.

Critics, though, are a bit too quick to invoke the old saw that says, "That government is best that governs least." With a population of almost a quarter billion, upon each of whom the Constitution confers equal rights, to whom each the Congress attempts to grant equal opportunity (and most of whom exercise the freedom to demand those rights and opportunities) proliferating rules and regulations and the executive agencies to administer them are almost necessary. The cynics are wrong: The system was not created to keep white-collar incompetents off the streets and out of trouble. On the contrary, of course, the government *intends* to give the best and most efficient service to the people. It's unfortunate—and perhaps inevitable—that it works so poorly.

The more government we have, the more bewildered the public is. The more benefits available and regulations promulgated, the greater the likelihood of bureaucratic gaps and gaffes.

Ours is a representative government, but the barriers that exist between 225 million people who aren't in Washington and those few who are there, supposing to represent them, often seem like iron curtains. This is especially true for individuals (as opposed to interest groups) who need or want something done "by the feds." Yet it is not unusual even for skilled attorneys to find it stupefyingly frustrating to deal with government bureaucracies, some of which seem to be in direct competition with one another. Trying to reach a bureaucrat by telephone can be a time-consuming ordeal: He is likely to be "in a meeting," "on a long-distance call," "at a conference," "out to lunch," "out of town," "out of the office" or "no longer with us."

In addition, the public is made amply aware of governmental scandal in high places and inefficiency everywhere, from an overpurchase of 99,000 paper cups (as happened one year in a certain small agency), to a $168,000 appropriation for development of a safety belt that was never used, to a $900,000 grant for studying "whether college students are capable of gathering information," to billion-dollar cost overruns, which almost seem built into defense contracts. We are told the Social Security system is bankrupt, yet we learn that millions of dollars are being paid to those who are cheating the system. We hear about the Navy confiscating acres of private property and beautiful homes so that it can build a runway that will not interfere with the *fairway* on one of its air bases' golf-courses. We read about the Department of Agriculture prohibiting a potato farmer from shipping his crop in interstate commerce because it feared a crop pest called the golden nematode—despite the fact that tests over the ten-year period failed to produce any evidence of infestation.

To make matters of public confidence worse, the government couches its masses of rules, orders, and regulations in a virtually incomprehensible form a bureaucratic gobbledygook. Parachutes become "aerodynamic personnel decelerators," empty oil drums "impact attenuation devices" and organization charts "systems concepts." Memoranda are strewn with words like "interface," "maximize" and "infrastructure."

On the other hand, diligent and conscientious public servants are frequently shunted aside and neutralized by their own agencies. A meat inspector in the Department of Agriculture is wrongfully indicted for taking a bribe when he was offered (but didn't accept) a Christmas turkey by a meat packager. A Department of Transportation specialist is assigned to promote bicycle travel, but is rendered powerless (and virtually penniless) to buck a national policy designed to bolster (and bail out) the automobile industry. A whistle blower in the Defense Department loses his job for doing his job. A physician at the Food and Drug Administration is ignored when he tries to expose a drug company that falsified test data on laboratory animals (and that was later convicted of criminal fraud). Not all public servants, of course, are martyrs to the system. For every quiet but heroic civil servant, though, there are others who go through the motions of public service but add nothing to the nation's productivity, who fully understand the paucity of their contribution but who cannot afford to leave the government because the pay and benefits are too good.

If the federal bureaucracy is the object of the public's rancor and scorn, the Congress as an institution does not fare much better for its performance. Professional critics maintain that it is too obese, arthritic, parochial, non-responsive or over-responsive. But even the average citizen, who does not possess a doctorate in political science, is frustrated or disappointed about the workings of Congress—even if he is not quite sure why.

Time after time I have watched visitors sit in the House and Senate galleries with a look of mild panic in their eyes. Their facial expressions are twisted into question marks—"Where is everybody? Why is there only one Senator on the floor speaking to an empty chamber? Why aren't the others there to listen to what he is saying?" Each time I see that look, it occurs to me that most people have little understanding about the activities of a Congressman or a Senator. It is a problem that we in Congress are partly responsible for creating. Our constituents read our press releases and newsletters or perhaps catch a fleeting television clip of us on the evening news, and an image takes shape in their minds of the two legislative chambers filled with men and women engaging in passionate exchanges of golden oratory. In fact, members of the House and Senate spend only a small portion of their time in the two chambers. Most of their days are consumed in committee hearings or briefings, legislative lunches or organized dinners. A considerable amount of time is devoted to meeting with constituents who come to Washington to lobby for a legislative program or who have brought their families to tour the nation's capital.

But if there is confusion about our legislative activity (or nonactivity, as the case may be), there is even less knowledge or understanding about one of the most important functions we serve as elected public officials—that of ombudsmen, of problem solvers for individuals who have been ignored, trampled upon or treated arbitrarily by the government itself. It's called "casework"—not a very glamorous name, but it's a service that can be more meaningful and rewarding than many of the laws we labor to write. An elderly woman's Social Security check has been stopped or stolen and she has no other means of support; an agency writes to say that you are no longer disabled and your compensation has been terminated; an IRS man without advance notice snaps a lock on the front door of your business; your visa has expired and cannot be extended, so you must leave the country. . . .

The cases of individual hardship inflicted by government practice or neglect are legion and, it seems, never-ending. While the work load and dedication of individual representatives and senators may vary, it is fair to say that most congressional offices devote as much as 40 percent of their resources to resolving conflicts between their constituents and the government. Nevertheless, many people are unaware that the service is available and oftentimes can provide relief.

Most of us who run for public office do so because we want to make our government work better; we want the people we represent to hold a higher opinion of the institutions that have, despite their deficiencies, provided us with the freest, most prosperous and generous society in history. And for all its inadequacies, the government is surprisingly successful at collecting revenues, passing needed legislation, and running programs.

It was with this thought in mind that I asked Kenneth Lasson to join with me in the project of describing cases where citizens have turned to Congress for assistance in resolving conflicts with, or grievances against, their government. The cases selected are merely illustrative and by no means all-inclusive. They are intended to suggest the variety and range of the difficulties people have experienced with government agencies and institutions. It should be noted also that the congressional assistance, while usually helpful, is not always successful. Even meritorious claims do not necessarily emerge vindicated from the quagmire of government rules and regulations.

The purpose of this book is to make the process of the federal government more clear, demands from it more productive and access to it easier. It is not intended as a blueprint for success in fighting the federal "city hall." Rather, we hope that by describing case histories in a humanistic and anecdotal style we can provide readers with some broad guidelines on how to make the system work even better for them—to tell them how they can, in fact, get more out of Washington.

—WILLIAM S. COHEN
United States Senator

GETTING THE MOST OUT OF WASHINGTON

☆ I ☆

CONGRESSMEN AND CASEWORKERS

Now and then an innocent man is sent t' th' Legislature.

—FRANK McKINNEY HUBBARD

The easiest and best way to get what you want out of Washington is this: "Know someone," preferably someone with both power and information.

Perhaps even more fundamental is to recognize that such advice is not limited to the landed gentry or useful only by established interest groups. The fact is that most Americans have at least several agent/advocates in Washington who are virtually ideal problem-solvers—who work long hours, pursue difficult situations to reasonable resolutions and do not charge for their services. They are skilled at penetrating the red tape of bureaucracy. Indeed, this book could conceivably begin and end with one thought: In an almost endless variety of circumstances, getting what you want out of Washington means calling or writing your congressman or senator. This is frequently the first, foremost and last action necessary.

Moreover, communication between an elected official and a constituent is mutually beneficial. The dialogue helps shape many issues and may affect the outcome of national legislation.

A surprising number of Americans don't realize that it's unnecessary to have a special relationship with their elected representatives—either by party affiliation, past campaign support or through family or friends—in order to get things done on their behalf. Most calls or letters to Washington will receive at least some response, usually quick and courteous. It is unlikely that the senator or congressman himself will handle the problem, but someone from his usually well-trained staff of caseworkers will. Even mass mailings of postcards advocating a particular position will often be answered if there is a return address. The only correspondence that is unlikely to be answered is hate mail.

The state of Maine, for example, may be 500 miles away

3

from Washington, but constituents there are active corre-
spondents. My Senate office receives more than 1,500 letters
from home each week. These, together with the tens of
thousands addressed to other senators and representatives, are
delivered four times daily to the basements of the Senate and
House office buildings. There they are sorted by hand—by
career postal workers and part-timers, usually young people
working their way through school. Even cards addressed to
"The Senator from Maine, Washington, D.C." will eventually
reach one of our state's two senators.

Not only do letter writers get a response, they also receive the
personal attention of a variety of aides. First, the assistant assigned to issues covered in the letter (for example, military
matters) reviews it. His draft answer must be approved by the
chief legislative assistant, who in turn shows it to the chief administrative assistant. The senator or congressman gives final
approval.

Writing your representative is generally a more effective approach than phoning. If the letter describes a problem you are
having with the federal government, make sure it is stated
clearly and concisely. It is important to provide all the relevant
details—name, address, phone numbers (day and evening),
Social Security number. Then give a complete chronological
explanation of the problem, including the agencies with which
contact has already been made, the names and titles of those
government employees to whom questions were presented,
their responses to date and exactly what corrective action you
seek. Of course, you should be legible. In some cases written
inquiries are a legal necessity: The Privacy Act of 1974 prohibits federal agencies from releasing information about an individual without his authorization in writing. (See Chapter IX.)

A caseworker may be forwarded a letter like this: "My
daughter is being held in a Mexican prison on charges of possession of marijuana. She's being mistreated. What can I do to
get her out?" The caseworker's first step is to respond with
what's called an interim: "Dear Mrs. Blank: We received your
letter and will contact the State Department on your behalf. We
will be in touch with you as soon as we have some information."
The interim is often sent by return mail. Then the caseworker
contacts the State Department, either by letter or telephone,
and lays out the problem. The State Department probably cables the embassy in Mexico, which contacts the Mexican government and finds out particulars. As the available facts are
known, the caseworker proceeds accordingly. He or she may

make follow-up phone calls, write follow-up letters or call the embassy in Mexico. The urgency of a particular problem will dictate what's done. Is the daughter in any physical danger? Is she likely to be subjected to mistreatment? On what basis was she put in jail? When dealing with the laws of another country, the caseworker may be told his subject will have to get a lawyer and go to Mexico.

Letters are most helpful when they reflect a balanced and realistic grasp of a particular issue—when they thoughtfully present the way things are and offer a feasible solution or another option.

In calling a congressional office with a problem or opinion, it is equally important to supply all pertinent information. Think about what you want to say before you pick up your telephone. Make notes if necessary. Organize your thoughts. If you are seeking a copy of a bill or want to know its status in the House or Senate, be as clear and specific as possible (provide both a description of the bill and its number, if you know it).

By all means take advantage of the services offered by an elected official's local (district) offices. They are equipped to deliver messages directly to the Washington headquarters and in many cases can save you the cost of a long-distance telephone call.

A senator himself ordinarily becomes involved in a constituent's problem when his staff is unable to handle it. On occasion real political clout is needed: A Cabinet officer will generally not talk to a staff member, nor will another senator or high White House official.

It's also wise to realize that, with 435 individual congressmen and 100 senators, the quality of service from office to office is likely to differ. Some are simply better than others. In gross terms, however, the great majority of legitimate problems submitted by constituents are solved to their satisfaction—sooner or later.

Not all constituents are free American citizens seeking help with a federal regulatory agency. There are, for example, the numerous prisoners who write long letters to law professors, civil liberties attorneys, newspapers and to their congressmen about their particular cases and conditions in jail. Many of them claim that their trials were legally flawed, or that new evidence has come to light, or that their parole applications have been mishandled.

Some of the pleas have merit, but they are difficult to resolve because coming to the aid of a prisoner usually pits the legislative caseworker against the entire criminal-justice system. Often the system cannot deliver what inmates are constitutionally due. But many caseworkers feel this is the sort of circumstance that makes helping so much more essential: These are people who have been locked away and forgotten, whose daily lives are filled with boredom, fear and the painful realization that even their own families don't visit them anymore, that there is no one who cares.

One day caseworker Terri Brennan found in her morning mail a letter from a prisoner in a federal penitentiary in South Carolina. Inside was a huge black dead roach, about four inches long. The attached note said that this is what the inmates wake up to every morning. The letter did prompt some action, including a phone call by the senator himself, and in a month there was another letter, this one a note of thanks. Some fumigation efforts at the prison had made things a little better.

Double celling is also frequently at issue. The "cruel and unusual punishment" clause of the Bill of Rights has consistently been interpreted by the courts as prohibiting more than public floggings and torture. It has come to mean that a prisoner is entitled to his humanity, that society is not interested in stripping away all vestiges of a prisoner's self-worth. The courts have insisted that the clause affects the living conditions of jails and penitentiaries. How many prisoners can or should be put in one cell? Many inmates complain to their senator of having to sleep on mattresses placed on the floor, or of being locked in a cell with an inmate they fear.

When she receives a letter from a prisoner who feels his life might be in danger because of double celling, Terri Brennan checks immediately with the appropriate prison authorities. If there is no imminent danger, the case is handled more routinely through the local correction agencies.

Other cases cannot be handled routinely, whether they deal with double celling or not. One prisoner-constituent was serving a sentence in another state, where he witnessed the hanging murder of a fellow prisoner. Risking his own life, he reported the incident to guards. In this sort of case, when word reaches the senator's office that someone's life might be in immediate danger, no one waits for a Privacy Act waiver to be signed. In this instance, the caseworker immediately phoned the warden, who at once placed the prisoner in protective custody.

And there are the cases involving prominent federal and state officials who have been convicted of various influence-peddling crimes. Letters come from both the public figures themselves and their former constituents. During ex-Maryland

Governor Marvin Mandel's incarceration following a conviction for mail fraud, the pressure for his early release was intense. Just as vociferous, it seemed, were voters expressing their opinion that Mandel should be forced to serve out his entire sentence, or transferred from a minimum-security federal camp to a county detention center in Maryland. Despite the volume of mail received, the staff of Senator Charles Mathias's office tried to handle the case as if Mandel were any other prisoner. (Later, though, the senator joined various other public figures in asking the President to order an early release for the former governor.)

Americans jailed overseas need a different kind of political support, as well as material assistance. The Department of State, through the Bureau of Consular Affairs, is charged with protecting the rights of all Americans in foreign countries. A special agency of the bureau, the Citizens Emergency Center, is specifically designed to provide effective 24-hour emergency help in a wide variety of situations—including (and especially) incarceration.

The center has several subsections. The Financial-Medical Services Division works with consular officers in cases involving deaths of Americans abroad. The Welfare-Whereabouts Division responds to public and congressional inquiries concerning Americans who are either presumed to be missing because they have not communicated with relatives or friends for an undue length of time, or who must be located urgently because a personal emergency has arisen in the United States requiring their notification. In cases of disaster abroad, the center will gather the names of the Americans involved and inform their families of their conditions.

The Citizens Emergency Center also regularly provides travel advisories on visiting certain areas where political or civil unrest, natural disasters, shortage of hotel space or other circumstances may affect the general welfare and safety of Americans. In addition, the center coordinates search and rescue efforts for missing or overdue planes or boats of American registry, or those carrying American passengers and crew.

But it is when Americans are arrested abroad that the center has the most contact with congressional staffers. In 1981, for example, some 3,222 Americans were arrested or detained in 105 foreign countries. There are now over 1,500 Americans incarcerated abroad, about 40 percent of whom have been arrested on drug-related charges.

Whenever an American mission overseas learns of the detention or arrest of a citizen, a consular officer will make every effort to visit the individual as soon as possible—usually within 24 hours—to discuss the nature of the charges, provide the arrestee with a list of local attorneys and gain assurances that there has been no mistreatment while in custody. The officer will also determine to whom the individual may wish to have information released regarding his arrest.

The arrested American will be visited regularly by a consular officer—at least once a month but sometimes more often, depending upon time and the severity of the situation. The consular agent cannot guarantee a release or favorable disposition of the case, but he can provide support, monitor treatment and deliver mail, food or messages from friends and family.

Oftentimes, of course, as in the movie *Midnight Express*, the matter is out of the hands of the United States. The State Department cannot intervene in the judicial process of a foreign country. The arrested American overseas is often on his own—which is why it is always advisable to be aware of the local laws, especially those involving the possession or use of drugs. Many countries are much more severe in punishing drug offenses than the United States.

Caseworkers also get involved in sticky passport matters, many of which can be frustrating and time-consuming. For example, a call came in to a senator's office from a constituent regarding his wife's passport. They wanted to go on a tour of Europe, a trip they had planned for years. And the passport in question had been returned because the original hospital birth certificate is necessary, they were told. The enclosed check was also returned. The couple contacted their senator. A caseworker went to work and was told that one of the problems with the application was that the check was predated. If another check were written, once it had been received a temporary passport could be issued under the absolute condition that the birth certificate would be forthcoming. All of this was done, and the trip to Europe went off in good order. The couple had learned what few people discover until they come face-to-face with the federal system: Things take very much longer than one might expect, and assurances that something will happen quickly are very unreliable. If a problem is not attacked persistently, it is likely to fade into the immense mound of paperwork that inundates every federal agency.

Sally Duncan is a permanent resident alien—someone who lives in the United States on a visa or a work permit but has not filed for citizenship. One day, as she was making plans to visit her native Scotland, somebody stole her purse. Inside was her alien card, an essential document for travel for resident aliens to and from the United States and abroad.

She called the Immigration and Naturalization Service and was told that she would have to apply for a replacement card, which she would receive in about six months. And then she could have her passport stamped to verify her permanent status, so she could get back into the United States. Well, Sally might have been willing to wait the six months, but that was before she was told that her whole file was missing. As far as the Immigration and Naturalization Service was concerned, she did not exist at all.

But what about the *facts* of her life? She had come to this country on the *Queen Elizabeth* with her sister and her parents. The family settled in New Hampshire, and Sally grew to love the state. It reminded her so much of Scotland—the climate and the scenery, the links with the past.

The caseworker in Senator Warren Rudman's office tried to find the file (or some duplicate of it) in a number of Washington offices. But it could not be located anywhere, not even in the National Archives. Then the aide checked the alien number listed along with Sally's name. Could it be that the name was either misspelled or somehow mislabeled? She would try a variation of the number and a variation of the spelling of "Duncan."

After about a week, part of the file was indeed found in the Archives—under another alien number. Among the missing data were Sally Duncan's fingerprints. She was told she'd have to have another set taken, and the office that performed this function was down in Boston.

Sally always wanted to visit Boston, but not like this. Because of some thief she had to make an unplanned six-hour trip, which she did. But then, when her new-found file was forwarded, another item was missing: her marriage certificate. The Immigration and Naturalization people said they needed a certified copy of the marriage certificate before they could stamp Sally Duncan's passport and let her visit Scotland.

Sally called the senator's office again. She had her own copy of the certificate, she'd been married in Scotland and she wouldn't be able to get a certified copy in any reasonable length of time. It just could not be done. Would the immigration office accept her copy, or a copy of her copy so she could start her trip? A couple of phone calls later, Immigration and Naturalization said that it would accept, temporarily, a copy of her marriage certificate, but once she was in Scotland she should make arrangements for a certified copy to be sent to the Immigration and Naturalization office. Then she would not have to go through this same process if she wanted to travel from the United States again.

Sally was told that she could work with the local office of the senator if she wished. She left a copy of the marriage certificate, which the caseworker copied, personally initialed and sent to Boston. Word came back of another problem: The certificate indicated that this was Sally's second marriage. Immigration and Naturalization needed the first marriage certificate *and* a copy of the divorce decree. Certified, of course.

At this point, Sally thought she was dealing with a collection of lunatics. She could not leave the country because she did not have proof that she was divorced. She spent the next five days tracking down the original divorce decree. That would do. The Boston Immigration and Naturalization office sent back approval and her stamped passport within three days. If she had had to wait any longer before receiving her passport, she would never have made it.

There are times when the snafus are more consequential, the personal problems more severe and the bureaucracy more intractable. Take the case of Bobby Tilson. He had been in the Navy for five years and would have liked to make it his career. He liked everything about the service, even the food. But Bobby's mother had multiple sclerosis, and there was no telling how long Bobby could be with her. He had lost his father in an auto accident.

There was a Navy program, however, that allowed a serviceman to be assigned to a Navy facility near a dependent family member if there was a need at the facility for his particular skill. Bobby was a radio operator—a needed position—and he tried to get the Navy to reassign him nearer his mother. But the red tape was too tangled. Eventually, a little desperate, he visited the local office of his senator.

After routine checking, it was determined that the necessary paperwork was not being sent to the proper command stations, that it had already been lost in transit. The service would be willing to consider another application, but Bobby would have to wait until he got his next overseas assignment before he could initiate it—since it would have to be approved by his current commanding officer. Bobby did not want to wait that long; he wanted to be with his dying mother.

This matter was handled by the senator himself, who firmly informed certain Navy recruiting and command officials about his constituent's problem. Word soon came that the facility where he wanted to be assigned did have a shortage of good radio operators; he could travel to that base immediately and talk to the personnel officials there. Within a week new orders were issued, and he started his assignment at that facility the following Monday.

Marylyn Moss is a veteran of thirty-five years as a case-worker on Capitol Hill. Most of her service during those years—and all of it now—has consisted of helping constituents cope, communicate and resolve disputes with federal agencies. She is currently employed by a senator from a small seaboard state, his only staffer in Washington exclusively handling constituents' cases.

Her workshop is the federal bureaucracy, a giant maze which, as if its nooks and alleys were not complex enough, is constantly being redesigned. To map it is frequently more than any citizen can handle, much less make it work for him. But that is precisely what Marylyn Moss gets paid to do.

Her low-key manner belies a stoic dedication to her task. Though diminutive in physical stature and subject to a Samaritan's vulnerability, she leaves no doubt that she can be tenacious and assertive when the situation demands. Her eyes reflect a mixture of sensitivity and steel; they rarely wander. She speaks of her job with conviction, seasoned pride and (though less readily) well-contained frustration. She does not savor the limelight. ("I don't need any publicity, just an occasional 'thank you' from a constituent.") She is somewhat uncomfortable with the popularity she's accumulated in her employer's home state, but she's proud her office has a reputation for providing responsive, professional assistance.

Marylyn Moss's career had an inauspicious beginning. When she arrived at Washington's Union Station from the Midwest on New Year's Day in 1947, the city was inhospitably snowbound, and by the time she reached Capitol Hill, the congressman with whom she was to have an interview that morning had gone for the day. Washington was full of holiday tourists and dignitaries; with lodgings scarce, she settled for a room at the YWCA. The next day she met her future employer—a member of the Armed Services Committee, a World War I veteran, a coauthor of the GI Bill of Rights and a friend of her family—who told her he was receiving a growing volume of letters and calls from

constituents asking assistance in dealing with the military bureaucracy. Marylyn's husband had fought and died in the recent war, and she knew something about the services; in addition to sundry other responsibilities, she was hired to handle
those cases.

Since that time Marylyn Moss has worked steadily on the
Hill. Her original employer retired from politics in 1960. Her
present employer, her third in succession on the Hill, took her
on in 1966. As the years passed, her responsibilities began to
focus more exclusively on casework, a job for which she had no
particular training. It was not long before she discovered there
was no better training possible than the work itself.

In recent years, as constituent service has matured into a
specialized field, prospective caseworkers have been offered
one-day training seminars (for a fee of about $150), which meet
at the beginning of each session of Congress. "For people who
want to come work on the Hill," says Marylyn Moss, "—and
most everybody coming to Washington does—it's a guide, an
outline. But once you get in here, you'd better have some feeling of wanting to help people." The primary reason special
training is of limited value rests in the disparity among congressmen in their policies toward constituents, because "each
office reflects the personality of the boss." Those employed by
representatives and senators who believe most strongly in services for constituent usually find their jobs demanding and extremely time-consuming. Those who provide what Marylyn
calls "routine service" enjoy routine hours. And, few though
they may be, there are congressmen who feel their only proper
obligation while in office is to represent the voters in legislative
matters; casework to them is money and time misspent. "After
all," Marylyn points out, "there's nothing in the Constitution
that says elected representatives will do anything but legislate."

Most congressmen and senators, though, believe casework to
be a natural adjunct to their representation. Their services differ in procedure and organization. Many prefer that all cases be
handled by their home-state offices; a minority direct casework
from the Hill. Some assign to each caseworker a specific area of
concentration, such as Social Security problems, while others
assign cases alphabetically according to the constituent's name,
thus requiring each caseworker to be versed in all fields. Marylyn supervises all her senator's constituent services, using the
home-state staff as both investigators and for liaison with constituents.

The size of a congressman's budget makes a difference, but
perhaps not as much as does a state's population. Congressmen

from smaller states can often afford to provide more personal service, even though they are allocated smaller budgets. On the other hand, some offices, especially those of congressmen representing populous areas in states such as California or New York, are forced to handle much of their voluminous casework by form letter.

The disparity does not end there. A congressman must decide when (if ever) he is willing to use one of his ultimate legislative weapons—the private bill—on a constituent's behalf. There may well be as many different approaches to the use of private bills as there are congressmen. Some find it a distasteful tool: Its very power is its poison, in that it provides special treatment to one constituent while others may be equally in need. Moreover, Congress is loath to allow private bills to clog the legislative agenda. In 1969 there were so many private bills to resolve immigration disputes that Congress was forced to amend its rules, disallowing them in such matters except when absolutely necessary to aid immigrant orphans.

Finally, the kinds of cases a congressman receives will depend on both his committee assignments and the demography of his home state or district. A congressman representing an elderly population is likely to receive many Social Security cases. A senator from an agricultural state is likely to sit on an agriculture subcommittee and be more familiar with farmers' problems.

Cases typically coming to Marylyn Moss's attention involve the military, immigration and Social Security. During the Korean and Vietnam conflicts military cases, many of them engendered by the separation of servicemen from their families, dominated her time. She'd frequently make "health and welfare requests"—inquiring about a soldier's health or asking an explanation of his silence—and trace missing packages or allotment checks (military pay that has been directed to a dependent). Congressmen could also assist in having sons or daughters brought stateside for family funerals, and would be asked to investigate failures to arrive home while on leave. The war in Vietnam was especially traumatic. "There were wives and mothers writing, calling, crying, demanding," says Marylyn. "We had boys over there who were unhappy, who felt lost, who had affairs. We had lots of problems."

Over the past several decades casework has undergone two fundamental changes. Until the 1960s, the manner in which congressmen first learned of constituents' problems was usually indirect: A family needing help would first appeal to a local politician or religious leader, who would in turn get in touch

with the congressman. This screening at the local level provided a useful verification that grievances were legitimate. But
times have changed; now people feel closer to their elected
representatives, who speak to them directly through news
broadcasts and interviews and make pitches for votes in television commercials and debates. "They feel very free and comfortable now to pick up the phone and call here and ask for
help," says Marylyn. The screening of most cases today must
therefore be at the staff level.

The huge volume of constituents' requests for information
about their relatives in combat during the Vietnam War, together with a growing concern about the government's stock of
personal data on individual citizens, has brought about the second change in constituent services. The Privacy Act, passed in
1974, prohibits federal agencies from releasing information
about an individual without his written authorization. Although
congressional offices can officially bypass the act (by virtue of a
federal regulation promulgated in 1975 allowing federal agencies to forgo the written-authorization requirement if the inquiry comes from a constituent's elected representative), some
agencies persist in requiring written consent in all circumstances. The casework process thus is often slowed to a
crawl, and constituents become impatient. "The people calling
in for urgent help are very bitter about the Privacy Act," says
Marylyn Moss. "They've never heard of it. They've only heard
that Senator So-and-so will help them if they call. (The call is
just to allow us to tell them what they must write us about.)"
While some constituents grumble about the inconvenience,
there are others who would complain if personal information
about them were released without their knowledge or consent.

Military enlistment contracts are cases in point. Little can be
done on behalf of a constituent who joined the military because
of financial hardship but has become disillusioned with military
life—not a rare problem. "Parents are saying, 'My son is unhappy. I urged him to enlist. He's getting into trouble so they
will court-martial him and send him home!' " Marylyn pauses to
emphasize her point. "I can't help them. Only the son himself
can authorize an investigation into a court-martial."

In peacetime, although nettlesome military and immigration
cases still pour in through the mail and over her telephone
hook-up with her senator's two home state offices, the bulk of
Marylyn's work involves problems with the Social Security Administration.

Constituents reach her any number of ways. Many know her

already. Others walk into a state office, call someone there—or even call the senator's home. "Our name is very familiar in the state now. We have a service record. If they don't find my number one way they'll find it another way." Although it's up to her to screen out frivolous requests, she cannot turn away any cases that appear legitimate. There are several important exceptions to this policy. As a matter of professional courtesy, no senator will assist a colleague's constituent who lives in another state, unless the citizen is a close friend or a relative. "Members are human beings, and they're jealous. They don't like to think their own constituent didn't contact them." Such cases are referred to the appropriate delegation. Caseworkers from different offices "work very close together on things like that, regardless of party affiliation. It's not a political thing." Nor is a caseworker likely to intervene if the constituent is represented by an attorney. After all, they feel, the lawyer is getting paid for his representation and can do the work himself.

Once a case is started, however, it's followed through. This too is part of the ethics of casework, and it's a rule that occasionally causes difficulties. This is especially true where a constituent has not been entirely honest. "I grit my teeth pretty hard when I've tried to help someone and discover he was not truthful, which I do find more and more. But once you start taking a case, you've got to finish it." Misrepresentations cannot be passed on to government agencies; wrong information must be set straight, and the case won or lost on its corrected merits.

The discomfort involved in having to apologize to an agency makes it necessary to investigate carefully all requests for assistance—much the same as a newsman confirming facts. This is often done by means of a form that constituents with problems are asked to complete. Marylyn Moss may have to speak with a constituent several times before she's convinced his case is "authentic." She recalls the time several years ago when a young man stationed in West Germany was reported AWOL for failure to return to base following stateside leave. His mother, concerned about not receiving letters or allotment checks—and convinced that her son was not the type to shirk an obligation—asked for help. Marylyn questioned her carefully over the telephone, testing the mother's conviction that the Army had made a mistake. In the meantime, her staff found the woman to be hardworking and reliable. Finally confident that the case was worth pursuing, Marylyn contacted Army representatives (they keep a liaison office on Capitol Hill), who vindicated the worried mother's faith. The mixup had resulted from travel delays, which had caused her son to return to base five days late; an overly eager sergeant had wrongly reported him AWOL.

Careful screening assures a caseworker that he or she will not strain the valuable rapport developed over a career with a particular federal agency. While a constituent's persistent expressions of faith in his or her cause might contribute to Marylyn's confidence in its legitimacy, she is careful not to commit herself too hastily. "You have to make allowances, for example, for the fact that much of what a mother tells you is what her son has told her. But not all boys tell their mothers everything, and in many cases unfortunately boys tell their parents what will make *them* look good."

The point at which constituents bring her their problems "depends on how mad they are, or how confused, and on their educational background." The more educated constituents tend to make at least one effort on their own to resolve the problem with the agency before seeking congressional help.

Some constituents have been referred by an attorney. Few lawyers will take cases for nothing; congressmen, of course, will serve free of charge. But Marylyn Moss is quick to point out that a caseworker is not an attorney. Her power is one of inquiry, or at most of tactful insistence. She may find the right ears to bend, but she does not twist arms. If a legal appeal is the proper step, she will educate the constituent on the necessary forms or evidentiary requirements; the constituent does the paperwork.

The number of cases coming to Marylyn's attention that could also be handled by an attorney for that constituent depends not only on a constituent's financial resources but also on the availability of qualified legal help in his or her area of the state. Rural areas, for example, tend to have few attorneys knowledgeable in immigration law. Moreover, even an expert attorney has nothing short of a court decree to rival the power of the private bill. Occasionally an unscrupulous lawyer seeks to collect fees from an unwary client for having referred him to a congressman who sponsored a private bill for the client. (The client, of course, could have made the same contact on his own.) Marylyn's office now requires that persons who desire private legislation write the senator personally—not through an attorney.

A caseworker's rapport with agencies and knowledge of the structure of the federal government are her stock in trade. If either skill deteriorates, she is of little use to the constituent.

Marylyn's small office is lined with bulletins and guides, major national and home-state newspapers, the *Federal Register*, the *Congressional Record*, the *Congressional Directory*, the *United States Government Manual* and a card catalogue of agency contacts. On her schedule of chores she lists government and private publications that she must continually peruse for new laws and regulations, changes in agency personnel, and nominations for and confirmations of executive appointments. She must keep abreast of current events. Political turmoil in any particular country may augur restrictions on visas and passports. A State Department guide helps keep her up-to-date on travel requirements. It is not uncommon for a visa or passport to be renewed on less than twenty-four hours' notice. The expansion of multinational corporations has increased international business travel, and some countries, though lenient with tourists, are strict about not letting a businessman off the plane unless he has the proper paperwork.

An equally important task for the congressional caseworker is the review of trade publications, through which business and industry express many of their concerns and ideas. The reviews are compiled by trade representatives—lobbyists—in Washington. "Lobbyists are very important for us if they're good, factual, sincere people," says Marylyn Moss. "They're experts in their fields, and caseworkers cannot be experts in all fields." In addition, special-interest literature (such as veterans' publications) occasionally trigger mail that can be very helpful in monitoring readers' concerns. Similarly, home-state newspapers are often accurate barometers of constituents' problems. "If people are unhappy with us, or especially with an agency, they'll write a letter to the editor. We'll read it and then try to find out why they're critical and sit down and work it out with them, so that maybe they'll have a better taste in their mouth for the federal government." Some years ago, one constituent—a military officer stationed overseas—found venting his frustrations in a letter to the editor more to his liking than contacting his senator who, he claimed publicly, had not responded to a written complaint that he had been stationed in an area devoid of schooling for his handicapped child. The senator involved happened to be Marylyn's, and his office procedure is nothing if not meticulous. All of his mail is carefully logged, numbered and assigned to a staff member; none of it showed receipt of the officer's complaint. The man's anger abated after Marylyn convinced him his complaint had not come through. Then she persuaded the Army to reassign him to an area appropriate for his child's needs. Had she not seen the letter or not followed up on it, she points out, her office's reputation would have been damaged.

Several agencies—namely, the Social Security Administration, the Immigration and Naturalization Service and the Defense Department—conduct seminars at the beginning of each year designed to bring congressional caseworkers up-to-date on changes in agency routine and organization. Since all three agencies draw a large volume of constituent requests and complaints, and since a caseworker's effectiveness is largely measurable by the quantity and quality of the government's telephone numbers in his possession and to which the public does not ordinarily have access, knowing and treating such contacts with respect is invaluable.

A citizen calling the local Social Security or Immigration and Naturalization office is likely to be greeted by a busy signal, a recording or a series of transfer references often ending with the message that the bureaucrat with the necessary information is "not available at the moment." A trained caseworker can make inside connections, usually with what is called a congressional liaison office, established within each federal agency especially to assist caseworkers and legislative aides. A constituent's complaint, after screening, is first routed to the liaison staff. Even then, according to Marylyn, a caseworker might want to go beyond the first contact. "If you find that the liaison office is giving your request slow handling, or that its lines are so busy you can't get through, then you've got to go around them—and you'd better have some good contacts in back. These," she says, pointing to a foot-long card file behind her, "are my contacts." Backup contacts might also be used to verify agency responses the caseworker has reason to question.

Having such special access is a privilege the caseworker can ill afford to abuse. Hence the screening process and the carefully honed attitude of deference. "We don't pound an agency on the head and make demands. We respectfully request that they review the facts and advise us if there's any help possible."

On the other hand, it is in the agencies' interest to keep lines of communication open and to give professional consideration to caseworkers' inquiries. Their purse strings, after all, are pulled by Congress. Three large bureaucracies—the Defense Department, the Veterans Administration and the Office of Personnel Management—have deemed it necessary to maintain liaison office space on Capitol Hill itself. Marylyn Moss finds this especially useful: On occasion she takes cases over personally rather than calling or writing. She has found that inquiries by mail bring responses by mail. Inquiries by phone or in person might bring responses immediately "if they trust you and you've got a good working relationship." And speed is important: "The quicker we can get answers to constituents, the quicker we've made them feel less suspicious or bitter about the federal government. And that's the name of the game for casework: Get the answer back to them as quickly as you can."

Of course, things are not all that simple. The steadily increasing turnover rate for agency personnel strains the rapport between agency staff and congressional caseworkers. "The majority of the people in federal agencies are still very sincere in their efforts to help us, but times are changing. There was a time when they would fight like tigers to help, because it would defend their agency." Agencies are losing talented staff (many of whom had become Marylyn's best contacts) through attrition largely brought about by the concurrent pressures of overwork and bad publicity. Budget cuts under Presidents Carter and Reagan have depleted their ranks. Seasoned caseworkers find it a chore to deal with neophyte agency personnel who are less knowledgeable than they. To make matters worse, the liaison office positions have recently been classified "Schedule C"— political appointments—resulting in staff turnovers with the arrival of each new administration. "There are many people in the liaison offices who might want to help you, but they don't have the necessary background, and they become so frustrated that they build a wall around themselves. This is human nature, really."

The reshuffling of agency personnel and "RIF's" (reductions in force) also create difficulties, as do constituents' heightened expectations. Staff veterans like Marylyn Moss take pride in rendering what they perceive as a special and necessary service. Many remember a time when government services were not so readily taken for granted. "In my grandparents' day," says Marylyn—her conservative bent showing through just enough to suggest that caseworkers are political animals, too—"a family cared for its own. You never went on welfare or begged or asked the state or the federal government for anything if you weren't entitled to it." Her own family emigrated from Europe, acquired farmland in the western United States and lost much of their bounty during the Depression. "But even the neighbors wouldn't have known they were having a struggle." Since then, she feels, the degree of publicity given entitlement programs (such as Social Security retirement and disability insurance) has distorted the original intent of the legislation. "People don't realize," Marylyn Moss insists, "that the Social Security Act is supposed to *supplement* your savings. It was never intended to support any individual or any couple." She concedes, however, that inflation has eroded the savings and buying power of the pension dollar: "Now there's no place for many of these folks to turn. Now they say, 'I paid my taxes. I want my Social Security.' They demand. And they're not always nice about it."

Misconceptions about retirement benefits may promote less rigorous financial planning by many citizens—and cause bitter disappointment for those who expect a nest egg but discover they have barely enough to pay the rent. For these people, in the absence of evidence that the Social Security Administration miscalculated the amount of the benefit, Marylyn can only patiently explain the situation. "I try to walk them through it slowly, so they'll fully understand. It's an educational process. It takes an awful lot out of me."

Other cases involving benefits can be solved to greater financial satisfaction, but the constituent's bitterness, having festered over the course of the struggle, remains. Marylyn recalls a retired doctor who in 1978 reported that he did not receive a Social Security check of $350. He carried on a fruitless battle with the agency for three years before finally contacting the senator's office. Marylyn went to work. Social Security records indicated that the benefits check had been sent, that the Treasury Department was in possession of the canceled check and that it had been endorsed with the recipient's signature. Marylyn knew from experience that such checks are occasionally stolen and forged, even by members of a recipient's own family, so she contacted the Lost and Stolen Checks Divison of the Department of the Treasury. It promised to send the doctor a photostatic copy of the canceled check; if he would sign documents alleging forgery of his endorsement, the government would investigate further. If it found that the check had been forged, the Social Security Administration would replace it. In the end the man recovered his money, but Marylyn was awed by the lengths to which he went—the time and energy spent—before he sought help from his senator.

Caseworkers are particularly sensitive to financially desperate constituents. Those ineligible for Social Security benefits can be directed to other federal and state benefits programs, or local and national charities. Generally caseworkers follow up on complaints, making certain if they can that needy citizens are getting the assistance required.

Hungry constituents can be particularly demanding, but the expectations cut across various lines. Calls tend to become more insistent during election time. Marylyn's employer, as well as many other (but not all) congressmen, feel strongly that the services they render to constituents should not be to solicit votes. The Senator's instructions to his staff on that point are clear: Voting posture and party affiliation are irrelevant. On occasion she must take pains to ensure that agencies understand the nonpartisan nature of the cases she brings to them. For example, she recently had to edit a constituent's letter—one the Army liaison office would see—so that the following plea (in italics) would be deleted: "Sir, I fought for this country that I love and believe in, *just as I voted for you. . . .* Please help me." The constituent's thinking might be simplistic but the editing remains scrupulous. "I don't want the agency to think that the only reason we're going to help him is because he says he voted for us." Likewise there are letters in which obscenities must receive the same tactful censorship. Even bland denunciations of an agency must be deleted, because under the Privacy Act the agency ordinarily requires a copy of the complaint in writing. "Do not damn the agency," Marylyn warns constituents when she gets the chance, "because I have to send your letter to them." Were it not for an experienced caseworker's careful editing, constituents might sometimes sabotage their own cases.

Whether it is a young man barely shy of Air Force height requirements who wants to fly anyway or an elderly couple struggling to make ends meet on a fixed income, assuaging bitterness and disappointment is one of the more draining and emotional chores the caseworker faces. Immigration matters can be especially daunting. A three-inch-thick folder on Marylyn's desk contains the paperwork generated by one case, still active after two years. "I shudder every time that family phones me," she says. It's another crisis that's been triggered by economic and political conditions in a foreign country. Many American citizens have relatives in troubled regions of the world, such as Poland, and they want to bring them to the United States. Conflicts arise when our government, having granted foreign families temporary asylum here, feels that it is now safe for them to return to their homeland. Parents with young children bitterly resist being forced to leave when they are certain they're being sent back to an atmosphere of political unrest or violence. Such cases become more complex when State Department representatives stationed in the home country report that other families are returning to the area.

Still other immigration problems arise when foreigners studying in the United States on temporary student visas become "so Americanized they don't want to leave" and don't want to forgo the employment opportunities they find here.

Illegal aliens who work on farms present a special predicament. The experience in Marylyn's home state is that such people are not troublemakers but a source of cheap, reliable labor. They become attached to the farms, and the farmers to them. Often the farmers request the senator's help in keeping their alien workers, some of whom have already taken American wives and begun to raise families by the time the government wants to expel them. "It's a hard knot to untie," Marylyn says. "It's possible to keep them here, but it takes a long time. And there's an awful lot more emotion involved in these cases now than there was in 1947. You didn't have people so daring that they would swim the river to get here. Immigration is a heartache for me."

The relationship between the caseworker and the employer he or she represents is just as important as the relationships carefully nurtured with his or her constituency and with the federal agencies. Proposals to pool Capitol Hill caseworkers into one office have been rejected in the past, on the theory that casework improves in proportion to the staff member's loyalty to his employer—a loyalty affected by politics as well as personality. Party affiliation, and certainly political philosophy, can bind the caseworker to the congressman. Marylyn Moss's politics are well settled. "I was a Republican before I came here. I was very active in Young Republicans. I grew up in a Republican family and I'm comfortable in a Republican atmosphere." Her loyalty means she is privy to the senator's political situation. "I know what his thinking is. I know what in the state is important. I know where our weak points are and where we're strong." It also means that her politics, settled as they are, may limit her job opportunities on the Hill: "For sure, only a Republican would hire me," she says (more with pride than concern), "because I've always worked for Republicans. I have been approached by a Democrat—a new member coming in—who wanted me to set up his office, but I declined, because he would always question my philosophy." There would come a time in each case, she told him, when he "would probably ask whether I had done everything that possibly could have been done."

Marylyn's loyalty to her present boss was amply demonstrated several years ago when she was hospitalized for major back surgery. Not wanting the senator to worry, she scheduled her operation for a period during which he would be working overseas. "I respect my current employer a great deal (and work well with his wife, too, which is important). I went into the hospital on Wednesday, they tested me on Thursday, Friday they operated on me, and Monday I was doing casework from my bed. One day I handled fourteen calls lying flat on my back with an eight-inch incision and twenty-two stitches." Secretaries in the senator's office took and reported her calls, and she called the constituents back, giving them no hint that she was speaking from a hospital bed. "There was no reason for them to know."

Casework on the Hill is likely to undergo further changes. It has already been affected by modern computer technology. Originally used on an experimental basis, computers have been installed in many senatorial offices to maintain records and to keep track of all cases. Some offices use computers to write letters to constituents. At least one congressman (Representative James Coyne of Pennsylvania) permits constituents with home computers to contact him directly on his office video terminal. Marylyn uses her senator's system solely to log cases. She feels that the computer "is not earning its keep" for caseworkers in small offices, who by and large never use form letters in communicating with constituents.

"There's nothing in the Constitution that says that elected representatives will do anything but legislate. Our job is an outgrowth, because people need help. I am a liaison between an individual in the state and a federal agency. My responsibility is to cut red tape.

"Some voters have the attitude that there are too many laws on the books now—don't pass any more laws, just give me service. The bottom line is what you promise them when you run for election or reelection. Some congressmen have already begun to shift budget funds in order to hire fewer legislative aides and take on more constituent-service personnel.

"You either like to do casework or you don't, and I wouldn't hold it against anyone who didn't. In fact," she adds, more calmly candid than bitter, "these days I'd say you were pretty smart not to get involved in it, because it's becoming increasingly hard to have good people to deal with in the agencies. And if you don't have someone down there who trusts you or cares they won't give you the time of day, and there's nothing you can do about it.

"Sometimes this job can be a little overwhelming, even to me. I shed tears over some of these cases. And many nights I wake up in the middle of the night and try to think of some way to help them when I've tried everything and I think, Is there just any one other thing to be done?

"But I probably learned this work because I like people. I like the satisfaction I get from trying to help a sincere person who has a problem. I've got people up and down the state I'll never see but whom I feel very close to."

GETTING THE MOST FROM A PROFESSIONAL CASEWORKER

DO's and DON'Ts

- DO put your complaint or request in writing, and sign it personally. (Your parent's, pastor's, or neighbor's signature will not suffice.)
- DO include all relevant identifying information—such as your name, address, telephone numbers and where you can be reached when away from home or office.
- DO describe your problem clearly, concisely and candidly.
- DO outline the steps you have taken so far to solve your problem.
- DON'T misrepresent or conceal any relevant facts.
- DON'T suggest that your political support for the congressman or senator you're contacting is contingent upon his solving your problem.
- DON'T write to more than one congressman or senator about the same problem.
- DON'T wait until the last minute if it's clear that solving your problem will take some time.

ASSISTANCE WITH APPLICATIONS FOR GRANTS

A caseworker will need to know to which agency the application was sent, under what program funds are sought in that agency, when the forms were formally submitted, for what purpose, in what amount, how long the project would run, if it previously had federal funding, the project's contact name and a telephone number where the applicant can be reached.

KEY FACTS

Both the House of Representatives and the Senate have their own post offices.

The way to reach your congressman by mail is by sending the mail to:

>The Honorable (name of your congressman)
>United States House of Representatives
>Washington, D.C. 20515

The way to reach your senator by mail is by sending the mail to:

>The Honorable (name of your senator)
>United States Senate
>Washington, D.C. 20515

The proper salutation on letters is "Dear Congressman" or "Dear Senator." Telephone numbers for congressional districts and senatorial offices remain the same from one election to the next. The easiest way to reach your congressman or senator by telephone is to call the Capitol switchboard at (202) 224-3121 and ask for him or her by name.

Local phone numbers and addresses of your senator or congressman are in your local telephone book under "United States Government."

For a complete list of Federal Information Centers (including addresses and telephone numbers), see Appendix A.

☆ II ☆

BUSINESS IN THE BACKWOODS AND DOWN ON THE FARM

Genius is mainly an affair of energy.

—MATTHEW ARNOLD, *Essays in Criticism*

"The state of Maine is made up tinkerers—they'll tackle anything—and maybe that's what the world needs now. Everybody is more qualified than he thinks."

So says salty Charlie MacArthur, who is less tinkerer than backwoods Renaissance man—a slow-talking testimonial to the spirit of dogged American individuality and stubborn New England self-reliance. He may be eclectic and eccentric, but he's nobody's fool. He has been a successful businessman (he founded a company that makes sophisticated copies of engineers' blueprints), licensed pilot and balloonist (he sailed over the Arctic Circle in a homemade basket), promoter (each spring he stages an Alternative Vehicle Regatta to the top of Mount Washington, New Hampshire), teacher (at college he studied English, which he taught at the high-school level), naval officer (he helped navigate a destroyer), and inventor (he's created various items, small and large, from a hiking stick with a built-in compass to an electric automobile, and he's sponsored those powered by everything from charcoal to chicken fat).

But most of all—especially when the government is either unresponsive or on his back—Charlie MacArthur is a dedicated curmudgeon.

It was one thing that the Department of Commerce and three other federal agencies would not answer his numerous applications for support of experiments with alternatives to the internal-combustion engine; after all, he could take some pleasure in reminding the bureaucrats that there is, in fact, an Electric and Hybrid Vehicle Development Act on the books, about which all they have done to date is send out press releases. But it was quite another thing for the government to

26

harass him with a barrage of picayune rules, regulations and forms when it discovered he hadn't applied for a license to run his little hydroelectric plant in the small Maine town of Dover-Foxcroft (population: 4,000).

It all started when MacArthur and his wife, Annie, sold their house and industrial-photography business in Connecticut to buy an aging and vacant power mill on the Piscataquis River in Dover-Foxcroft. He was returning home (he was born in Lewiston, Maine, in 1928), but there was more to it than that. Charlie had always wanted to own a power plant—maybe because when he was about to be born his mother hailed a cab and hurriedly told the driver "Central Maine" and was driven to the Central Maine Power Company instead of the Central Maine Hospital—or perhaps because he is dead serious about mankind's excessive consumption of energy ("We'll all starve if we lose our mechanized agriculture, dependent as it is on oil for both fuel and fertilizer.").

The MacArthurs took over the plant, called Brown's Mill, in 1976. It was more than a century old and consists of six buildings sprawled across 26 acres of remote land 35 miles northwest of Bangor. Besides a huge (92,000 square feet) wooden main structure, Brown's Mill's only visible asset was a pair of small hydroelectric turbines (totaling 600 kilowatts) built in 1949—and one of the turbines wasn't working.

The first thing Charlie MacArthur did was spend $123 converting an oil furnace to one that burned wood. Then he repaired the broken turbine and started making electricity, enough of which he sold to the Central Maine Power Company to supply 85 percent of Dover-Foxcroft's needs. And finally he began renting out space in the massive old mill—nine-by-13 cubicles, with heat, light and water included—for one dollar a day to any cottage industry with vision and gumption enough to experiment with new production methodologies. So far he has a dozen-odd tenants, from a one-woman barrel company to a producer of hydrophonically grown lettuce (three bushels a day from a three-by-six-foot area illuminated by surplus lights from a highway) to the proprietor of "the only water-powered African violet farm in the world."

MacArthur generally steered clear of the government, perhaps because he wanted to show a world starving for alternative sources of energy that "if a stupid, aging person like Charlie MacArthur can do it, anyone can," or perhaps because of earlier frustrations. "We are laboring under the misapprehension that the government knows what it is doing. From my one-to-one encounters, I know that what the government is doing is not what the people think it is doing."

In April 1978, when a bulkhead burst at the tiny generating station, he called Washington hopefully: He'd been encouraged by the Carter administration's loudly proclaimed support of hydroelectric projects, and he knew that new plants no bigger than his were being built at a cost of $6 million or more and he was asking for a repair loan of a mere $30,000. Nine more days and $114 worth of phone calls later, he hung up. His request, he'd been told, couldn't even be *considered* until it underwent a two-year study to determine the feasibility of generating power at his site. This, in regard to an existing facility. "Trying to deal with the government," concluded Charlie, "is like having a hippopotamus for a ballet partner."

But Charlie MacArthur's real problems began in January 1981—or, he thinks, several months after an article appeared in the *New York Times* about the first modest successes at Brown's Mill. The report had been complimentary, quoting liberally from Charlie's down-home philosophy of initiative and independence.

> "Buying local wood from local wood cutters keeps our local economy running, which is the key to regional self-sufficiency," he said. But to prepare for the time when wood becomes scarce and expensive, MacArthur is making plans for installing "the world's largest" solar-energy collecting panels on the immense roof of the mill building. Naturally, he won't use those expensive copper and glass models, but a recently developed, very cheap variety of extruded rubber.
>
> The hydroelectric turbines are now, after years of unproductivity, running at about 75 percent efficiency. . . . Since Brown's Mill is not licensed as a utility by the state, MacArthur has to sell the electricity to Central Maine Power, which, in turn, sells it to local consumers.
>
> "We're doing a little better than breaking even, depending on how you figure it," Mr. MacArthur said. When he isn't spinning valves in the hydroelectric plant's control room, taking orders for the life-sized inflatable whales he markets, or organizing barn dances, a health club and buses to out-of-town movie theatres, he tends to his Museum of Transportation. "I'm deeply interested and deeply depressed about transportation," said MacArthur, who drives an electric car.
>
> Situated in the mill's unprepossessing ground floor, the museum houses about 18 vehicles that use alternative power. Included in the collection are a covered wagon, a Chevrolet

station wagon that runs on charcoal ("It won't leave rubber, but it has hit 55 miles an hour"), a three-wheeled buggy that runs on waste fat from the mill's restaurant ("It gets 25 miles to the pound and smells like fried chicken when it goes by") and a solar-powered two-seater.

On January 22, 1981, MacArthur received a telephone call from a man at the Federal Energy Regulatory Commission (FERC), telling him that it would be necessary to license his hydroelectric plant on the Piscataquis. Smelling a rat, MacArthur decided his best defense was a good offense. On January 23 he wrote to the chairman of the FERC, inquiring about the agency's source of information:

> The caller indicated that he had learned of our existence through an article published in the NEW YORK TIMES in November. He advised me that he was not aware of the article on original publication, but that it had been provided to FERC sometime in early December. I am under the impression that the donor of the article was not on the FERC staff.
>
> In accordance with the "Freedom of Information Act", I would appreciate your furnishing me with a copy of the communication to FERC from the donor of the copy of the article.

MacArthur anticipated that he'd need the support of his elected representatives in Washington, so he sent copies of his letter to Representatives Olympia Snowe and David Emery and to Senator George Mitchell and me.

On January 28, the FERC supplied him with a more detailed request for data—this time in a communication from its New York regional office:

Dear Mr. MacArthur:

> Your efforts to restore the hydroelectric power station at Browns Mill has [sic] recently come to our attention. We encourage and support all interest in developing potential hydroelectric sites. However, hydroelectric projects proposed by non-Federal entities must be licensed by the Federal Energy Regulatory Commission (FERC) if they either: (1) occupy Federal lands; (2) are situated on a navigable waterway of the United States; (3) affect interstate of foreign commerce; or (4) utilize surplus water or water power from a government dam. The authority of the Federal government to regulate certain aspects of hydroelectric development is contained in the Federal Power Act. Your project may be subject to our jurisdiction under items (2) and or (3) above.

The requirements for an application for license are contained in the Regulations of the Federal Energy Regulatory Commission, as set forth in Title 18, Parts 1-149, of the Code of Federal Regulations. Copies of the Federal Power Act and of 18 CFR Parts 1 to 149 are available by mail from the U.S. Government Printing Office, Washington, DC 20402. Enclosed is a copy of our Hydro Power Licensing Manual. Also included are new regulations for exemption from licensing for small hydroelectric projects.

When an application is received by the Secretary of the Federal Energy Regulatory Commission, it is examined by the Commission staff to determine whether it contains all of the information required by the Commission's Regulations. If so, details of the application are transmitted to various Federal, State, and local agencies for their comments. The Applicant is then given an opportunity to respond to these comments.

Based on the information gathered through the above processes, the Commission staff prepares its recommendations to the five members of the Federal Energy Regulatory Commission. The Commission then reaches a decision as to whether a license should be issued, and whether any special conditions (as to minimum flow releases, recreation facilities, etc.) need be included.

As a minimum please submit a statement of your intentions (we enclose a copy of Part 24 of FERC regulations) regarding application for FERC license for the Browns Mill project. Your response by March 6, 1981 should be addressed to: Secretary, Federal Energy Regulatory Commission, 825 No. Capitol St. Washington, DC 20426.

Enclosed was a photocopy of the federal regulation requiring a "declaration of intention" by the applicant for a license. It read, in pertinent part, as follows:

§ 24.1 Filing.

An original and ten conformed copies of each declaration of intention under the provisions of section 23(b) of the act shall be filed. The declaration shall give the name and post office address of the person to whom correspondence in regard to it shall be addressed, and shall be accompanied by:

(a) A brief description of the proposed project and its purposes, including such data as maximum height of the dams, a storage capacity curve of the reservoirs showing the maximum, average, and minimum operating pool levels, the initial and ultimate installed capacity of the project, the rated horsepower and head on the turbines, and a curve of turbine discharge versus output at average and minimum operating heads.

(b) (1) A general map (one tracing and three prints) of any convenient size and scale, showing the stream or streams *to be* utilized and the approximate location and the general plan of the project.

(2) Also a detailed map of the proposed project area showing all Federal lands, and lands owned by States, if any, occupied by the project.

(3) A profile of the river within the vicinity of the project showing the location of the proposed project and any existing improvements in the river.

(4) A duration curve and hydrograph for the natural and proposed regulated flows at the dam site. Furnish references to the published stream flow records used and submit copies of any unpublished records used in preparation of these curves.

(c) (1) A definite statement of the proposed method of utilizing storage or pondage seasonally, weekly and daily, during periods of low and normal flows after the plant is in operation and the system load has grown to the extent that the capacity of the plant is required to meet the load. For example, furnish:

(i) Hydrographs covering a 10-day low water period showing the natural flow of the stream and the effect thereon caused by operations of the proposed power plant:

(ii) Similar hydrographs covering a 10-day period during which the discharge of the stream approximates average recorded yearly flow, and

(iii) Similar hydrographs covering a low water year using average monthly flows.

(2) A system load curve, both daily and monthly, and the position on the load curve that the proposed project would have occupied had it been in operation.

(3) A proposed annual rule of operation for the storage reservoir or reservoirs.

MacArthur was perplexed. "They gave us a month to get all this together," he noted. "It would take years!"

On March 6, 1981—the due date for the declaration of intention—he fired off instead a pointed letter to FERC headquarters in Washington:

Ref: James D. Hebson, FERC New York Regional Engineer ltr of 1/28/81

Dear Commissioners,

Mr. Hebson's letter refers, in its first paragraph, to a New York Times article concerning my "efforts to restore the hydroelectric power station at Browns Mill", and that "hydroelectric projects proposed . . . must be licensed . . ." *This dam has been producing mill power since 1867, with the last known change in dam characteristics completed by 1920 without any change in the power capacity of the site.*

1. The mill does not occupy federal lands.
2. The Piscataquis river is not navigable to Dover-Foxcroft. Last year I attempted to canoe down river and could not escape from our tailrace pond in a boat with a draft of 2½".
3. Power produced here is consumed locally.
4. We do not utilize surplus water or water power from a government dam.

Drawings of the dam and power station do not exist, nor am I aware of the likelihood of "blueprints" being made in the post Civil War period. An acquaintance who applied for a license in another state has told me he spent $14,000 in surveying, drafting and legal fees when attempting to document a similar historic mill site for a FERC license. After five years of investment of his time and money, FERC informed him that a license application was not necessary as the stream was not navigable at his site. During the waiting period his equipment, idle, deteriorated and I believe at this time he has no interest in attempting a second restoration.

Your agency efforts in encouraging the development of new hydro sites are commendable. I do not feel you can help us any more here, and I do not wish to burden your staff with studies of a 114 year old accomplished fact when so many new sites need your servies.

I am sorry that the New York Times article you read was not fully explanatory of our situation. I have decided that after next weeks appearance on Good Morning America that I will discourage the press from reporting about this site. It tends to give the public a false hope that the energy problem is easily solved.

This is a small "mom & pop" plant. We have all our life savings invested here, so our backs are to the financial wall . . . no staff, no secretaries. All the money we can acquire is needed to build an inventory of spare parts, brushes, hydraulic oil for the governors, replacements for ancient carbon pile voltage regulators (the only regulators we are looking for at this time.)

(Constructively defensive,)
Charles E. MacArthur

This time, besides sending copies to Maine's congressional delegation, MacArthur wrote directly to me:

Dear Senator Cohen,

The Federal Energy Regulatory Commission has suggested that it may be necessary to license our 114 year old power station. Such a license will add nothing to our ability to produce power, and will in fact decrease the time we have available to maintain the plant at peak performance.

In a telephone conversation with FERC staff, I understood the representative to say that it is likely that we are exempt from license because:
1. Our history before 1920 "grandfathers" us.
2. We are not on a navigable waterway.

BUT, I am fearful that the enclosed letter, once in file, will lead to further reviews each time it is accidently encountered. I would hope that some positive recognition of our non-licensable status might be forthcoming from FERC. This will save both FERC and Brown's Mill staff time at a later date, allowing each of us to concentrate on:
1. FERC contributions toward *new* stations.
2. Our devotion entirely to the production of low head hydro power.

We have an adequate supply of snags floating down the river into our intake screens, and do not need distracting regulatory snags to further diminish our ability to produce.

We feel our site is secure against fire, flood and all other acts of God . . . but do feel threatened by acts of the Legislature.

Please ask your staff to look into the enclosures. I would like to have your thoughts on this instance of excessive attention.

Pleadingly,

Charles E. MacArthur
Owner/Operator
Brown's Mill

Our office staff went to work immediately. Tom Heyerdahl, my chief legislative assistant, contacted Charles Lord in the FERC's Office of Applications, Electric Power Regulation. Then he called MacArthur, who made his reluctance even to apply for a permit abundantly clear: He was worried about the time and costs involved, and he felt that his limited resources should be devoted to repairing the facility at Brown's Mill and not filling out a slew of federal, state and local forms. Finally, after numerous conversations with both Lord and MacArthur, Heyerdahl convinced the latter it would be in his best interest to apply for either an exemption or a license. Later Heyerdahl noted in a memo that "Lord (or someone at FERC) commented that MacArthur could fill out the application while watching *The Waltons* one evening, it was that simple."

In late April, following a number of further discussions with Lord, Heyerdahl arranged to have the FERC's "short form" license application forwarded to MacArthur, whom he told to "call me if any problems developed."

The next Heyerdahl heard from MacArthur was in November 1981. It had obviously taken more than a full season of *Waltons* reruns and some coin of the realm for Charlie to complete the short form, but he had, and he had sent it along to Lord at the FERC with a covering note:

Dear Mr. Lord,

Enclosed is our application for Short Form License (minor) on the existing Brown's Mill hydro-electric facility. We have done our best on it over two months, and have set aside work on the power station in order to expedite it. Telephone calls during one three day period amounted to $55.00 . . . so I hope that we have it right. . . .

Firmly,

Charles E. MacArthur
Owner, Brown's Mill
cc: Tom Heyerdahl

On February 18, 1982, MacArthur called Heyerdahl. MacArthur was very agitated. He said that he'd heard nothing from the FERC, that he was fed up with the application process because it was costing him a fortune ($10,000 to date) as well as his precious time, that he was through playing the game and that he wanted Senator Cohen's help in obtaining a permit to picket the White House legally. He also suggested that Mr. Lord might be amused if MacArthur showed up at the FERC with Mike Wallace (the inquisitor from CBS) in tow.

Heyerdahl called Lord, who as usual was pleasant and professional. Lord had even come to like and respect Charlie MacArthur and hoped that Brown's Mill would not go broke or otherwise out of business. But he said he wouldn't be amused by a visit from Mike Wallace. Lord told Heyerdahl that on December 21, 1981, in accordance with established procedures, the FERC had notified two Maine agencies (the state's Department of Environmental Protection and the Atlantic Sea Run Salmon Commission) of MacArthur's application. If no adverse comments were filed by March 1982, the FERC said it would proceed to issue the operating license without any conditions.

Then Heyerdahl spoke with a contact named Dana Murch at the Department of Environmental Protection, who said that after some problems had been resolved to MacArthur's satisfaction regarding water-quality certification, a permit from the DEP would likely be forthcoming.

But then Heyerdahl hit a snag—in the person of "a consummate bureaucrat" at one of the various state commissions in Maine. The man struck Heyerdahl as "terribly combative and defensive" on the phone. "He was none too friendly to me, suggested that MacArthur was 'trying to get rich at taxpayers' expense' and had increased his interest in the Brown's Mill facility 'to the point of a malignancy.' I took that to mean that in his eyes MacArthur was greedy and bent on mucking up the 300-square-mile watershed (the Piscataquis River Basin) so that the Atlantic salmon will not survive in the upper watershed. He also informed me that this 'fly-by-night operator' (MacArthur) was going to have to build an expensive fish passageway before the Atlantic Sea Run Salmon Commission would approve his application. (I have never talked to Charlie about the fish passageway, but I suspect that he will be very upset when informed officially of the requirement, which he obviously can't afford to meet.)"

In short, Heyerdahl concluded, the commission man "would like Charlie more if he were a salmon."

By April 1982, MacArthur still had not heard from the FERC. He estimated that he had now spent more than $14,000 on the application process and an "incalculable number of late-night hours."

Not that Charlie MacArthur is afraid of hard work. It's just that there are too many physical things that need doing around the mill and house to put in a lot of time filling out forms. MacArthur has worked hard all of his life. His family had little money, and Charlie, supported by loans, went to Bates College in Lewiston. He worked at a variety of jobs before buying a business. "At one time I was going to be a minister," he says, "but I had a religious experience and was saved." He and Annie "went through hell to get our first photo business started. We ate cereal three times a day. For five years we lived in dread fear of the telephone, of bills we couldn't pay. That's one of the reasons I want to help young businesses." So at

Brown's Mill he's supporting an indoor trout farm, a food-freezing plant and three commercial greenhouses.

MacArthur and his wife live in what was once the carpenter's workshop, a two-story clapboard building with big doors and many windows, situated a few feet from the Piscataquis River. He's had some successes in his own businesses and some failures, and a lot of colorful publicity to go with both. The State Department has featured Brown's Mill at the United States Embassy in Moscow as an example of American free enterprise.

All MacArthur really wants is the freedom to solve, cheaply and innovatively, serious local problems with broader national significance. And all he really needs to achieve that freedom, he feels, is for the government to get off his back.

American revolutionaries, he's fond of pointing out, used to say (and said in the Declaration of Independence) that King George III " 'has erected a Multitude of new Offices, and sent hither Swarms of Officers to harass our People, and eat out their Substance.'

"I would race down to the harbor to toss in a box of tea," says Charlie, "but now that too requires a license."

Sam Thurston is a different kind of small-businessman—a farmer—in a different kind of predicament: He wants the government to get involved and help him out.

Being a farmer in Texas means being constantly at the mercy of the elements. There is no predicting, or controlling, the weather, which has its direct and indirect effects on the sprouting of planted crops, infestation, oil chemistry and market fluctuations. But though it's a hard life, farming has always been part of Sam Thurston's blood—his father owns acreage too, in Lubbock—and Sam feels the nobility of his labor as well. Farming, after all, is at the heart of civilization, having transformed man from a tribal wanderer to a stable developer of communites—a domesticator of animals and planter of food crops.

But the number of Americans who remain wedded to the land is dwindling, as huge agribusinesses using space-age technologies have taken over. The owner of a small farm is often squeezed out by high interest rates, the price of land, the need to capitalize equipment, inflation—and the inability to withstand the vagaries of the weather.

Sam Thurston grows cotton and peanuts on his three thousand acres of Texas farmland. Although cotton is no longer King—its market share has been cut drastically by modern synthetic fabrics—it is still a mainstay crop and is grown in nearly every southern state. Peanuts, too, remain a staple. But prices for both of these commodities fluctuate heavily, making what a farmer can reasonably expect for his work all the more speculative.

From 1979 to 1981 the weather played havoc with the cotton and peanut crops: drought, sandstorms and hail took turns sweeping across the countryside. In June 1980, Sam turned to the Small Business Administration for help, applying for a loan under the SBA's Farm Disaster program. If a farmer can demonstrate that his enterprise is promising but that it has been hurt by unforeseeable market or environmental difficulties, he may qualify for a low-interest loan from the government. He also has to show a likely ability to repay the loan—perhaps with letters of recommendation from banks and fellow farmers.

Sam was turned down. Feeling he needed stronger references, he wrote to Senator John Tower in July 1981. It was not just an idle letter, Sam said. His business was in real trouble, caused by, as a bank official in Brownfield, Texas, attested, "disastrous production conditions." Largely as a result of weather problems, Sam had not been able to show "a positive net profit." Nobody would say it would be different this year, but at least there was some cause for optimism. Sam had integrated his operation, had managed to raise some loan capital to improve his irrigation system and had kept a closer watch on his yields. In so doing he had incurred what the bank officials said were "a high amount of fixed annual obligations" but "given decent to good production and an adequate price," he should now have "no problem showing a positive net cash flow."

The Small Business Administration had been dubious. After all, Sam was asking for $290,000, and he wanted to spread the payments out longer than usual, and some of his land had already been pledged to banks as collateral.

It was pledged dearly, too. In June 1981, the Brownfield State Bank wrote to the SBA that it would be glad to have Sam borrow from Peter to pay Paul but that it could not lend any more money to Sam Thurston.

Senator Tower's office did what it could, which apparently was not enough. The SBA again turned Sam down, claiming that his cash flow was not sufficient to repay existing fixed annual payments, which totaled $54,997, or to clear up another delinquency at the Farmers Home Administration of $17,268, or to pay out the loan monies of $162,000 owed to the Brownfield State Bank. The actual cash flow that Sam showed to the SBA were $27,800 in 1977, a deficit of $7,000 in 1978 and a deficit of $3,000 in 1979. The SBA found no reduction anticipated in Sam's fixed obligations for at least four years:

> Your financial condition is critical with assets being highly leveraged. Credit history with some lenders is not satisfactory. At this point in time, you have no operating commitment which leaves you with inadequate working capital for this crop year. The above factors indicate that you may not be able to comply with the terms of a loan agreement.

The SBA wanted Sam to work out a payment plan with all his creditors. But Sam had tried that and the creditors were not too sympathetic. He felt that his only recourse was a low-interest loan, with assurances of absolute repayment. On what could those assurances be based? All Sam had to sell was optimism about the future. Hope can't be amortized or make crops grow, but Sam was undaunted. Nor was his father. Writing to the SBA on his son's behalf, John Thurston had said, "The whole area is in the best shape moisture-wise it has been in 10 years. Also, Sam's total operation is in the best shape moisture-wise since 1976. As of this date he has 100% of his peanut crop up and growing and 50% of his cotton crop up and growing. He also has two circles of irrigated wheat which should be harvested, some of the best wheat I have ever seen in Cass County. I truly believe that Sam's gross income could exceed $500,000 in 1981." John went further. "Because I believe that Sam has unlimited potential built into his farming operation, I will submit the Southwest Quarter, Section 23, Block G, Cass County, to further collateralize the loan. This property is owned by my company. I own 100% of the stock." But John Thurston was really not offering much more than his son's hope: The property he described had already been heavily mortgaged. His plea ("Please reconsider the application and give it your approval") was turned down.

Later in 1981, Sam wrote to the SBA disaster office in Lubbock:

> I have the best cotton, wheat and peanut crop growing I have ever had. Since my operation is about 75% dryland, the adequate moisture supply in this area this year really makes my crop prospects look extremely good.
>
> I understand only too well that my assets are highly leveraged. This is due to not producing dryland crop since 1977. Again the prospects look much improved this year. With just an average

crop on an operation this size of mine, my indebtness could be greatly reduced in a mere 6 to 8 months.

My father has agreed to put up another ¼ section of land as collateral. He is a good businessman and if he did not believe in my operation, he definitely would not do this.

Since my problems at this time are largely of cash flow, I cannot stress too much how much assistance your approval will be. I believe that under decent conditions (which have not existed since 1977) my highly integrated farming operation can do nothing but produce and grow in the future.

The SBA would still have none of it. The disaster office was not prepared to take this kind of gamble.

But Sam kept plugging away, almost defiantly, with still more letters to the government. He was a good farmer with a good farming operation, he could handle his debt and he did not owe that many people that much money. "Another point I would like to make," he wrote, "is that my annual liabilities will decrease rather rapidly. FHA will be paid off in four years, the others in nineteen. Given average crop prospects my equity position would become stronger rapidly. This loan would help tremendously. If I should run upon trying times again 5 or 10 years down the road, I should generate enough equity in my property to make some sort of refinancing available. I was reared on a farm. I realize farming presents special problems requiring huge financial risks, but I have the resolve to overcome these problems."

Maybe Sam also realized he was desperate, willing to pledge anything, claim anything. He was a farmer at the end of his line. He had to improve his crop yields, but to do so would take the sort of capitalization he didn't yet have. In order to plan for the future he had to have more in front of him than a collection of bills. Perhaps it was little more than despair that prompted letter after letter to an impersonal agency that had already said no three times. Maybe his persistence was like the twitching of an animal already dying.

The SBA responded in cold, businesslike terms:

The basis for reconsideration of a loan application that has been declined requires the applicant to furnish information that will substantially overcome the reason for the original decline. A review of your loan application reflects that it was declined for reasonable assurance of repayment ability. A careful review of your request for reconsideration, along with your supportive documentation, has been made. We regret that we cannot be of assistance to you.

Your fixed annual obligations are twice the amount of cash flow from your best year. We cannot add another payment to your existing burden in view of this disproportion even in view of the 1981/1982 projections. We would suggest that you explore restructuring your debt load to ease the payment burden if possible.

More stubborn than a mad mule, Sam wrote back:

I received your letter declining my SBA farm disaster application. I am sorely disappointed! Admittedly, I have strung together four poor years due to wind, hail, drought, and poor financing. However I have an opportunity this crop year to remedy many of the problems. Your approval of this loan application can only enhance this opportunity!

His father also wrote another letter. Essentially it repeated the same things that he or Sam had told the SBA.

The SBA, properly as ever, responded in kind.

Sam turned once again to Senator Tower, who said again that he would be happy to contact the appropriate officials on his constituent's behalf.

About a month afterward, near the end of 1981, the disaster office reported to the senator that it was requesting "additional research by our Lubbock Disaster Branch." Finally, the glimmer of a positive reply.

And in September 1981, Senator Tower was able to inform Sam Thurston that his loan application had been favorably reviewed. Sam did not receive all that he asked for, but it would be enough to put him in a position to turn a good crop year into a profitable future.

The government had finally gotten on his back.

GETTING THE MOST OUT OF THE SMALL BUSINESS ADMINISTRATION

What a Caseworker Needs to Know

The maximum amount that the Small Business Administration will guarantee is $500,000 on a $1 million bank loan. It depends on the type of industry involved, the number of employees, yearly income, etc. A caseworker needs to know if the business is new or established, if there are any delinquent loans (if so, with whom and how far delinquent), the business's current financial status and if you are seeking disaster assistance.

KEY FACTS

SMALL BUSINESS ADMINISTRATION
1441 L Street, N.W.
Washington, DC 20416
Phone: (202) 658-6365

The fundamental purposes of the Small Business Administration are to aid, counsel and protect the interests of small businesses; to ensure that they receive a fair proportion of government contracts; to make loans in situations involving natural or marketplace disasters; to improve management skills of small-business owners; to study economic conditions; and to license and regulate small-business investment companies.

The SBA was created by an act of Congress in 1953. The SBA is an independent federal agency.

FEDERAL ENERGY REGULATORY COMMISSION
825 North Capitol Street
Washington, DC 20426
Phone: (202) 357-8055

The Federal Energy Regulatory Commission is an independent agency within the Department of Energy, which is charged with coordinating and administering national energy policy. The FERC has retained many of the functions of the former Federal Power Commission, such as setting rates and charges for the transportation and sale of natural gas, for the transmission and sale of electricity and for the licensing of hydroelectric power projects. In addition, the Interstate Commerce Commission has assigned to the FERC the authority to establish rates for the transportation of oil by pipeline.

The secretary of energy is represented in each of the ten standard federal regions by regional representatives, whose duties include speaking for the secretary in all regional DOE activities; working with state governors to set up regional energy advisory boards; providing feedback on the regional impact of DOE policies and programs; and performing various functions in conservation, energy resource development and data collection.

The field activities of FERC are separate from other DOE field activities, although office are generally shared.

FERC coordinates the operations of the following power administrations:

- Bonneville Power Administration (1002 NE Holladay Street, P.O. Box 3621, Portland, OR 97208), serving the Pacific Northwest.
- Southeastern Power Administration (Elberton, GA 30635), serving West Virginia, Virginia, North Carolina, South Carolina, Georgia, Florida, Alabama, Mississippi, Tennessee and Kentucky.
- Alaska Power Administration (Federal Building, P.O. Box 50, Juneau, AK 99802), serving all of Alaska.
- Southwestern Power Administration (Page Belcher Federal Building, Tulsa, OK 74101), serving Arkansas, Kansas, Louisiana, Missouri, Oklahoma and Texas.
- Western Area Power Administration (P.O. Box 3403, Golden, CO 80401), serving California, Arizona, Nevada, Montana, North Dakota, South Dakota, Iowa, Colorado, Wyoming, Minnesota, Texas, New Mexico, Utah and Nebraska.

For further information contact the Department of Energy, Washington, DC 20585. Phone: (202) 252-5000.

"YOUR CHECK IS IN THE MAIL"

Governments can err, Presidents do make mistakes, but the im-
mortal Dante tells us that Divine Justice weighs the sins of the
coldblooded and the sins of the warmhearted in a different scale.
Better the occasional faults of a government living in a spirit of
charity than the consistent omission of a government frozen in the
ice of its own indifference.

—FRANKLIN D. ROOSEVELT

Approaching the Woodlawn headquarters of the Social Security Administration, just off the I-70 Security Boulevard exit
from the Baltimore Beltway, one is immediately struck by the
Kafkaesque massiveness of the complex's five huge buildings.
Each of them is nearly the area of a city block; they are jux-
taposed close by one another in a gigantic plaza. More than
10,000 federal civil servants work here. The buildings appear
to be eternally occupied—they are lit twenty-four hours a
day—as if Social Security was and always will be here, rising
above the clear flatness of Security Boulevard and dwarfing
everything around like a man-made mountain range. Acres
of parking lots are filled several times a day by the various
shifts of employees who maintain records, process claims sent
by various other offices, keep work histories and attempt
to distribute billions of dollars in benefits to millions of participants.

A visitor must get off the Beltway at Security Boulevard, go
up Perimeter Drive, pass Access Drive, make a left on Interior
Road—and then hope to find a parking place among the
thousands in the lots. Next to be negotiated is a huge maze of
offices, all camouflaged by initials. One of the buildings is
marked HCFA—Health Care Financing Administration. On
the third floor are the Improvements Management Staff, the
Improvements Promotion Division, the Corrective Action
Projects Division, the Bureau of Program Policy, the Bureau of
Quality Control, the Office of Systems Analysis, the Division of

44

Systems Support and the Division of Payments Operation. A typical door is marked "IM 24a." The labels are likewise codified: "OMBP, OMR, DMS Facilities Branch" or "OMBP, OMR, DPUM Management Branch" or "EDP Drop Point, SSA Approved Personnel Only." Everywhere there are computers and copying machines, and people holding files, folders, clipboards or cups of coffee.

With this degree of enormousness, it is virtually inevitable that benefits are misplaced, wrongly denied, inadequately processed or inordinately awarded. And sometimes it takes more than a letter or a phone call to have error corrected.

Then, the resources usually available to the average Social Security recipient are pitifully short of those necessary to produce expeditious results. The combined efforts of friends, relatives and even privately retained lawyers are often to little avail.

Of particular poignancy are the thousands of recent cases where, in the crusade initially ordered by Congress to trim the federal budget, disability benefits have been wrongfully discontinued.

Between March 1981 and April 1982, the Social Security Administration ordered reviews of more than 430,000 files and summarily terminated benefits in more than 40 percent of them—far above the 20 percent figure originally predicted by the General Accounting Office. In the state of Maine alone, benefits for more than a thousand individuals were ended, despite the fact that in a number of cases the claimants appeared to be severely disabled and unable to work.

We received similar reports from all over the country of truly disabled individuals being dropped from the program. A disturbing pattern emerged of inadequately documented reviews, incomplete medical examinations, misinformation and erroneous decisions. We discovered that the claimant's medical history is sometimes disregarded in making the decision on his present disability, and that beneficiaries often did not understand that they must again prove their eligibility for the program.

If an individual is mistakenly eliminated from the program he can appeal the decision, and his chances of eventual reinstatement are rather good. In fact, the administrative law judges who were hearing appeals from claimants were revising the decisions for over 65 percent of them. That's an astounding rate of reversal.

But the road to reinstatement is very arduous and lengthy,

and in waiting for a final decision, the claimant may be without benefits for many months, due to the tremendous backlog of cases. Many individuals had been forced to turn to welfare, since their disability benefits had been their only source of income.

Now, the principle of regular reviews of eligibility is a sound management tool, necessary to identify people who are no longer disabled and thus not in need of assistance. The federal government spends some $17 billion a year to provide benefits to disabled workers, their spouses and their children. And unless we eliminate from the program those individuals who no longer require this assistance, we limit our ability to provide fully for those who urgently do.

But the Social Security disability program is a promise to working Americans who contribute to and support the system that they will be protected in the event of accidental injury or serious physical disease or mental disorder—conditions that can befall any one of us without our control.

This promise had really turned into a nightmare. Many people were severely sick, with definite disabilities, and could not—perhaps would never be able to—secure substantial gainful employment. If the reversal rate was any indication, for every one weed that Social Security was plucking, it was crushing two flowers. There were cases that we knew of where individuals committed suicide, apparently because they were either terminated from the program or were denied Social Security disability benefits.

What we should remember about the disability program is that it is not a charity, it is not a handout. Each worker pays for his or her right to be protected every time he makes Social Security payments.

Again, the real injustice occurs during the appeals process: From the time that the disability termination decision is made by the state agency to the time that the administrative law judge (ALJ) issues a reversal, the claimant is not entitled to any disability benefits or disability medical insurance under the Social Security system; and the appeals process can take anywhere from nine months to a year.

If the reversal rate were to continue through 1982, Social Security would have terminated (and ALJ's subsequently reinstated) 232,000 individuals. That's an unconscionable amount of financial and emotional hardship.

So here was a situation that required much more than the efforts of individual caseworkers. The Senate's Subcommittee on Oversight of Government Management called hearings to determine what could be done to prevent further injustices. Requiring reviews is fine; it's appropriate. But not unless and until there is a fair system in place.

The Social Security Administration did not want us to hold the hearings and, when we insisted, did not take kindly to them.

The public sessions took place in late May 1982. The deputy commissioner of Social Security was the first witness. He conceded some inequities in the system but placed the blame squarely on Congress—in the process implying that our own hearings were political in nature.

> DEPUTY COMMISSIONER: The time has long since gone for demagoguery on this issue, and we are still getting a lot of it in some quarters. I think it's high time that we had some constructive, creative action. It may well be good theater, good television and good headlines to blame this administration as some have for the problems, anomalies and mistakes. That's a bum rap. If there are errors and failures in this program, they are not this administration's—they are the errors and failures of the United States Government over time.

> SENATOR COHEN: I'd just like to comment about your statement about demagoguery.
> Let me assure you, first, and everybody here in this audience, that you won't find any demagogues sitting up here on this podium. Senator Levin, Senator Pryor and others who are concerned about the issue certainly have gone to some lengths to make sure that we reduce this capacity that we have in the Senate and the House for theater.
> What we really want is a discussion—an intelligent discussion—of the issues involved. Now, everybody's for eliminating fraud, waste and abuse—so I can assure you that no one here is going to seek to exploit the very volatile issue dealing with people's disability payments for the purpose of any political gain.

Senators Levin and Pryor and I went on to point out what we thought were vital deficiencies in the disability-review program:

- The letters from the Social Security Administration announcing that a review is about to take place fail to inform veterans that the burden will be on *them* to *reprove* their disabilities—that past evidence is irrelevant and would not be considered.
- There is no face-to-face relationship between the government and the benefit recipient, only a quick and imper-

sonal determination by a government claims examiner looking at a limited file.

• The detailed findings of a beneficiary's physician are
often ignored completely.

The Subcommittee also took the occasion to rebut the
suggestion by some of Social Security's witnesses that the
administrative law judges responsible for reversing so many
bureaucratic decisions were not very well trained. After all,
most of the appellate reviewers were highly practiced attorneys and judges with many years' experience!

The first phase of the hearings was summed up eloquently
by Senator Levin:

> We know there are hundreds of thousands of folks out there
> who are going to be eliminated from those rolls, who are going
> to be reinstated on appeal to the ALJ's. We know it. It is coming
> for sure, and we have a chance to do something about it. Let's
> work together and do something about it. That is my plea.
>
> I am not pointing blame or trying to make political hay or
> taking partisan advantage. It would be to me despicable for
> anybody to take political or partisan advantage on that misery.

The next witness to testify was Ethel Kage, a soft-spoken
woman from Reed City, Michigan, whose husband had been on
Social Security disability since 1974. Before that he had worked
for the Michigan Department of Transportation as a surveyor.

> MRS. KAGE: Friends had stopped over. When they left, my
> husband went out to bring our car around, and that's when it
> happened. He began honking the horn. I went out, and he was
> paralyzed on his right side, he could not see at all and was con-
> fused, and his speech was slurred. He had had a stroke.

The Kages applied for and received Social Security disability
without any problems. In 1981, however, the benefits were
abruptly terminated. Mrs. Kage then gave a revealing account
of how callous the bureaucratic process can be.

> MRS. KAGE: We received a Notice of Disability Examination
> Form on April 21. We received the Notice of Pending Cessation
> Form on May 14, saying that they were advising the Social Secu-
> rity Administration to cease payments within the two-month
> frame. We heard nothing from the Social Security Administra-
> tion itself until July 30, saying they were discontinuing our
> payments with the July payment. We had no previous notice

from the Social Security Administration that they were accepting the report of the Disability Determination Service.

On August 10, I sent the reexamination request in. On September 25, I sent additional data in from the doctors to support our claim.

On October 8, I called the Social Security office in Mt. Pleasant to find out—we had heard nothing—that they had received our request or anything at that time. Mrs. Wilson in that office said she would return my call after checking the file. I never received a call.

A week later, I called the Social Security office, and she said they had requested the file from Baltimore and as soon as it was received she would send it to Traverse City. She sent us additional forms that we needed to sign. I signed them and sent them back.

On October 30, I again called the regional office and asked what the status was, because we still had heard nothing. And she reported that the files had not been sent out from Baltimore. It was tied up in their computer process somehow, and they did not get the file.

All this time, we had been without any income. And Dick had been in the hospital. He had a toe that was gangrenous, and they thought it was going to have to come off. Fortunately, antibiotics stopped it at that time, so he only spent a week's stay in there.

I sent that additional information, also, to the Social Security Administration. By November 5, I still had heard nothing. That is when I contacted Senator Levin and our other representatives for our district.

On November 25, we received another Notice of Disability Examination Form from the Disability Determination in Traverse City, setting another appointment with the same doctor in Mt. Pleasant for another visual exam that we had gone through before.

Two days after that, Dick died. He took sick on Thanksgiving evening, and by seven o'clock the next day he was dead. He had two massive heart attacks.

I talked to the doctor on Monday who performed an autopsy. He gave me the results. And he said at that time that the pressures that he sustained, the stress from this cessation of benefits, was definitely a contributing factor to his death.

I called the Disability Determination Service to tell them that we would not be keeping the appointment and why, that Dick had died. And they made no comment whatsoever. They just said, "All right," and hung up.

I think I would like to speak to that, because any time people are working with people and trying to be helping people, I think there could be a little compassion shown.

Through Senator Levin's work on our behalf, we received a

letter and a phone call at the end of January saying that our
Social Security disability was being reinstated from the time that
it was cut off until Dick's death. We received nothing from the
Social Security Disability Determination or anyone else until
April 5, no correspondence saying, "We have received your re-
quest and it is being processed." We got nothing.

CHAIRMAN: Mrs. Kage, one of the reasons I suggested that
perhaps it would be a wise policy to have a face-to-face interview
at the very initial stage is to try and deal with that very problem.
In this case, when Social Security talks about us as a society,
we've moved to the age of the computer, all we have to do is
factor in the age, benefits, when they began, entitlements, push a
button and out comes a sheet. And that's not good enough.
Then they do the same thing, and they say, "Here are 40 cases or
440,000 cases. Now, we're going to determine how many people
should be continued and how many should be discontinued."
Again, there's no face-to-face dealing with those people.

You look at the file and you look at the docket report, but you
never see the person. And in an effort to insulate the hearing
examiner from the passions of the people, we calcify our indifference. We just remove people from the process and deal with
it on a file-by-file, number-by-number basis. People like you and
your husband fall through the cracks in the computer. That's
what happens.

MRS. KAGE: It's interesting, I think, to note that the same
doctors who first supported our disability claim and whose reports were accepted, those same doctors were completely ignored on the review.

Dr. Viney, who had been our doctor for some 17 to 20 years,
states in his letter: "I believe that the disability determination
service standards for disability are erroneous, false, and mis-
leading.

"When a physician who has been entirely in charge of a patient's medical care states that a patient is totally disabled, it
seems totally unrealistic and completely ridiculous for any
physician seeing him one time on a brief examination to coun-
termand a statement of disability on the part of an experienced
physician on the basis of a single visual field determination. On
Mr. Kage's residual vision, he was claimed to be no longer disabled and was directed to return to work by the Disability Determination Service."

I note with interest Senator Pryor's question on this very
thing, whether the family physician's reports were considered or
whether it was strictly for the government doctor. In our case, it
was strictly the government doctor.

Senator Levin then asked to comment further on that first letter from Social Security.

> SENATOR LEVIN: It keeps you in the dark. It treats you like a child, to your own detriment, because ultimately what's happening to you is that you're in the process of being cut off the rolls.
>
> What's also happening, not only are you not told that you're going to have to prove all over again that you're disabled, but you're going to have to prove it according to new rules, and that's a fundamental unfairness as well.
>
> Finally, after all that is done to you without adequate knowledge, you may then appeal. Most of the people who are wise enough or informed enough or whatever to appeal, or are alive to appeal, are going to win. But during that nine-to-12-month period of that appeal, they're going to lose and they're going to lose hard because they're going to be cut off the rolls. Benefits will not be paid during tht period of appeal, although two thirds of the people appealing are going to win.
>
> I can't get that fact out of my craw. No government, it seems to me, should tolerate that kind of injustice. It's a massive injustice.
>
> I'm not a doctor, but let me read what a doctor said, and doctors don't say things like this very easily. He says, after your husband was notified that he was now capable of working and in the process of attempting to do so, that "under the stress created by the termination of his disability benefits, Mr. Kage had an acute myocardial infarction and died."
>
> Now, I've been to a lot of doctors in a lot of courts, and know doctors do not readily reach those kinds of conclusions. . . . Multiply this one case by hundreds of thousands of cases and we have an added dimension; but in one very real case, most real to you, you're familiar with it, we have a doctor who said that under the stress created by the termination of his disability benefits and attempting to work because he was totally incapable, he had a heart attack and died.
>
> This doctor says, and his rage comes through the letter not as well as it would in person, but my gosh, he said, "I don't care who up there realizes that I feel this way. I will say it now and I will say it publicly, that this service is a disastrous failure. I don't care who up there knows it."
>
> I think these letters should be made part of the record, not just as to what they say as to a specific case, but also because of the frustration and rage that's reflected in here.
>
> By the way, Mrs. Kage, would your husband have liked to have worked, if he could?

MRS. KAGE: Would he have liked to have *worked?* Very definitely. He sat home for seven years, confined. It was very frustrating to him.

There were two other witnesses of note that morning in May—Kathleen Grover and Jonathan Stein, both of them attorneys experienced in disability litigation. Ms. Grover noted the difficulty of interpreting the Social Security Administration's guidelines for determining pain and impairment. She noted a particularly glaring case of a 36-year-old man who had had three disc operations on his back. None of them had been successful. The only medical evidence in this claimant's file were from the treating orthopedic surgeon and the neurosurgeon who performed the consultation. Both physicians claimed him to be totally disabled with a very poor prognosis and neither one recommended any further treatment. Based solely on this medical evidence, the claimant had been denied continuing benefits.

MS. GROVER: The list of impairments also fail to deal with persons who have multiple severe problems, none of which are in the specific listing but when taken together cause the person to be totally disabled. These people simply cannot be fairly adjudicated under the list of impairments, and yet at the first two levels of review, that is the only criterion applied to determining the degree of impairment. These are the people who will never fit within the list of impairments and the strict instructions listed by the state agency. They will always be terminated from benefits when their claims are reviewed. In most instances benefits will be reinstated, but only after pursuing the full administrative procedure. This process means an average of 10 to 18 months without benefits.

A striking example is a middle-aged woman who suffers from residuals from a stroke as well as a heart condition and circulatory problems. Again, the only evidence in the file was from the claimant's treating physician, who stated that the claimant was totally disabled and that the condition had deteriorted during the period of review. This claimant was denied benefits until she appeared at the hearing. She was without benefits for 20 months, during which time she lost her home and car because of her inability to remain current on payments. This woman's disability condition stems not from one impairment but rather from several, no one of which meets the criteria on the list of impairments. Because she is disabled by many, rather than one impairment, she will never be found disabled at the initial two stages of review.

Problems with the high volume of reviews ordered by the Social Security Administration were further articulated by Mr. Stein—particularly the cursory review of evidence. The state adjudication process could only be described, he said, as "arbitrary and completely failing in due process." The Pennsylvania Office of Vocational Rehabilitation, which oversees the DD agency in Pennsylvania, has called the process "dehumanizing and frenzied."

MR. STEIN: Which brings me to my second point, that the state agencies, under guidelines from SSA, are totally excluding treating physician medical evidence. The high volume of cases causes the state adjudicators to cut corners and not even to seek out such evidence.

An example in Pennsylvania is a policy that they won't even write to VA Hospital doctors to get evidence. In one case, Robert Astrove, a 60-year-old client, a World War II veteran, with multiple disabilities, including severe arthritis, angina, high blood pressure, diabetes and a psychiatric condition, had two treating physicians at a VA Hospital, a neuropsychiatrist and an orthopedist. He found out that the DD agency wouldn't even write to them because if they did their explanation was the processing time was so severe on them that they couldn't wait to get treating physician evidence from any VA doctor.

So as a matter of policy, so that every veteran in this practice being reviewed in our area would be subjected to this policy. Their treating physicians at VA were ignored.

We have heard, of course, this morning [the deputy director of Social Security] gloat over his processing time goals, but he never revealed at what cost those goals resulted.

Not all of Social Security's disability cases, of course, involve termination of benefits. Many people have trouble with the initial application.

Take the case of Christine Garrettson.

In May 1976, everything seemed to be coming up right for Christine. She had just graduated from a vocational course in bookkeeping and accounting, and her husband, Mark, had a good job as a welder for a steel construction company in Baltimore. Married for three years, living in a small home in the blue-collar suburb of Glen Burnie, the Garrettsons were beginning to think their luck had changed. It was about time. Mark and Christine had worked hard since their teen years, and even after they met in high school in Glen Burnie they often had to postpone dates because they both had jobs—Mark at a factory and Christine as a teller at a drive-in theater. Mark's father had died only a year before, and Mark did not know if he would ever get over that; the two of them had been very close. And Christine's mother had been in the hospital for major surgery three times in eighteen months, and the doctors couldn't say how long she would live. Christine and Mark wanted to start planning a family. They hoped that Christine's mother would live long enough to see her first grandchild. The thought of a new family excited them in other ways. After one more Christmas alone together, they would be able to share the rest of their lives with their children. Sometimes they even thought of retirement.

There were some beautiful days in May 1976—clear, bright, sunny and warm, with none of the oppressive mugginess that comes later and characterizes Maryland summers. On May 15 it had rained but now, a day later, the streets were mostly dry and Christine was tooling around the neighborhood on the little Honda motorcycle she had managed to save enough money for, and which she rode when Mark was away at work and there was little in the house for her to do. Out on the motorcycle, she had a chance to think about their plans for the future and about some things in the past.

Her mind wandered back five years. She had had to deal with a difficult romantic dilemma: Mark had been her high-school sweetheart, but when school was over they had begun to drift apart. Christine had taken another job, as a secretary and receptionist for a used-car dealership, where she met Bob Henley, one of the owners. He seemed to have everything that spelled success and excitement. He was a smooth talker and he was even going to get a master's degree in business administration by going to night school. He was a college graduate, ambitious, likely to be very wealthy—and Mark was still living at home, going to school to be a welder, thinking no farther than across the street.

The courtship had lasted only five weeks. In August 1971, when Christine was 21, she married Bob, 34, and she was gloriously happy. She was also—she would realize later—very naive. Bob was always at the office, and he seemed to have little interest in her or what she wanted to do with her life. The marriage ended in court with a divorce decree in her favor.

For Christine, the saying that a second marriage is the triumph of hope over experience could not have been more true. Mark was much more of a husband to her.

It was probably her daydreaming that caused the accident. As Christine turned a corner she did not see the puddle of water in the road, and by the time she hit the puddle, at about

30 miles per hour, it was too late. The helmet she wore was of little use. The motorcycle slipped out from under her, as if it were attached to a rope tied to a pole at the other end of the street and had been yanked away. The motorcycle slid and caught her leg, wrenching her body around with it, and dragged her along for about 25 feet before finally coming to rest. The whole accident could not have taken more than 10 seconds.

She regained consciousness after an hour in the hospital emergency room. The doctors did not give her the word until Mark had arrived, having been called off his construction site: The accident had done more than tear her clothes and skin— there was also extensive neurological damage. Christine Garrettson was paralyzed on one side. She would not be able to move her right arm, and flexibility in her right leg would be minimal at best. The prognosis was not good; the damage could not be repaired. The doctor, a nurse at his side, began quietly talking about wheelchairs, her stay in the hospital, physical therapy to keep the arm and leg from atrophy. When the tragedy finally dawned on her, Christine began to cry. She did not stop sobbing for two days, no matter how long Mark held her and told her it would be all right.

She would eventually learn how to dress herself again, how to move about and to cope. It was an entirely new existence, with an entirely new set of plans. What she and Mark would do now would have to be taken day by day. Little else could be said or done. They fully expected that Christine's long-term participation in the Social Security program—her contributions from the time she began working at the age of sixteen—would at least help pay for medical expenses and provide her with a monthly disability check. There should be no problem with that, they thought, once the claim forms were sent into the district office.

That was in 1976. Christine was confined to home, where she watered her plants, read, watched TV, sometimes moved about in the kitchen trying to make dinner on stoves and countertops that made her feel like a six-year-old again. It was not a kitchen made for someone who had to be in a sitting position all the time. *Nothing* was! Sometimes it got to be too much. She tried walking, but she could not keep her balance. Taking six steps in a row was a major accomplishment, moving across the room on two legs a victory. Going down the stairs was a task to be performed under only the gravest of circumstances: The dangers of falling were just too great. But the worst part of all was the waiting.

For four years, there were no Social Security disability benefits. Every month Christine tried to contact somebody, but either her phone calls were not returned or she was told that her case was being looked into. Nothing more. She had to postpone medical treatments. She wanted to get into more extensive physical therapy, to enroll in a course designed to help people deal with permanent disability. It took nearly all the money the young couple had to fix up the car so that Christine could drive it and to pay for lessons in driving a specially modified automobile. Now she could visit her mother, but without the use of her right arm she could find little employment. Concentrating on anything beyond meeting medical expenses and trying to make dinner, she thought, would be so much easier if those benefits would finally come through. She could not imagine why she was being singled out, or what the Social Security Administration could possibly be doing with her case after four long years.

Then another blow: Mark awoke one day to find that he was urinating blood. It was a fundamental shock; after everything else, he thought he had some terrible cancer and was going to die. The Garrettsons barely had the funds to pay for the expensive series of tests, but to their relief it was determined that Mark had developed a relatively minor dysfunction of one of his kidneys. No operation would be needed, but a strict diet—and an extended period of home rest—were recommended to prevent a kidney failure of the kind that would require costly dialysis treatment. Mark had to leave his job as a welder, with no guarantee he'd be able to get it back.

This time, however, the Social Security Administration came through. Within three weeks of the official report on Mark's disability, he began to receive supplemental security income checks—each one for $208.20. Every month, without fail, they came in. They were hardly enough to pay for all the expenses, but they helped. And Christine's mother appeared to be getting better. As much as Mark and Christine knew that he would have to go back to work, perhaps on a less strenuous schedule, they enjoyed that summer of 1980 and the opportunity to live it, in a way, like a summer vacation from school. But not really, with Christine in a wheelchair, Mark bedridden with his kidney ailment, and the bills never-ending. Strange what a few years would do, Mark would say. Christine thought things would be a little better if her own disability payments would finally arrive.

By the fall of 1979 Mark Garrettson was well enough to begin looking for welding work. Although homebuilding was at a near standstill, the office-construction business was still moving along, and construction foremen knew that good welders are as critical to an operation as they are hard to find. By the end of the year Mark had been hired by a firm in the process of building warehouses and office buildings in the industrial corridor along U.S. Route 1 between Baltimore and Washington. It was even closer to home than his previous job in Baltimore had been. He went back to work in January 1980.

Christine, although she knew they could use the money, decided to tell the Social Security office that Mark was no longer eligible for SSI benefits. She did not want to go to jail for defrauding the federal government. Now if they could only work on her own case. The Social Security Administration told her that they would discontinue SSI for Mark Garrettson.

But the checks kept coming. Repeated phone calls would not stop them, nor letters to SSA. It seemed like something out of a twisted administrative fairy tale: Woman in wheelchair denied disability benefits while husband who is working continues to receive checks for being out of a job. Christine had been putting the checks in the mail and just sending them back, hoping that their return would trigger something within the massive headquarters of Social Security—just twenty minutes from her own home. The irony was not lost on her. It increased when Mark started to receive even larger checks.

The problem seemed to be with work records. SSI benefits help the aged, blind and disabled, but with no work history required—if there is a temporary disability, there is no need to supply complete work records. The benefits are discontinued once work begins again. But in Christine's case—a total disability—there is a requirement for a complete work history, with proof that she worked for ten quarters in occupations covered by Social Security in which she made payments to the system. She had been working at least that long, but some of her records apparently had been lost.

Christine, now 30, considered hiring a lawyer, but she wondered whether he would be able to accomplish anything for her that all of her calls and letters and so forth had not. And she hardly has the resources to fight a system that claims her records are incomplete. How does one make one's life complete?

Finally, sadly, the Garrettsons decided they would have to give up their home. They could not be sure if the benefits Christine claimed but was not receiving would have helped with the finances enough for her to get her medical treatment and maybe get a job that would allow them to maintain their two-bedroom place in Glen Burnie. Now it had gone way past the point of uncertainty. Mark's job was giving him a steady salary, but it was not enough. Christine had $3,000 worth of medical bills outstanding, including $2,000 owed to an orthopedist. The mortgage and utility bills were climbing. And in September 1980 she fell down the stairway—one of the worst falls she had. She knew that she must have cracked a couple of ribs—it hurt for weeks afterward—but she could not even think of what the medical bills would be or how they would afford it. The fall put her in bed for nearly four weeks. It looked like another tense Thanksgiving, and now one with a change of address. So the precious home was sold and the Garrettsons moved into an apartment with no steps.

Social Security had now become a frustration beyond endurance. The only response she got from the agency was a snappy phone call from a claim representative wondering why the agency was not notified of the Garrettsons' change of address so that the checks for Mark could continue. That was it. She decided that something else had to be done. This time she called the local newspaper, the *Baltimore Evening Sun*. Within a week a reporter came to talk to her. Soon a story appeared, with her picture, entitled, "Stop the Checks, She Pleads; Social Security Sends a Raise." It gave details of her story: the benefit checks for Mark and none for Christine. She was quoted as saying, "This can't be right. Something must be wrong."

At about this time Christine also decided to meet with a representative of the office of Paul Sarbanes, Maryland's junior senator. She found Dolores Rottman, one of the senator's legislative assistants, and told her the entire story. Rottman worked on the case for two solid months. Finally, in December 1980, near to Christmas, the news came through: Christine's file had been straightened out, and her disability checks would be forthcoming. It was news she never thought she'd hear.

It appeared that one of the jobs she had worked in had not been credited to her because her employer had scrambled her Social Security number—on *his* records. A painstaking search of all the records of each of her former employers had unearthed that difficulty, but no one at Social Security could figure out why more than two years of Christine's work record was not available in her file. It was Dolores Rottman who came up with a solution to the puzzle: Her W-2 forms would reflect Christine's name from her previous marriage and would not be filed under Garrettson. The computer, looking at that name only, would not have any record of her work history under the name of Henley!

Christine and Mark finally had something to celebrate after the pain and the sadness of seeing Christine face the rest of her life in a wheelchair and forced to give up a profession she wanted to build a future on. And, though the celebration could not take place in the home they started out with, at least now the medical expenses could be covered—and then some. Moreover, Christine would also have the option of two years of retroactive Medicare insurance—another benefit discovered by Dolores Rottman and Senator Sarbanes' office but not by anybody at the Social Security Administration.

By the end of the fall, Mark's case also had been straightened out and Christine no longer had to send back checks improperly issued to him.

Now she could keep the checks that came in the mail.

A cynic might say that the secret to gaining Social Security benefits is not being eligible, but being persistent.

Josephine Ashworth had been a seamstress all her life. Even as a girl she loved to help her mother make family clothes. It was a vocation of joy she carried with her through all the years she spent at the garment plant in Tiverton, Rhode Island. The factories of many major garment companies are scattered throughout the New England area. In some population centers they remain the largest employer. The International Ladies' Garment Workers' Union began in this New England area and is still the strongest union there, providing some of the best benefit packages available to union members, including a very positive retirement plan. But since the advent of Social Security, the retirement plan has also been keyed to Social Security payments, or at least to Social Security records.

Thus, when members of the ILGWU retire, they must obtain an earnings report from the Social Security office in order to become eligible for retirement benefits from the union. It is usually a routine matter, ready for the process of reviewing the benefit application weeks, sometimes months before the date of actual retirement. For steady or fixed-income employees like Josephine Ashworth, who has been shop steward for the past ten years, the estimate of earnings until the actual retirement date should also have run smooth as silk. She was finally ready to retire in July 1981. She planned a trip to see her family in Boston and to celebrate the Fourth of July in grand style. All it would take was the earnings report from the Social Security office, which she figured would be ready in May 1981.

But by June there was no report to be had and none in sight. Josephine, not the sort of person to worry a lot, took action.

Hers was the New England spirit: After all, she was from a line of people descended from some of the first settlers there. When it appeared that the Social Security Administration did not know where or how to find her records, she called the local office of her senator, John Chafee. She was put through to Vicki Riccio, a caseworker.

Josephine said that she had put her money into the system all those years and the least it could do was give her one form when she requested it. She had asked for the piece of paper on January 14, 1981, and her request was acknowledged on February 7, 1981. But it was now June. Something was wrong, and the senator's office in Washington might be able to find out what it was. The message was simple and direct: An earnings report form was needed from SSA at Josephine's retirement on July 1. That's it and that's all.

Thus began a series of phone calls among Josephine, Vicki and a woman at SSA, Carol Sanders, who was one of the claim representatives for the division handling work records and earnings reports at the huge office complex in Woodlawn. Josephine would call every other day to assure herself that people at the local or Washington office of the senator were working on her problem. And Vicki would call Carol three times a week to see what, if anything, was happening.

It would go on like that for nearly a month. At first Carol Sanders informed Vicki Riccio that the computers had broken down. Then Carol said that the claim numbers were not with Josephine's union's request for the form and that they would have to be traced. Then she said that she would be out of the office for a couple of days and that no one else would be able to take over the case until she returned. Then she said that the dates of the authorization and request were wrong and would have to be changed. Then she said that the files seemed to be located in another office and that she would send a requisition through. Then she said that the third page of the earnings report had been located but that the first two pages were yet to be found—but that all should be straightened out in a couple of weeks.

Sometimes Vicki's calls were not returned. Sometimes Carol was out of the office, at a meeting. Sometimes she was gone for the day. Often she was in but could only say, "Nothing yet, I am still checking on it." Vicki wondered if she should bother making further calls. She thought that if Josephine alone had been calling the Baltimore office, her phone bills might be higher than her retirement benefits. But she knew, too, that if

Josephine alone had been calling, she would be just another customer among many thousands who had complaints, that she was dealing with a superagency charged with processing miles of records and roomfuls of paper and forms. At least Vicki's station at the senator's office gave an air of authority to the request for the earnings-report form, and Josephine alone would not have been able to generate that.

By July 5—the retirement date for Josephine had come and gone—the calls still had not produced results. There had been several false fits and starts: On June 16 Carol had said she'd located the original request and it should already have been honored but was not and it would be "sent through to Central Operations." The next day, though, all she could say was that "it's in the computer" and that it "should be spit out any day."

Finally, on July 14, Carol called Vicki in the senator's office. Carol had news. The report has been found, completed and was on its way to Carol's desk. As soon as it reached her she would call Vicki and mail it to Josephine and to the union. The next day Carol called again: She had the earnings report in hand and would mail it that day. Vicki called Josephine with word that retirement with full benefits was no longer an expectation fading into a nightmare. The report was on its way.

By the third week in July Josephine Ashworth had the simple piece of paper that had been requested of Social Security way back in January. On August 4, Josephine walked into Senator Chafee's office and presented Vicki Riccio with an African violet plant in a brightly colored vase—a symbol, she said, of Vicki's help, the light that shone through the murkiness where 100 million people were each no more than nine digit numbers. Josephine said she could have sent a plant, too, to Social Security, but it would have to be one that could live in an office without sunlight.

Sometimes Social Security pays too much. Overpayment problems necessitate even more detailed record checking that wrong-program payments or the loss of necessary forms. The entire case history may have to be reviewed to discover the source of the overpayment. At times in such a review the very eligibility of the benefit recipient may come into question. Often the SSA requires a hearing in which the beneficiary is asked to justify the payments being made to him. And it is at these times, particularly, that he may need the support of his elected representative.

Edward Morrill's son Paul is not what one would call a problem child. He just has never seemed really to enjoy school. By the time he was beginning high school, his father had already retired from his job as a lumber-mill worker.

Paul loved lumber, which is still a big business in Cherryville, Oregon, in Clackamas County. He felt part of the history of his home state, a pioneer with a strong desire to keep the land as it was found, as much as it's possible. He loved to be able to look up and see Mount Hood and to meander along Oregon's long coastline. For Paul, formal education was secondary to forestry and camping and hunting.

But Paul Morrill is receiving education benefits from Social Security. With his mother unable to work (since she is caring for other children in the family) and his father retired, Paul is eligible for benefits to help offset the cost of formal education. But when he is missing from school for weeks at a time, or even for a term, the Social Security Administration is notified. Whatever checks were sent during that period are deemed to be an overpayment. This has been going on for two years, but the checks keep coming.

Meanwhile, Edward Morrill has been notified that his retirement benefits are also subject to review. The SSA wanted to know more about the disability problem that forced him into retirement five years early. It had to do with a lumber saw, the sort that can cut whole timbers in half. Edward Morrill does not like to talk about that accident. Suffice it to say it was an awful experience which nearly cost him his left leg. Only quick action by his coworkers, and the fact that a hospital was a mere 30-minute drive away, at 75 miles per hour, prevented an amputation. But the reports as to his accident and earnings records keep getting reevaluated. He received several letters from Social Security as to the nature of his benefits, and in 1975 he was finally informed that they had been "refigured" and that he would now be receiving a lower monthly check, together with some bureaucratic hints that he would be liable for the overpayments supposedly made.

Edward Morrill's own attempts to get some satisfactory results on these cases met with little success. Finally, he went to the Portland office of Senator Mark Hatfield and explained the problem. The explanation took a lot less time than straightening it out. The senator's aides worked on the case for more than three months, dealing with district and regional offices from Oregon to New York and finally with the headquarters' office in Baltimore. The most nagging problem was tracing all the times that Paul had been in and out of school. In the end, the

Social Security Administration refused to take the position that it had made overpayments in Paul's case, but at least it was determined that the conflicting information was not the result of any deliberate act on the part of Edward Morrill or of his son—Paul just hadn't wanted to go to school.

As to his own benefits, several payment centers had to be contacted before an accurate calculation could be made of the supposed overpayments for Edward Morrill's retirement benefits. They came to $1,200. Due at least in part to the work of the senator's office, this amount has been waived by Social Security: The agency will not attempt to hold Edward Morrill or his employers liable for any of it. Edward Morrill would receive a lower monthly check, but at least his retirement benefits from the Social Security Administration are secure.

Ku Ling-hei is ordinarily a passive man, a demeanor common to the Chinese peasant he once was. Born in Soochow in 1918 and orphaned at the age of five, the lines of his well-weathered face reflect the hard life he's led. Ku is now a blue-collar worker whose slight build is kept all the more trim by the rigors of survival in a new land: the United States of America. When he says the words he smiles, his face gleaming beneath thin strands of neatly combed gray hair, and he does not think of hardship and toil.

Ku Ling-hei was looking forward to his retirement. The mortgage on his small home was nearly paid off, and he would have more time to spend with his wife and four grandchildren. The house is on a quiet street in a neighborhood that used to be considered suburban but has long since been part of urban Detroit. All of the houses on the block are either white clapboard or shingle, and many of them have lawns littered with children's toys.

It was late summer, the afternoon sunlight filtered by oak and sycamore, the ground lime-colored and the air heavy. Ku's daughter was preparing supper in the kitchen while her young son hung onto her apron with a grip that blanched his fist. In the den, reclining on a threadbare sofa, Ku sipped ice water and mused about the circumstances that had brought him to the United States and to a dream that was almost shattered a year earlier, when he discovered an error he had made in his Social Security records.

He had only a vague recollection of his parents. They died when he was too young to form any lasting impression of them. For most of his childhood his sister Leichi looked after him, tenuously holding together the family of seven brothers and sisters. She was the oldest, he the second youngest.

It was a way of life in China, where age—at least as it is measured in cold numbers—does not seem to matter as much as it does here. Leichi inherited the responsibilities of their parents when she was a teenager. The fishermen who hired Ku and his brothers to haul their heavy nets and their buckets laden with carp cared little about how old their employees were. All that mattered was earnestness and strength.

As time passed, Ku grew tired of the fisherman's life and yearned for something better. He was a young man in search of adventure. From Soochow the port of Shanghai was a modest trek, and he headed for the bustling wharves of the big city with the idea of securing work on a freighter. But the year was 1938: Japan was menacing East Asia, and navigation of the Pacific shipping channels was becoming perilous. For Ku, the protective shoals of his boyhood were far behind him; the world was engulfed in war. He signed on. In 1942, his ship was sunk on its way to San Francisco.

American rescuers brought the surviving crew to the United States, where most of them, including Ku, stayed. For three years he worked as a milling-machine apprentice in a New York repair shop, until in 1945 the Immigration and Naturalization Service issued him an ultimatum: Join the military or face deportation. As a noncitizen, Ku had little recourse. But he faced a dilemma. He had no desire to return to China, a wartorn country, and at twenty-seven he was ineligible for service in the U.S. military. So Ku did what many men had done in similar situations: He lied about his age. Of the armed services, the Navy attracted him more, for his experience was at sea. Having no birth certificate, there was no way the Navy could discover his real age. Consequently, in September 1945, Ku joined the Navy at—according to naval records—the age of twenty. After two months of Navy duty, a tour that seemed to satisfy the authorities at INS, Ku headed back to civilian working life, honorable discharge in hand. But his new age lingered in government records. To camouflage the discrepancy he continued to represent himself to government authorities as being seven years younger than his true age. When he became a United States citizen in 1948, his naturalization certificate carried the altered birthdate; so eventually did his Social Security card and driver's license.

For years the lie persisted, mingling with Ku's identity, but it gave him little reason to be concerned. He settled in a small southern town and began to raise a family. His younger brother and older sister, the only members of his immediate family who survived the war, immigrated to the United States and became U.S. citizens. His children grew into adulthood, married and began to raise families of their own. Ku knew that he was getting up in years, and at age 63 he contemplated retirement.

But suddently it struck him: As far as the government was concerned he was only 56. Unless something was done, he would not be eligible for full Social Security benefits for another seven years.

He did not know where to begin to correct the mistake. The error, after all, was his own, and it caused him some embarrassment. Although lying about his age had seemed a proper thing to do at the time, he never anticipated it would cause anyone trouble. He had to lie to join the Navy. He served well. He was not sure what would happen to him when the government found out. Were his actions illegal? Would he be punished?

Ku's son-in-law, who was born and raised in the United States, doubted very much that Ku would be in serious trouble. The son-in-law offered to call his United States senator on Ku's behalf, and he did so. Over the telephone, a caseworker took down the necessary information and said she would look into resolving the problem. That was really all there was to it— except for the paperwork. The caseworker found out that the change in government records could be made if Ku could prove his actual age to the Navy and to the Social Security Administration. Because the error originated in his naval records, the first step was to arrange for those to be corrected. The lack of a birth certificate could be surmounted by means of affidavits made out by Ku, his brother and his sister. The caseworker mailed Ku a form titled "Application for Correction of Naval Records." In a follow-up letter, his senator explained that "there are often lengthy delays in processing this type of application through the Board of Naval Corrections, and I would like to be of assistance in seeing that it receives expeditious action."

Ku and his son-in-law began to prepare the paperwork. His brother wrote, "I was born on August 3, 1921. It was always told that Ku was three years older than me. The first I can remember, my brother was much larger than I was and much older. He started school a long time before I did. He would do a lot of helping with my bringing up. I remember how he would help me talk and do things for myself. He has always been my big brother."

Ku's sister similarly explained the facts in her own affidavit. "I was born on October 3, 1909," she wrote. "I know of my own personal knowledge that my brother Ku Ling-hei was born on March 14, 1918. At the time he was born I was eight years of age and all of us were so proud of him. We did not bring any papers to America, so I had to write all this information down to keep a record. This record is all in Chinese and was made by me after I came here."

In his own affidavit, Ku admitted to the lie that kept him in the United States, explaining, "I wanted to stay in the U.S. and I heard that I could join the Navy if I wasn't too old. I lied about my age so I could be sure I could get in. I reduced my age by seven years." On his Application for Correction of Naval Records he wrote: "I made an honest mistake in my birth date. I wanted so badly to join the Navy and I did not know it was important to keep my true birth date. In China, it was not important. I know now that it is important in the U.S. I made the mistake and did not know it would cause trouble."

After contacting the Navy by telephone and explaining the problem, the caseworker sent Ku's application, along with the affidavits, to the Naval Personnel Command. Attached was a letter signed by the senator, urging action. "Because of my desire to be of all possible assistance to my constituent," it read, "I would appreciate your giving his request every consideration, of course within existing guidelines."

The Navy was convinced of the authenticity of Ku's evidence and proved cooperative. Normally, processing such an application through the Board of Naval Corrections takes as long as a year. But with the aid of the senator's letter, Ku's records were corrected in about six weeks. All that remained was to send the corrected naval record to the Social Security Administration.

At the huge headquarters complex in Baltimore, it sometimes takes months before even relatively simple cases can be unraveled. Ku Ling-hei would recognize such delay, perhaps, as the price to be paid when "providing for the general welfare" is a billion-dollar business.

GETTING THE MOST OUT OF SOCIAL SECURITY

What a Caseworker Would Advise

When writing to your senator or congressman, be certain to include your full name, address and Social Security number. If you are writing about benefits derived through a deceased spouse or parent, note his or her name, Social Security number and date of death. If you are writing about a disability claim, mention the date it was filed or (if being appealed) the dates of the original adverse decision and the appeal.

Many people try to locate an old friend or missing relative through the Social Security Administration—which will not release addresses. The best that can be hoped is that the SSA will forward a letter to the missing person's last known address, a courtesy that is afforded if the reasons for locating that person are compelling enough under agency guidelines. Write directly to the Social Security Administration, explaining why contact is imperative, and enclose an unsealed letter to the addressee. If it is forwarded, it is accompanied by a notice that the addressee is not required to respond. Likewise, delivery of the letter is not acknowledged by Social Security. The lesson to be learned is that not even a court order can force open Social Security records.

KEY FACTS

SOCIAL SECURITY ADMINISTRATION
6401 Security Boulevard
Baltimore, MD 21235
Phone: (301) 594-1234

When Social Security was established in 1937 to ensure minimal subsistence for millions of unemployed workers still suffering the effects of the Great Depression, it applied mainly to laborers in industry and commerce—that is, it covered only about 60 percent of all working Americans. Since then, the growth in the population and labor force has caused both the program and the benefits paid under it to rise at a near-exponential rate. Coverage has been extended to self-employed persons, state and local government employees, household and farm employees, members of the armed forces, members of the clergy, families with dependent children, and persons with nonwork-related disabilities. In July 1940 there were 26.8 million workers covered by Social Security, as opposed to 19.6 million (42 percent) who were not. By 1978 the number of workers covered had risen to 91.1 million, with only 8.2 million (8 percent) not covered.

The panorama of benefits has also grown so that it presently includes at least eight major programs, including retirement insurance, survivors' insurance, disability insurance, Medicare for the elderly, supplemental security income, unemployment insurance and public assistance and welfare services.

Although Social Security is intended only as a replacement of a portion of earnings lost as a result of old age, disability, retirement or death (and, now, to cover a portion of expenses caused by illness for aged and/or handicapped persons), the program budget is staggering. As of June 1979, more than one of every seven Americans was receiving monthly Social Security benefit payments in some form—over 35 million beneficiaries in all. Total cash-benefit payments amounted to over $160 billion.

To be eligible for benefits, especially disability coverage or supplemental security income (SSI), a claimant must satisfy several requirements. If a claim is unfavorably reviewed and benefits denied, the applicant must submit to an administrative hearing to challenge the review. This generally calls for hiring an attorney and gathering evidence to demonstrate that the claim is valid and should be granted. Delays can take many months, even if the result of the hearing is to reverse the earlier decision. But the sheer size of the program often presents the biggest difficulties.

Social Security is administered by both the Social Security Administration (SSA) and the Health Care Financing Administration (HCFA). Each is part of the Department of Health and Human Services; in 1979 they accounted for roughly 60 percent of the department's total employees and 75 percent of its total expenditures. Even more important, they accounted for approximately 27 percent of total expenditures by the federal government. The Social Security Administration governs the old-age, survivors and disability insurance program, supplemental security income, and aid to families with dependent children. (Determination of eligibility for disability benefits is handled by state agencies under contract to SSA.) The Health Care Financing Administration governs Medicare—both hospital insurance and supplementary medical insurance—and Medicaid, a program providing hospital and medical expense benefits for the needy.

The Social Security Administration has some 1,325 district and branch offices in operation around the nation. They are supposed to issue Social Security cards, process benefit claims, provide information about the program and help resolve participants' problems. The local offices are supervised and assisted by ten regional offices. There are also about 30 "tele-service" centers, which give information and assistance by telephone if possible. The Social Security Administration's national headquarters are located in two primary locations near Baltimore—one in the downtown area and one in a sprawling suburban complex known as Woodlawn. Both feature huge glass-enclosed buildings housing thousands of workers and millions of miles of computer tape and information on benefit packages, personal data of participants, income figures and work histories. To operate these offices and administer the benefit programs there is a staff of more than 80,000 people, including about 20,000 in the central offices. The programs are so pervasive and far-reaching that they touch nearly everyone's lives, as the benefit packages continue to grow in size and complexity.

For further information, contact the Social Security Administration, 6401 Security Boulevard, Baltimore, MD 21235. Phone: (301) 594-1234.

☆ IV ☆

OLD SOLDIERS
AND PAPER BATTLES

As for us, our days of combat are over. Our swords are rust. Our guns will thunder no more. . . . Whatever of glory yet remains for us to win must be won in the council . . . never again in the field.

—OLIVER WENDELL HOLMES, JR.

Old soldiers never die, according to the familiar military proverb, they just fade away. Nevertheless, at the foot of the page on many letters from the Veterans Administration is printed another quotation, this one from Abraham Lincoln: "To care for him who shall have borne the battle, and for his widow, and his orphan." The VA had taken that quote as its motto; for millions of former servicemen, their families and survivors, VA benefits have helped to nurse them back to health, educate them for productive careers and assure that their old age will not be poverty-stricken. But because the Veterans Administration serves so many people, like Social Security it has also spawned a gigantic bureaucracy—one that deals more in forms than faces, is devoted more to procedure than to personalities. The tens or hundreds of thousands of veterans and their dependents who have been trapped in the maze of federal regulations or frustrated by the recalcitrance of unresponsive bureaucrats would probably find more appropriate the legend that appears on many other pieces of VA correspondence: "Show veterans's full name, VA file number and Social Security number on all correspondence." Abraham Lincoln never said that.

When people run up against a VA regulation that doesn't seem to fit their circumstances, or reach an impasse in negotiations with an unyielding administrator or VA office, they frequently turn to their elected representatives for assistance. Sometimes it comes to light that an individual has met all the criteria for benefits that are nevertheless denied them because of a misunderstanding between the applicant and the VA about the *sort* of benefits being applied for or the specific paperwork required.

This was the experience of Virginia Welles, a widow in Farmington, Maine, who applied to the Veterans Administration for survivors' benefits after her husband died in 1971. Oliver Welles had served in the Army for 25 years, and though his death was not service-connected, Mrs. Welles rightly believed that she was entitled to a pension. But when she wrote to her local VA office, she was told that she was eligible for nothing but a token payment for a gravestone.

Mrs. Welles had never applied for benefits based upon a service-connected death, in fact had specified that her husband's death was *not* service-connected. Nor was she told that in order to be considered for a pension for a nonservice-connected death she must complete two different VA forms (21-4100 and 21-8049). Instead, she continued to make inquiries in person at VA offices in her area, first in New York State and then—after 1973—in Maine. After seven frustrating years, she wrote to my congressional office asking for help.

We contacted the Togus, Maine, branch of VA, which explained that Mrs. Welles had never been considered for benefits because she had failed to submit the two necessary forms, but assured us that Mrs. Welles could file for benefits at any time. This she did, and—nearly eight years after her husband had died—her pension application was approved.

Veterans attending school on VA benefits often have difficulty satisfying bureaucrats that their programs of study meet the requirement set by law—that is, that they are full-time students in a degree-granting program. Robert Little, who retired from the Army after 28 years of service and enrolled in a program in French civilization at the Sorbonne, in Paris, found himself in this difficulty. He had fully expected to receive educational benefits, since the program led to a degree from a renowned university and conformed to VA requirements, but he was turned down. At my office's request, the VA reconsidered its initial decision and granted the benefits.

Another VA regulation pertaining to educational benefits requires that students attend all sessions of an academic year. If they don't, they lose their benefits during the period between terms. At many universities, however, offerings during the summer term may not be of use to students in specialized programs, or to those so far along in their education that they must take mostly specific courses in their major fields. This was the situation at the University of Maine several years ago, where a number of veterans discovered they would lose their VA benefits over the summer unless they enrolled full-time in not one but *two* summer sessions—even if these sessions offered them no useful courses.

Keith Morton's was a case in point. An upper-level student in electrical engineering, he found that there weren't enough courses in his field during the summer term to permit him to take a full load. But if he were to register for less than a full load or not attend the summer session, he would lose his benefits for the entire summer.

The University of Maine Veterans Association (UMVETS) turned to my office for help, and we were able to work out a compromise with the local VA office. Students who attended at least eight weeks of school at the university during the summer would receive benefits without interruption, as would students who attended a shorter session if their university considered them to be in full-time attendance. All others would receive partial benefits for the summer. UMVETS estimated that under this plan some 90 percent of their members would be able to qualify for full benefits.

The temporary loss of educational benefits would not ordinarily work a hardship on veterans, especially if they are able to find employment during periods of ineligibility. But for some people the checks they receive from the VA are their only means of support. When their benefits are cut off or their applications denied, they may be (quite sadly but literally) without the means to feed, clothe and shelter themselves.

One such man is Harold Norton, an aging citizen of Maine who lives alone in a modest cabin. He is unable to work due to a respiratory condition that has reduced the functioning of his lungs to about 10 percent of normal; for years, he has received a complete disability pension.

Harold Norton supplements his modest pension by finding and returning soft-drink bottles for the deposits. He has never thought of it as anything more than a sideline—in a good week he might earn $10. One day a photographer for the local paper, the *Kennebec Journal,* asked to take a few pictures. He told Norton they were for his personal use, and Norton believed him. But a few days later one of the photographs turned up in the *Journal* with a story that asserted that Norton made $4,000 a year scavenging for bottles.

As it happened, the article caught the eye of a VA administrator in the Togus, Maine, regional office, who immediately stopped paying benefits to Norton until the case could be investigated—thus leaving him with virtually no income.

Norton appealed to my office for help. A staffer was told that several weeks would pass before the necessary investigation could be started, and a much longer time before the determination of whether to restore Norton's benefits. However, when we explained Norton's dire plight, stressing his complete dependency on the VA pension, the VA officer agreed to expedite the process. Norton started to receive his VA checks again within three weeks.

Norton's condition makes it clear that he is unable to work, so his level of benefits can be incontrovertibly placed at 100 percent. But many people suffer from conditions that are much harder to assess. On the surface they seem physically healthy and well equipped for work, but they may be emotionally unable to seek and hold a job, or even—as in the case of a former Army WAC—unable to leave the house alone.

In 1955, Alice Smith, then a 19-year-old WAC, was raped by a group of servicemen at an Army base in Texas. They also threatened to kill her. She was so traumatized that she did not report the rape but instead tried to resume a normal life as if nothing had happened. She thought she had succeeded, after having married and raised a daughter, but Mrs. Smith has for years been beset by fears: of open spaces, of automobiles, of blood, of doctors and hospitals. She cannot leave her house unless someone accompanies her, and several years ago, after her husband died and her daughter went away to college, she became a virtual recluse.

For over 20 years, Mrs. Smith had tried to live as if nothing were wrong, but in 1977 she finally admitted she needed help. She began to undergo psychotherapy with a psychologist in Bangor, Maine, near her home. She came to understand that the trauma of her rape in 1955 had disabled her, and she applied for VA benefits. She was awarded compensation at the level of 50 percent disability, but since she cannot work, the payments do not permit her to meet her expenses while she tried to continue her rehabilitation. Mrs. Smith believes that the Army doctors who hospitalized her after she became despondent and attempted suicide in 1955 should have provided her with counseling she needed then. "I could be working now," she says, "but instead I can't even go out to buy myself a box of tea bags."

The case has already set precedents at the Veterans Administration, since veterans had not previously received benefits for noncombat traumas. But Mrs. Smith has persisted, appealing the initial ruling from the VA, and hopes that the Board of Veterans Appeals will increase the level of her disability payments to 100 percent.

If Mrs. Smith's case seems a rarity, that of Bill McFarland is much more familiar. A combat veteran of the Vietnam War, McFarland was diagnosed as suffering from "delayed-stress syndrome," characterized by symptoms of depression, feelings of guilt, difficulty sleeping, anxiety, alienation and mistrust of other people. During his combat service he had been wounded in the leg and head and was hospitalized at Walter Reed Army Hospital in Washington, D.C. When he was discharged from the service, he had a decoration for bravery, a small VA pension and a drug habit. He drifted around the country until he landed in prison in California for manslaughter. A prison psychologist recognized that McFarland was suffering delayed-stress syndrome and recommended that he be paroled.

McFarland was released. He settled in Colorado and, because he could not work, his VA benefits were increased to the level of complete disability. He married, took up residence in the mountain town of Hotchkiss, had a daughter and began to make friends. No one is sure what went wrong in the summer of 1981. He again showed signs of strain and—after learning that the VA was going to reevaluate his disability status—began to take large amounts of tranquilizers. Whatever the cause, as he was driving toward Denver, his van went out of control and crashed into a retaining wall. McFarland was crushed to death inside the crumpled van.

Many veterans are haunted by the arbitrary power of the VA to change and even cut off benefits completely. Once the final appeal within the VA has been exhausted, a dissatisfied applicant has no recourse. For several years, Senator Gary Hart has wanted to change that—to open up VA decisions to judicial review in cases where applicants disagree with the rulings in their cases. He has introduced a bill to that effect. This would guarantee the same rights to veterans that are now available to citizens who disagree with Social Security or IRS rulings. As Bill Holen, staff aide to Senator Hart and himself a Vietnam veteran, says, "This is a simple issue of justice, a constitutional rights issue. There are several court cases that call into question whether there is due process within the agency." It is impossible, of course, to say whether due process within the VA would have given McFarland the confidence that he would be treated fairly.

Everyone who meets John Ross notices his grin. Some find in the smile a reflection of his desire to please. Others (like Roger Berlin, the doctor who examined Ross in a Topeka, Kansas, mental hospital in 1966) have perceived it as a "worried" smile, an attempt to mask the fact that all is not well in his life.

According to Ross and many of those who have gotten to know him since he was in the Army in 1961 and 1962, his problems stem from an adverse reaction to nerve gases administered to him during a drug experiment for which he had volunteered. But it took him more than 15 years to convince the Veterans Administration that the psychological problems he had were the result of his reaction to the nerve gas GD.

When Ross was growing up in his hometown of Atchison, Kansas, in the northeastern corner of the state, what people found most remarkable about him was his persistence in the face of adversity. John's mother had deserted her husband and family in 1945, when he was four years old, the youngest of five children. His father obtained a divorce and placed John and one of his four brothers in an orphanage. About five months later, however, Ross returned to Atchison and lived with his mother until he volunteered for the draft upon graduation from high school.

From the time he was 12 years old, Ross had more or less supported himself by doing odd jobs around the neighborhood. Although he enjoyed school, he often stayed home because he was ashamed of the soiled, torn clothing he had to wear. He did not have many friends in school, nor was he a good scholar, but he was a good athlete and was determined to get his diploma.

John Ross's Pentecostal religious beliefs forbade him to bear arms, so when he was in the Army he volunteered for the Medical Corps. Because he felt that his status as a conscientious objector protected him from the risks that his comrades in the service would be compelled to take in the event of war, he volunteered for a medical experiment: In 1961 he was transferred to the Army Chemical Center at Edgewood, Maryland, to participate in a nerve-gas experiment.

Subjects in the experiment apparently were not screened beforehand to determine whether there were psychological or physical reasons to exclude them from a particular chemical experiment. Neither was it likely that they were warned beforehand about possible aftereffects (not that Ross would have asked to be excused if they had been). But it is almost certain the volunteers did not fully understand what had taken place.

Ross recalls, "They were testing nerve gases on me and something funny happened. My neck got all tight and my left arm wouldn't move." After being given an injection, Ross was able to resume control of his head and arm, but he continued to show signs of agitation and restlessness. He moved around constantly, squirming in his chair, changing position, pacing back and forth, even lying down on the floor. At times he anxiously expressed a desire to save the souls of his fellow soldiers; at other times he desperately asked the attending physician for help.

He was sent to Walter Reed Army Hospital in Washington, D.C., where he stayed for nearly three weeks. Doctors at Walter Reed found Ross to be mildly depressed and anxious, but they attributed his condition only tangentially to the nerve-gas injection. He rebounded quickly from the acute state of physical and psychological loss of control that he had displayed at Edgewood, although he continued to show signs of extreme religiosity, preaching to others and speaking of his desire to preach the Gospel. He also assisted the medical corpsmen assigned to the hospital and expressed a desire to return to his post and complete his tour of duty. His anxiety reaction was traced equally to his chaotic childhood and his reaction to the nerve gas. Finally, he was released from the hospital.

At the time, Ross was reluctant to apply for a medical discharge, fearing that it would besmirch his Army record and make it difficult for him to find civilian employment. It would be, he felt, as if he had been given a dishonorable discharge. He therefore returned to Fort Bliss, Texas, and was discharged soon after.

Ross had married his hometown girlfriend while he was still in the Army, and upon his discharge he returned to Atchison, where the first of his two daughters was born. He was able to find work, first in a nursing home, where he made use of the skills he learned in the Medical Corps, and later at the local foundry. Apparently he had abandoned his ambition to study for the ministry, but to all intents and purposes Ross's life was stable and unremarkable.

However, by the time the second child arrived, Ross and his wife had reached an impasse, one precipitated by his recurrent bouts of drinking, jealousy accompanied by sporadic attempts at infidelity, and several gestures of suicide. In the spring of 1966, after an argument, Ross's wife took their children and moved back with her parents. Ross turned on the gas and lay down on the living-room couch. He was found several hours later, barely alive, by his father- and brother-in-law. Ross claimed at the time that he did not wish to commit suicide but to prevent his wife from leaving him. In part to satisfy her wishes, he sought help at that time from the psychiatrists at Topeka State Hospital, but doctors there were unable to treat him. One of them did perceive great rage and apprehension, however. Although they were aware of the incident at Edgewood in 1961, they drew no connection between it and his chronically troubled state.

In 1966 Ross applied for VA benefits, but his application was eventually rejected after he missed a scheduled medical examination. He did not pursue the matter, but left Kansas for Colorado. There he began working as a meatcutter, and in 1972 he married for the second time.

In 1976 Ross was injured in a freak accident and lost four toes on his right foot. Unable to continue working or to subsist on the slightly more than $200 per month he was receiving in unemployment compensation and welfare payments, he applied again to the VA. Again he was denied, this time on grounds of his failure to satisfy the VA that his problems were service-connected.

Without a job or sufficient income to support himself and his family, he eventually found his way to the Denver office of Senator Gary Hart. Staff assistant Bill Holen took a particular interest in Ross's case. With Holen's help, Ross began to substantiate the claim that his psychological problems had either been caused or were worsened by the exposure to the nerve gas. He appealed the earlier negative decisions.

But because the experiments with nerve gases had been a classified defense study, the Army had not included the records of Ross's participation in his regular file. It was therefore necessary to secure details of the research and Ross's part in it. In addition, Ross's reaction to the chemical had been called "an unusual physiological response" by both Army physicians and the VA. Eventually Ross and Holen were able to produce evidence that shows a strong correlation between exposure to drugs like the nerve gas used and exhibition of symptoms of depression and schizophrenia such as Ross had shown intermittently from the time of his first reaction to the experiment.

After further psychological testing (at the request of the VA), the appeals board agreed that Ross's condition was very likely the result of his reaction to the gas and awarded him a 50 percent disability status. By the end of 1977, he could begin rebuilding a life that had begun to unravel more than 16 years

earlier in a laboratory room at Edgewood. And people who
meet John Ross today find that his smile is a little less worried-
looking than it used to be.

When Robert Williams completed high school in 1965—
before the antiwar feeling that was sweeping through college
campuses during the height of the Vietnam war had made its
presence felt at relatively isolated institutions—he matricu-
lated at the University of Maine in Orono. A few years later,
however, there was considerable antiwar feeling on the cam-
pus, and it bothered Bob Williams. So he dropped out of
college, where he had discovered an aptitude for foreign lan-
guages, and enlisted in the Army. On his induction in 1968, he
was assigned to Army Intelligence and sent to study Russian
at the Defense Language Institute in Monterey, California.
After completing his course of studies, he was shipped out to
Germany.

Shortly after New Year's Day in 1971, Bob Williams noticed a
small lump in his neck. It did not cause him any pain and grew
no larger, but neither did it recede. He decided to consult a
doctor. A biopsy revealed cancer of the thyroid; he would have
to undergo surgery for removal of the gland. The operation
was performed in an Army hospital in Berlin at the end of
June. According to the surgeon, the removal of Bob Williams'
thyroid was "technically difficult" but accomplished "without
complications."

Although a cancer operation is always traumatic, the prognosis for full recovery from a thyroidectomy and extended
survival is generally good. Besides, Bob Williams was young—
just 25 at the time—and otherwise in good health. To replace
the functions of the thyroid gland, however, he would always
have to take medication: a thyroid hormone, calcium lactate,
and Vitamin D.

Williams had only two months to go on his Army tour when
he was released from the hospital in late July 1971. Despite
his condition, though, the Army apparently did not consider
granting him a medical discharge. The physician who examined him and adjusted his medication several times during his
hospital stay said that after convalescing he would be able to
resume a normal existence.

Williams therefore was in an optimistic frame of mind when
he left the Army and returned to the United States. He expected that after a brief further convalescence he would be well

enough to resume both his college education and an active life. He particularly looked forward to being able to hike and climb again in the Longfellow Mountains, a chain that runs just north of Houlton westward to the Canadian border. He'd spent countless boyhood hours rambling the trails and climbing the peaks of these familiar mountains, sometimes camping out along the way.

Even before Williams left Germany, however, he began to suspect that he would not bounce back as quickly as he had anticipated. He grew tired easily and could not exert himself without feeling weakness and fatigue. His limbs often felt numb and lifeless; and at other times they would tremble. He had periods of insomnia during which he'd lie exhausted in bed, unable to sleep except fitfully. And sometimes he would sleep for half a day or longer without stirring. In addition, he frequently felt nervous and irritable, and he began to suffer migraine headaches and dizziness.

But Williams was determined to continue his education. Because of his cancer operation, he was automatically entitled to full disability benefits from the VA for at least one year. He could not do physical labor, but he could study. He decided to enroll at McGill University in Montreal. It had a first-rate language institute, and since the fees were lower in Canada than at a comparable institution in the United States, Williams hoped to get by on the VA benefits he would be receiving. He was an honors student at McGill, where he majored in Russian language and literature and from which he received a B.A. degree in 1975.

Williams' disturbing symptoms persisted, however, and he sought help from the McGill health service. There it was discovered that, besides his thyroid gland, his parathyroids also had been removed in the 1971 operation. The parathyroids are extremely small and are often embedded in the thyroid gland—itself so small that it weighs no more than an ounce. Whether it was their minuscule size or the camouflaging effect of the adhesions to the thyroid (mentioned in the Army surgeon's report) that led to the removal of Williams' parathyroids is not clear. But the implications of the loss of both thyroid and parathyroid functions—the need for lifelong hormonal therapy and the likelihood that he would never be able to engage in any sort of work that might be physically fatiguing—were not fully made known to him until after he had consulted a physician in Montreal in 1973.

Nevertheless, Williams remained optimistic. "I realized that this meant no more backpacking or things like that, but I could still swim and jog a little, things like that. Besides, I was in school, studying Russian, as I'd wanted to for a long time. So I figured that since I wouldn't be able to get any kind of teaching job until I had my master's and couldn't do any unskilled work to speak of because of my condition, this meant I'd be able to keep my VA benefits until I'd finished by M.A. or even my Ph.D."

For nearly a year the VA seemed to concur in Williams' assessment of things, for his benefits remained intact at the level of 100 percent disability—meaning that he was unable to do any remunerative work—and they were sufficient to cover his expenses as a student. Early in 1974, however, the VA advised Williams that his benefits were being reduced to a disability level of 30 percent—this in spite of the fact that his condition had not improved and could not be expected to improve. Williams appealed the decision on grounds of the severity of his medical condition and his inability to work until he had received further training in his field (at the time he was still an undergraduate). Acknowledging the validity of his claims, the VA restored his benefits to their original 100 percent level. And there the matter stood—until 1977, when Williams was preparing to write his master's thesis.

It is easy to see why, after the VA once again notified him that it had reduced his benefits to 30 percent, Williams grew despondent. In the interval since his first series of appeals of VA actions in 1974, he had a number of achievements to his credit—he had graduated from McGill's language institute with a B.A. with honors and had completed course work for his M.A. at McGill. In addition, he had become engaged to a young Canadian woman he had met when they were both undergraduates. Martine del Giudice was a Montreal schoolteacher, and they had planned to marry as soon as he was assured of earning a living, at the end of his M.A. or Ph.D. studies. But the stress caused by the loss of benefits, added to the persistent insomnia, nervousness and headaches that had Williams suffered from all along, were apparently more than the couple could bear. They broke off in the fall of 1977.

During the summer of 1976 Williams had tried to do light work for a few weeks at the suggestion of his physician, who thought that some light physical activity would be a good idea. A Montreal businessman had offered Williams a job, but after only a few weeks Williams developed sciatica and tendonitis. He had found that a day's work left him exhausted until the next morning, and after a week he would have to sleep through the weekend in order to have the strength to report the following Monday. So he knew that the reduction in benefits would be devastating.

Williams therefore embarked on a series of appeals to the VA and a round of letter-writing, hoping to find some high-placed government official who might take an interest in his case. Someone would appear on the *Tomorrow* television program and profess sympathy for the problems of veterans, and Williams would write him a letter seeking support for his case. He also wrote to Rosalyn Carter, then the First Lady. None of his efforts produced any concrete results. In September, a VA appeals board affirmed the decision to maintain the level of benefits at 30 percent.

In the meantime, though, he was making some medical progress. An endocrinologist in Montreal had switched his medication from a thyroid extract to a safer synthetic hormone, which, it was hoped, would prevent the dangerous buildup of calcium that was thought to have caused his tendonitis and the extensive dental problems he had.

Williams' plight came to my attention when I was still a congressman.

Under present law the final body to which a veteran may appeal an adverse VA decision is the Board of Veterans Appeals, in Washington, D.C. I offered to appear before the board on Williams' behalf, along with his father, Jim. (Bob Williams himself could not afford to make the trip from Montreal to Washington.) At the hearing we stressed the seriousness of Bob Williams' condition and explained that it would be next to impossible for him to find any work until he had completed his graduate training. His job would have to permit him to rest frequently, to be of such a nature that he would not be exhausted by it. I explained,

> Outside the academic field there are relatively few jobs that would permit him the necessary rest periods and also represent substantially gainful employment. So Mr. Williams is left in a *Catch-22* dilemma. On the one hand, he is told by the VA that he is well suited for an academic career. On the other hand, he has to complete his graduate requirements in order to qualify for that career. It think it's clearly essential that he complete his degree requirements. The VA originally reasoned that Mr. Williams can't work because he's a student, but I think they've gotten things turned upside down. Mr. Williams is a student because unless he completes his advanced degree requirements,

he's never going to be able to undertake significant and substantially gainful employment.

What is even more striking to me is the suggestion made by some members of this board that this man might find work as a clerk or bank teller—that this might not be beyond his physical capacities and therefore he ought to do it. Now, why should we take an intelligent young man—with a really fine mind—and force him to do something he's overqualified for when he's training to do work that will be really productive in our society?

As a result of his condition, he is affected physically and emotionally. He can't do any exercise—can't play tennis or swim—can't even be treated with cortisone for the tendonitis in his elbow. How can we also deny him an education in a field in which he is so uniquely skilled and has a promising future?

The board may have been impressed with these arguments, but apparently not enough to restore Williams' benefits to anything more than a 60 percent level. And that is where it stands today.

Senator Hart's efforts to increase the accountability of the Veterans Administration for its decisions on benefits have already achieved concrete results, and further progress is expected in the area of judicial review of decisions by the Veterans Appeals Board. But even under the best of circumstances, the road from an entitled veteran's first application for benefits to his receipt of them can be extremely long.

Few cases in the recent past illustrate this fact more poignantly than that of Robert Palmer. As a Marine in 1956, Palmer participated in Operation Redwing on the Marshall Islands in the Pacific, measuring radiation levels on Bikini Atoll immediately following hydrogen bomb tests there. Almost twenty years later, in 1977, he discovered that he had lung cancer. In addition to fighting the disease, he immediately began the process of applying for VA benefits—since he believed the cancer was connected to his exposure to high levels of radiation during the Marshall Islands operation. The VA, however, thought otherwise and rejected his claim. Palmer persisted, despite failing health. Assisted by his parents and Senator Hart, he undertook the arduous appeals process, rebutting the VA assertion that the cause of his cancer could not be traced to his exposure to fallout from the nuclear bomb.

Of course, Palmer knew that he was dying—that even if he had been awarded a VA pension while he was still alive it would do him little if any good. But he had two children, aged nine and 11, who were entitled to survivors' and education benefits. So it was for their sake—and for the sake of others in similar positions—that he persisted.

Robert Palmer was just nineteen when he was shipped with other Marines to the Marshalls, to an island near Bikini Atoll, where the hydrogen bomb was being tested. During the tests the Marines waited on the flight deck of an aircraft carrier—until it was time to fly over the site of the blast in a helicopter, to conduct the measurement of levels of radioactivity. The usual waiting time after a bomb had been detonated was about one hour.

The helicopter crews of which Palmer was a member performed several operations, including dropping devices to measure radioactivity and visually overviewing the blast site and nearby areas to determine the impact of the explosions on standing structures. Although they would not land on the atoll during these operations, the crews visited nearly every other island in the Marshall group, usually to ferry scientists. When the helicopters returned from a test mission, the crew would go through decontamination procedures. These included washing down the helicopters while wearing a sort of raincoat that left the head, hands and parts of the legs exposed. As a matter of course crew members were splashed by water bouncing off the helicopter bodies. Palmer and his buddies were told by their superior officers that if they thought they might have come in contact with radioactivity, they should take showers.

Each of the Marines wore a round black monitoring device, about an inch in diameter, during his entire tour of duty on the islands. Palmer's device indicated he had been exposed to 800 millirems of gamma radiation. A doctor suggested that he leave the island on which the men camped and return to the aircraft carrier. No one offered any other precautions.

Over a period of three months, six bombs were tested at the Bikini Atoll site. How much of the radiation Palmer absorbed during the operations and how much from the atmosphere in the area of the tests is uncertain. Palmer recalled that the radioactive cloud formed by the bomb blasts customarily traveled in a path that passed over the island on which the Marines were stationed, adding, no doubt, to their exposure. Although this island was considered to be at a safe distance from the test site, Palmer reported that on several occasions the force of the explosion was so great that the Marines' tents were blown down as a result.

So little was known at the time about the dangers of radioactive fallout, and under what conditions an individual might be exposed, that Palmer and the other Marines naively believed that the work they were doing in the Marshall Islands posed little if any risk. "I didn't think they'd do anything to jeopardize us," he told a newspaper reporter later. As it turns out, other test sites in the middle and late fifties did have signs posted warning about the risks of radioactivity, but there had been none at Palmer's.

What if anything would constitute a "safe" level of radiation was and still is controversial. At the time, at least, the 800 millirems to which Palmer was exposed seemed high enough to warrant his removal from the immediate area. Because the results of radiation on the human body may appear long after the event, little was known at the time of exposure of the myriad possible effects on health. Moreover, it is extremely difficult, even now, to isolate with certainty the specific cause or causes of cancer in a single individual. For large groups of people, the weight of scientific evidence is heavy: Exposure to gamma radiation is likely to cause cancer in some individuals, just as some cigarette smokers will contract cancer. But for a single victim of cancer it is usually impossible to pinpoint the cause.

In addition, because the risks to servicemen who like Palmer were exposed to potentially dangerous levels of radiation were unknown (or ignored), no records were kept by the armed services of their later medical histories. The badgelike devices they wore measured only external radiation levels and are no longer thought to be accurate. Internal radiation is much more important when assessing the health risks of exposure. One expert suggested that someone like Palmer, whose badge had indicated a dose of 800 millirems, might in fact have absorbed an internal dose of 100 times that level, or 80 rems, which would be far above *any* scientist's estimate of a safe level. A government spokesman, on the other hand, claimed that less than 1 percent of the servicemen exposed to radiation absorbed doses above five rems and that nine out of 10 were exposed to less than 1,000 millirems.

When someone in Palmer's position claims VA benefits for a cancer that he thinks was caused two decades earlier, he may not find an especially credulous Veterans Administration at the other end of his application. Some servicemen give up after being told that there is no evidence to link their illness to their earlier exposure to radiation. At first Palmer himself was told by the VA that there was only a "remote possibility" of a connection between his exposure to radiation while in the service and the cancer he had contracted. But Palmer had the active support of his parents, of an officer of the Veterans of Foreign

Wars named Ed Glade, and of Bill Holen of Senator Hart's staff. All of them felt that he had been used as a guinea pig by the people responsible for nuclear testing in the 1950s, and they wanted to make that fact known, not only for Palmer's sake but also for the sake of others who had been similarly exposed.

For two years they fought through the established process of appeals. At least for Palmer, it was too long. Sadly, in May 1979, he died.

But the Board of Veterans Appeals, prompted by the unusual circumstances of his case, took the unusual step of reconsidering the evidence even after his death, and in June it finally agreed that although over twenty years had elapsed between Operation Redwing and the day Palmer found he had cancer in 1977, his exposure in the Pacific had probably caused his disease. The board raised questions about a number of the assumptions that had led to earlier decisions in such cases. It pointed out that the film badge that was suppoed to record exposure to radiation very like reflected only part of that to which Palmer had been exposed. It omitted, for example, all radiation but gamma rays, as well as radiation contained in the food Palmer ate or the dust in the air he breathed. Reversing its earlier finding, it concluded that Palmer had most likely been exposed to higher levels of radiation than indicated on his badge. Furthermore, it reasoned, since there was no evidence of Palmer's having been exposed to radiation in any of his other activities, either in the service or in civilian jobs as radio announcer, bank employee, truck driver or government worker, the probability of his exposure during the Bikini Atoll tests having contributed to his cancer was great enough to justify a finding in his favor.

Robert Palmer did not live to hear those words, but his family and friends know it was his courage, confidence and persistence that inspired them.

GETTING THE MOST OUT OF THE VETERANS ADMINISTRATION

What a Caseworker Needs to Know

For a disability claim, a congressional caseworker will need to know the full name of the claimant; his VA claim number, Social Security number and address; whether the disability is service-connected; and the nature of the problem (Are benefits being cut? Has an application been unanswered? etc.). If the claim is on the account of a deceased spouse or parent, note in addition his or her name and date of death. A caseworker must also know if, after a claim has been denied, a formal appeal has been made to Washington.

Medical service records are kept in St. Louis. If you seek yours, note your branch of service, when and where you served and the date and type of your discharge.

For educational benefits, tell your caseworker how long you have been out of the service and what school you plan to attend.

KEY FACTS

VETERANS ADMINISTRATION
810 Vermont Avenue, N.W.
Washington, DC 20420
Phone: (202) 393,4120

Established by an executive order signed by President Herbert Hoover in 1930, the Veterans Administration sought to consolidate under a single agency responsibility for various veterans' bureaus and programs enacted by Congress over the years. The administrator of veterans' affairs is appointed by and reports directly to the President. Today, the VA is the largest of all independent agencies, and its 1982 budget of about $25 billion is the third largest in the federal government. In the number of its employees, the VA is smaller only than the Department of Defense and the Postal Service.

HEALTH CARE

During fiscal year 1982, the VA health-care system provided medical and dental services in 172 medical centers, 226 clinics, 98 nursing homes, and 16 domiciliaries. In the year ending 1981, the VA cared for approximately 1.36 million inpatients, 41,800 nursing-homes residents, and some 15,000 others. There were more than 15.8 million outpatient visits to VA facilities, and 2.1 million visits to private physicians that were authorized by the VA.

The VA also assists in education and training of physicians and dentists, and with the training of many other health-care professionals, through affiliations with various educational institutions. In fiscal year 1982, the VA's Department of Medicine and Surgery operated with a budget of over seven billion dollars and employed over 193,500 persons. The Veterans Administration Health Care Amendments Act, enacted by Congress on August 26, 1980, provides special pay provisions that have enhanced the government's ability to retain both high-quality physicians and dentists. The VA's current nursing shortage will be alleviated by enactment of the Senate-passed Health Care Programs Improvement and Extension Act of 1982, which offers enhanced pay and work schedules and a scholarship program.

BENEFITS

Compensation and Pension

The Compensation and Pension Service programs administered by the VA fall into five categories, including:

1. Dependency and indemnity compensation (DIC) and
death compensation, which provides benefits to dependents
of certain veterans who died of service-connected causes on
or after January 1, 1957. Dependents of veterans who died
before that date are entitled to death compensation, or may
elect to receive DIC.

2. *Disability compensation,* which entitles a veteran to compensation for disability incurred or aggravated while on active duty. Compensation is based on the degree of disability.

3. *Disability pensions* for veterans who suffer from nonservice-connected disabilities and are either indigent or
over 65.

4. *Death pensions* for the surviving spouse and children of
a war veteran for nonservice-connected causes, subject to
specific income limitations.

5. *Burial allowances* include a flag to drape the casket of the
deceased veteran.

The Compensation and Pension Service also has responsibility for automobile allowances and special adaptive equipment,
claims for specially adapted housing, special clothing allowances, eligibility determinations based on military service for
other VA benefits and services or those of other government
agencies, and claims for accrued benefits.

EDUCATION AND REHABILITATION

The VA administers two basic programs for veterans and
service-members seeking educational assistance. The GI Bill
applies to service before December 1976. A contributory plan
is in effect for those who have served from January 1977 to the
present. There are also programs available for certain spouses,
children, and surviving dependents.

LOAN GUARANTY

The VA loan guaranty program provides credit assistance whereby the housing needs of eligible veterans and active-duty servicemen may be satisfied by private capital on more liberal terms than generally available to nonveterans. Assistance is provided chiefly by substituting the government's guaranty on loans made by private lenders for that generally required in conventional home-mortgage transactions. The VA is also authorized to make direct loans to veterans living in areas where private lenders were not interested in loan guaranty programs, or who had insufficient funds for such mortgages. The VA is also engaged in appraising property values, determining the ability of the veteran to repay, supervising construction of new residences, managing loan assets, and counseling potential minority homebuyers in obtaining housing credit and discharging financial obligations.

LIFE INSURANCE

Life insurance protection is available for all service personnel and veterans through the VA, which completely administers five life-insurance prorgrams. In addition, the VA also supervises three other insurance programs through a contractual relationship with private companies.

United States Government Life Insurance (USGLI)

This is the oldest government-administered program, established in 1919 to handle the conversion of World War I risk term insurance. There has been a steady decline in the number of policyholders under this program, a decline that will continue to accelerate as the average age of the insureds nears 90 years.

National Service Life Insurance (NSLI)

This was established in 1940 to serve the insurance needs of World War II service personnel. The program is self-supporting except for administration expenses and for claims traceable to the hazards of military service, which are paid directly by the government.

Veterans Special Life Insurance (VSLI)

This was a means of providing postservice government life insurance to Korean conflict veterans for whom there was no premium-paying insurance during service. Effective January 1, 1959, legislation modified this program to permit exchange to a lower-cost term policy, which was nonrenewable after age 50, or to permit conversion to a permanent plan of insurance.

Service Disabled Veterans Insurance (SDVI)

This is the only government-administered insurance program remaining open to new issues. SDVI was designed to assure that service-disabled veterans could obtain life insurance at standard rates. Every veteran separated from service on or after April 25, 1951, who receives a service-connected disability rating for which compensation would be payable of 10 percent or more in degree, and who is otherwise insurable, has one year from the date of notice of his VA rating to apply for this coverage.

Veterans Reopened Insurance (VRI)

This was a limited reopening of National Service Life Insurance for certain disabled World War II and Korean conflict veterans who, because of their disability, would be unable to obtain commercial life insurance or could not obtain it at a reasonable cost.

Veterans Mortgage Life Insurance (VMLI)

This is supervised by the VA, administered by the Bankers Life Insurance Company of Lincoln, Nebraska and provides mortgage life insurance for any veteran who receives a VA grant for specially adapted housing—unless he or she declines the insurance, fails to furnish information to establish the premium or does not pay the premium.

Servicemen's Group Life Insurance (SGLI)

This provides insurance coverage for members of the uniformed services, is also supervised by the VA but is administered by the Prudential Insurance Company of America (as primary insurer). The serviceman is automatically insured for the maximum coverage in the absence of a request for less or no coverage. Members of the four service academies (U.S. Coast Guard Academy, U.S. Naval Academy, U.S. Air Force Academy and U.S. Military Academy) are entitled to full-time coverage.

Veterans Group Life Insurance (VGLI)

This provides for conversion of SGLI to a five-year non-renewable term policy and provides low-cost, government-supervised insurance to the veteran immediately following separation or release from the service.

VETERANS ASSISTANCE

The Veterans Assistance Service (VAS) offers information, advice and assistance to veterans, their dependents and beneficiaries, representatives and others in applying for VA benefits. In addition to cooperating with the National Alliance of Businessmen and other agencies to develop employment opportunities for veterans, the VAS provides benefit information and readjustment assistance to recently separated veterans, including professional guidance in resolving socioeconomic, housing and other related problems.

The Veterans Assistance Service also supervises benefit payments to fiduciaries on behalf of adult beneficiaries who are incompetent or under some legal disability and to minor beneficiaries, and provides information regarding benefits to veterans incarcerated in prison and/or to veterans residing in foreign countries.

DEPARTMENT OF MEMORIAL AFFAIRS

The Department of Memorial Affairs administers the National Cemetery system, which provides funeral services to veterans and others who may be eligible. Benefits include the headstones and markers, as well as plots in federal and state cemeteries.

☆ V ☆

CHEATS
AND BULLIES

The teaching of politics is that the Government, which was set for protection and comfort of all good citizens, becomes the principal obstruction and nuisance with which we have to contend.... The cheat and bully and malefactor we meet everywhere is the Government.

—RALPH WALDO EMERSON, *Journal* (1860)

The sun shines brilliantly through a pale blue sky, crisply outlining the figures below as if they were in a Passion play postcard—or a frieze in a terrorist docudrama.

Actually the scene is that of a small wholesale business operation in a middle-size American city. Inside and outside the offices are a swarm of men who, though they are plainclothes detectives, are armed with submachine guns, which they train on nervous executives and startled employees while the company's business equipment is removed from the building and loaded onto a waiting truck.

The panorama would be suitable for propaganda by *Pravda*—even though this is not a typical case of American Violence. In fact it is a picture of agents of the Internal Revenue Service of the United States in the process of confiscating the marketable property of a small-businessman in order to satisfy a tax liability. In this particular operation the equipment seized is worth about $18,000, though it will bring the government only $8,000 when it is sold—a good deal less than the back taxes owed. Moreover, the loss of the machinery may force the business into bankruptcy.

Such strong-arm tactics are not reserved exclusively for business. IRS agents sometimes subject individual citizens to cruel treatment, seizing personal property without warning and on occasion even threatening the safety of the people involved. In one notorious case in Alaska, a married couple adjudged delinquent in their taxes were set upon in their car by two agents, who broke the windshield, forcibly removed them and had the car towed away.

Even the IRS's harshest critics, though, will concede that such bizarre collection tactics are rare. Most of the forcible attempts to gather delinquent taxes are conducted against businesses, not individuals, and the sums involved are usually Social Security and federal income taxes that have not been withheld from employees' salaries. In fact, the great majority of tax delinquencies are settled amicably. A taxpayer may be asked (or allowed) to pay the entire amount due, or to arrange to pay in installments over a specified period (usually 12 to 24 months) while keeping current with all further tax obligations.

But the law is clear: When the IRS discovers that anyone—an individual or a corporation—is delinquent, it has the power to place liens on the taxpayer's property, to set a levy on anything he owns and to seize and sell any of his assets. The law does require that a delinquent taxpayer be notified of his liability and given a brief time in which to pay, but then any of these summary collection procedures—liens, levies and seizures—may be used at the discretion of the agency.

In the late 1970s the number of seizures rose sharply, and complaints from both sides—the businesses that suffered and the IRS agents who were pressured to seize—revealed a new policy: seizure for seizure's sake. Assets were sometimes taken after taxpayers had already entered into installment agreements. Many seizures forced small companies into bankruptcy, with the result that they would no longer produce tax revenues or provide employment, and they frequently led to recovery of much less than the amount owed—and that would have been produced by less drastic means of collection.

The congressional testimony of a number of a revenue officers disclosed a "get tough" approach by the IRS that both violated the agency's own national policy and left many revenue officers disgruntled, having forced them to use collection procedures even when their judgment and experience convinced them that to do so would cost the government money and cause businesses to close down. Cases arrived on revenue officers' desks with instructions that read: "First Action: Levy" or "This is a seizure." Agents found themselves directed by superiors to ignore the fact-finding process in favor of seizing assets and closing cases. As Joe Boyd, a St. Louis IRS officer, put it, "The name of the game has become seizure. The one thing a group manager does not want to have is a zero month in seizures."

Maurice Bishop started All-Time Pest Control in 1958, having moved from Detroit to Benton Harbor, Michigan. After 20 years of hard work he had built up his business to the point where it grossed about $350,000 a year, enabling him to move into a new building, which he built at a cost of nearly $250,000. Bishop was a firm believer in the American ethic and was pleased with his success. And he always paid his taxes—or at least so he thought.

Late in 1979 he began to receive notices from the IRS informing him that over $40,000 in taxes withheld from his employees' salaries had not been deposited with the government. Bishop discovered that his accountant had been responsible for failing to make the payments and fired him. He then came to an agreement with the local IRS agent: he would pay part of his delinquency immediately and the rest in installments, to begin a year after the agreement.

A few months later, he was called in to meet a second time with an IRS agent. Bishop was told that the original agreement had been rescinded, that the agent who had worked it out with him was no longer with the IRS and that he would have to pay his full debt immediately. It was even suggested that he fire some of his employees and sell part of his equipment in order to raise the needed funds. Bishop declined. So the IRS placed liens on all of his property (except his house), thereby preventing him from borrowing against the property to pay the back taxes. Bishop borrowed money from a former business associate, used all available receipts from his exterminating company and within seven months had paid in full the more than $41,000 he owed. More than two months later, the IRS finally released the liens on his property.

Richard Dyke is a former IRS agent who now owns an accounting firm in Portland, Maine. In the course of his work, he occasionally comes across a small company that is losing money but that he believes could be turned into a profitable business with new management or with an infusion of new funds. Dyke's firm likes to acquire businesses like that and try to turn them around. By 1980, he owned fifteen such companies (most of them in Maine) and employed nearly 500 people. This is the story of one of them.

In 1978, a year after acquiring one small business and hiring a new manager to run it, Dyke discovered not only that it still wasn't making a profit but also that the manager had embezzled the payroll taxes of all 25 employees. In short, the company owed $20,000 to the Internal Revenue Service.

Dyke still believed he could make the business profitable and did not want to declare bankruptcy. But in order to keep operating, it was necessary to work out arrangements for payment to all creditors (including the IRS). A revenue officer at the agency's Collection Department agreed to an installment plan: The company would pay $2,000 per month until all taxes, penalties and interest were paid, while at the same time keeping current on all new taxes. For seven months—until June 1980—the payments were made as promised. Then, suddenly and without warning, the revenue officer called to announce that the balance had to be paid immediately.

The new manager reminded the IRS agent of the existing agreement and pointed out that all payments had been made as promised. Nothing further was heard from the IRS until the manager discovered that $9,000—the entire balance due—had been levied from the company's bank account without notice or warning. Fortunately, the IRS action was discovered in time for the firm to take steps to protect the credit and good name that had been built up with suppliers and the public over the previous seven months. For its part, the IRS seemed to have been motivated by the desire to add to its tally of levies or closed accounts before June 30, an internal reporting deadline. In this instance, the full amount of the delinquency was recovered early—even though the agency had been assured of payment in another few months.

In 1979, Dyke found another small company that had already filed for bankruptcy. It had debts outstanding of about $350,000, of which $50,000 were for taxes. Its assets came to under $20,000. Thinking the company nevertheless had potential, Dyke arranged with the private creditors to pay 10 cents on the dollar as well as to continue buying from them when the company came out of bankruptcy. He then offered to pay the IRS the full $50,000 tax debt over a period of two years. The agency agreed, in part because the alternative would have been to recover less than 40 percent of that amount were the company forced to liquidate.

Once the agreement was reached, Dyke and his associates placed $100,000 in escrow in a Maine bank—for the purposes of paying off the private creditors, providing new capital for the company and reserving funds for the 24 installments due the IRS. But then the IRS began to equivocate, declining to approve the installment agreement first at the local and then at the regional level. Finally, although the IRS did not actually turn down the agreement, the new backers were discouraged enough from expecting that it would be approved in time to save the company that they withdrew. Dyke was forced to release the full $50,000 to pay the back taxes.

So instead of having approximately $60,000 in new capital,

the struggling company was left with $10,000. And instead of encouraging businesses (within the scope of its mandate) to become profitable in order to contribute greater tax revenues, the IRS seems to have become preoccupied with enforcement for its own sake. In Dyke's words, "It seems to me we have a two-headed horse, but the enforcement (or collection) head has chosen to feed itself in a way that threatens to starve the revenue-producing head."

Many congressional caseworkers are often stymied when faced with a constituent's legitimate tax grievance. The sequence of events often happens like this:

Mr. Taxpayer, who is having a problem with the Internal Revenue Service, calls the office of one of his congressmen or senators and complains to a staff assistant that certain travel expenses are deductible. The IRS disagrees. The caseworker prepares a letter to be sent to the IRS district office, asking why the specific deduction for Mr. T.'s travel expenses was not allowed. He also inquires of the secretary of the treasury if there are any pending policy decisions regarding travel deductions. And finally he calls a contact at the IRS to discuss the matter so that he can give Mr. T. a prompt answer.

As to the phone call, he'll be completely frustrated. The IRS will not discuss the specifics of any tax return by telephone— not even with a senator himself. The letter to the district office would likewise be futile, unless it were accompanied by Mr. T.'s written authorization. And the inquiry to the secretary of the treasury could wind up in the public record.

"No wonder," says the *Congressional Staff Journal,* "some congressional aides admit that they feel somewhat queasy at times when working on constituent problems involving the IRS. There are particularly rigid regulations to contend with; there is the Freedom of Information Act, which can occasionally inspire second thoughts for aides dealing with the sensitive subject of taxes; and finally, there is that persistent awareness that work with the IRS is not exactly the same as work with the Park Service, for instance."

But not all dealings between caseworker and IRS agent are futile.

"Sometimes a husband and wife will file a joint return and then get a divorce," says as aide from a southeastern office. "Afterward, when there is an overdue tax, the IRS might start going after the wife instead of the husband. In these cases, we can usually get the IRS at least to stop and look at the situation.

Then, if the woman is actually liable but is really struggling, some sort of repayment schedule can be worked out."

In general, inquiries and complaints fall into three categories: (1) routine problems involving lost or incorrect refund checks, harsh treatment by IRS agents or ordinary disputes about the tax laws; (2) requests about rulings; and (3) questions about policy.

Attempts to track down missing checks generally follow a well-established pattern. The caseworker first contacts the IRS service center where the taxpayer filed his return. No checks are issued by the center—they come from the treasury's Bureau of Government Financial Operations—but it does have a record of whether a check had been authorized. If it had been, the center requests a stop payment and authorizes issuance of a new check.

The IRS says that a taxpayer whose refund check has gone astray can expect to receive the requested duplicate within two to four weeks after the center has been notified.

All IRS district offices, as well as the service centers, have "problem resolution officers" who are supposed to be able to delve into any level of the agency, and many of them are known to congressional staffers.

If the taxpayer wants a ruling on the way the IRS will treat a particular transaction, whether prospective or completed, he must file a request in accordance with federal regulations. He is entitled to a conference with the IRS personnel handling the ruling request, and to withdraw the request if the agency's tentative finding is unfavorable.

Professional caseworkers are also familiar with the appeals procedures available to constituents who do not agree with original determinations of the Internal Revenue Services about their tax liability.

Whether the Internal Revenue Service deserves its reputation as the most ruthless federal agency in carrying out its policies is open to question. But it is certain that the IRS touches the lives of virtually every American year in and year out, through the collection of income and Social Security taxes. Many people who otherwise try to steer clear of any government agency besides the post office must maintain regular contact with the IRS. And when the IRS makes up its mind to seize someone's property for failing to pay back taxes, its agents often act with zeal that is unusual in civil servants.

Although IRS enforcement personnel are confident that they are within their legal rights in seizing the assets of a delinquent taxpayer, their tactics can be ruthless. Consider, for example, the experience of Richard Brasseur, who had built up an ophthalmology practice in a small town in Washington state, and as an adjunct to his medical practice decided to open an optical store and laboratory as well. During a slack period in the optical business, Brasseur told his bookkeeper to delay sending the taxes withheld from his 13 employees to the federal government: He simply did not have the cash to pay the taxes at that time, but he was confident that business would improve. What Brasseur did was clearly not legal, but he insists that he was motivated by a desire to save his business and the jobs of his employees.

The IRS, however, was less than sympathetic. It refused to permit him to pay off his debt in installments, even though it had reached a total of some $27,000. They seized his company's bank account (thus ruining his credit), impounded his automobile and locked him out of his ophthalmology office. Brasseur now had no way to earn a living, much less pay back taxes. He was forced to sell his house and leave town. Eventually, he was able to reestablish his practice—in Coldwater, Michigan.

Defending the actions of the IRS, a spokesman for the agency pointed to Brasseur's refusal to cooperate with agents assigned to the case. He wouldn't answer letters and phone calls, the spokesman said. But by seizing all of Brasseur's assets, the IRS realized less than it claimed it was owed, as has been the case in numerous other seizures.

Another man who would have seemed an especially unlikely candidate for the sort of rough treatment the IRS displays in selected cases of tax delinquency is Dwight Snyder. A cabinetmaker in Oakland, Maryland, Snyder is a member of the Dunkard Brethren Church. The Dunkards' beliefs are similar to those of the Amish, whose farms surround the countryside near Snyder's home. Snyder is thus not a worldly man, but devout, pacifist and hardworking.

For a long time he had also been wrangling with the IRS about taxes. The IRS claimed Snyder owed about $73,000, a figure he insisted should have been much lower. He also contended that portions of the tax law are "unbiblical" and that to conform to them would interfere with his religious beliefs.

During one meeting with an IRS agent, Snyder brought in a tape recorder. The agent abruptly canceled the session, saying he would not conduct it if he were recorded. Snyder pointed

out that IRS regulations permit a citizen who is being inter-
viewed by the IRS to tape-record the proceedings.

Snyder further contended that he was not a scofflaw. "If I
owe an honest and legal tax, I am willing to pay it. I am not
refusing to pay taxes. I just want fairness and justice."

But one morning, while the cabinetmaker and a single apprentice were at work in Snyder's shop, a small army of IRS
agents and special officer troopers and U.S. marshals—most of
them armed, some with automatic rifles—surrounded Snyder's
home and workshop and announced that they had come to
seize his property. They searched the house for cash, but also
departed with soap dishes and toothbrush holders—as well as
with all of Snyder's farm machinery and cabinetmaking tools.

Like Brasseur, Snyder was unable to continue earning his
livelihood. But that was not the worst of what the agents did.
The experience so traumatized the farmer's wife that she was
confined to a mental hospital for nearly a month.

The Snyders' neighbors rallied around them, bringing gifts
of food and other household items, providing tools and order-
ing his wares. In less than two weeks, Dwight Snyder was at
work again with cabinetmaking.

As resilient as Snyder has shown himself as a craftsman, he
has proven equally persistent in carrying forward his tax protest. In the fall of 1981, he stood trial for refusing to file and
pay taxes he owed throughout the decade of the 1970s. Appeals
are still pending.

We do not look to the Snyder case with sympathy for the
proposition that an individual's religious beliefs should exempt
him from the tax laws. Nor do we question the right of the IRS
to seize property for nonpayment of taxes. What is abhorrent,
however, is the nature and extent of the seizure here. While
Snyder's refusal to pay taxes in dispute called for action by the
United States government, it did not justify such overaction by
the IRS. Extremism in the pursuit of a legal claim is not necessarily a virtue.

The IRS, of course, does not confine its battles to members
of obscure religious sects. The Alaska case referred to earlier
was particularly bizarre. Stephen Oliver, a pilot from Fairbanks, and his wife, disagreed with an IRS claim that he owed
back taxes of $4,700. The Olivers filed a formal disagreement
with the IRS. Although ordinarily the dispute is resolved in the
courts, somehow the IRS determined to seize the Olivers'
property. So one day a number of armed agents surrounded
the Olivers as they were sitting in their Volkswagen in a Fair-

banks parking lot. Terrified, the couple locked the doors of their car, but this ploy served only to infuriate the agents. They smashed the windows of the vehicle and dragged Mona Oliver out of the car, across a pavement covered with the shattered glass. Then they towed the car away and eventually sold it for a few hundred dollars. (The IRS did not pay the couple's medical expenses.) The entire proceeding was photographed by a Fairbanks newspaper photographer who happened to be on the scene, and it made the front pages across the country.

Many figures in these confrontations with the Internal Revenue Service face their formidable federal opponent alone, but there have been cases where elected officials have succeeded in interceding with the IRS on behalf of a taxpayer and securing more humane treatment. Senator Levin, a Michigan Democrat, recalls a number of such instances. One of them involved the only ambulance company in a populous Michigan county; a private concern, it performed a vital health service in an area with a population of over 285,000. But the company owed the IRS nearly $250,000 in back taxes—mostly as a result of its failure to pay employees' withholding taxes when due. In truth the ambulance company was poorly run; however, it had also suffered inordinately long delays in receiving reimbursement for some of its patients from various government agencies (such as the VA) and programs (such as Medicare).

Had the IRS seized the company's assets for back taxes owed, it would have recovered far less than the debt and would have put the only ambulance company in the county out of business. A local hospital was interested in acquiring the service, provided the IRS would agree to accept an "offer in compromise"—that is, a payment of part of the tax liability. The rest of the liability—as well as most of the other debts of the company—would be canceled. In this case, motivated partly by reluctance to deny ambulance service to an entire county, the IRS agreed to the settlement, and the ambulances continued to roll.

Not every case of flexible behavior involves services as vital as ambulances. Another case where Senator Levin was instrumental in achieving a compromise between the taxpayer and the IRS involved a large Michigan bakery. Here again, the business had failed to remit its employees' withholding taxes, and the bakery had other debts as well, the result in part of undercapitalization. The owner agreed to pay off his back taxes at the rate of $10,000 per month. In return, the IRS agreed to subordinate its lien on the bakery's assets, so that the financing company could be assured the bakery would be able to operate until it was out of debt and making a profit.

The original IRS agreed to all these provisions, but during the week before Christmas, after the arrangements had been made, he fell ill and another officer took over the case. The second agent refused to keep to the terms of the original agreement and filed a lien against the bakery. This would have put the bakery out of business immediately, ruining the baker and leaving 100 employers without jobs just three days before the holiday. The desperate owner called Senator Levin, who persuaded the regional IRS commissioner to convene a meeting of IRS administrators, the company owner, his financial and legal advisers, and members of the financing company. The group was successful in restoring the original agreement, thus saving the bakery from bankruptcy. Since then it has successfully repaid its full tax debt.

Because confrontations between taxpayers and the IRS so rarely have happy endings, some members of Congress recently drafted a Taxpayer Protection Act. It was designed to protect the civil rights of taxpayers and guarantee that due process be observed in the collection process. The act would require that all tax-collection practices conform to those spelled out in the Fair Debt Collection Practices Act. (In other words, the tax collector could be liable for fines and damages if he violated the statute.) The IRS could not seize a taxpayer's property without first securing a court order, nor could it rescind arrangements providing for payments over time unless the taxpayer had committed fraud. In addition, taxpayers would be protected by statutes of limitations in all cases and would be informed of their rights as part of the packet of information they receive with their tax forms.

Except in rare cases, the IRS could not practice covert surveillance nor otherwise violate a taxpayer's civil rights without running the risk of a lawsuit. The agency would be required to give notice before seizing property and could not confiscate tax records without justifying a need for such records in court. In short, the act would reaffirm that the IRS is bound by the Bill of Rights with regard to each taxpayer.

Enactment of the proposed act would guarantee protection to every taxpayer, no matter how stubborn his temperament or unconventional his views. If it would not support Dwight Snyder's claim that the collection of taxes is in part "unbiblical," it would assure the safety of his property and his exercise of a livelihood until he has had his day in court.

One congressman received this letter of support from an agent of the Internal Revenue Service:

> Yes, there should be a strong clampdown upon the illicit activities of the IRS. I know of many such acts first hand because *I have worked for this institution for over six years.* I can tell you of *many more abusive acts* committed by some of my colleagues and supervisors (the latter probably being the worse of the lot). . . .
>
> The passage of H.R. 4931 may bring about changes which are long overdue to help alleviate the plight of the taxpaying public. Some legislation may also be needed to assist dissenting IRS employees from harassment from the Gestapo tactics of this institution as well.
>
> I sincerely hope that this letter will not jeopardize my employment. I wish you the best of luck in your efforts to have the immediate passage of H.R. 4931.

I supported a less stringent measure proposed by Senator Levin which would ensure that the IRS notify a delinquent taxpayer when a lien or a levy is imposed on his property or a seizure made. It would also require that the IRS promptly release any liens as soon as the tax liability (together with interest and penalties) had been paid in full. Both of these requirements are reasonable safeguards and would not impose any onerous burden on the agency.

Most taxpayers would assume that the IRS is already required to take such basic steps of fairness, but hearings before the Senate Governmental Affairs Oversight Subcommittee demonstrated that neither procedure is consistently followed.

The United States is considered to have the most effective tax system in the world because of its high degree of voluntary compliance. The great majority of American businesses and individuals report their incomes honestly and pay their taxes promptly. But perhaps the true measure of a tax system is how it treats those who appear to violate its precepts. We will surely jeopardize the success of our system if we do not assure that the agency charged with administering it operates equitably and efficiently.

GETTING THE MOST OUT OF THE INTERNAL REVENUE SERVICE (OR KEEP THE IRS FROM GETTING THE MOST OUT OF YOU)

What a Caseworker Would Advise

Caseworkers familiar with constituents' tax problems offer a number of practical tips for dealing with the Internal Revenue Service. Among them are to be as honest as possible, know your rights, don't be antagonistic, ask to speak to a supervisor if you're dissatisfied with the treatment you receive and obtain the services of a good accountant or tax lawyer. When those steps fail, contact your congressman.

If you write to your congressman concerning a joint account, make sure to have both taxpayers sign the letter and include both Social Security numbers.

KEY FACTS

INTERNAL REVENUE SERVICE
1111 Constitution Avenue, N.W.
Washington, DC 20224
Phone: (202) 566-5000

The Internal Revenue Service is one of eleven component parts of the Treasury Department. The Office of the Commissioner of Internal Revenue was established in 1962. Although the IRS performs many related functions, it is the agency that has exclusive responsibility for the administration of the federal revenue laws.

The goal of the IRS is supposed to be encouragement of the highest possible degree of voluntary compliance with the tax laws and maintenance of the highest degree of public confidence in the integrity and efficiency of the IRS. IRS activities include resolution of taxpayer complaints, providing taxpayer education and service, assessment and collection of taxes and issuing rulings and regulations to supplement the IRS Code. The IRS attempts to achieve consistency and uniformity of treatment of taxpayers by centralizing various functions in the national office and by establishing administrative policy for its various subdivisions. Published rulings and procedures, technical advice memoranda, private letter rulings and instructions as to policies to be followed by field offices emanate from the national office.

ORGANIZATION

The IRS consists of a national office in Washington, D.C., and a field organization.

The National Office

Office of the commissioner. The commissioner is the officer chiefly responsible for the administration of the IRS Code. Appointed by the President, he promulgates regulations, issues rulings and distributes all the directions, forms and other matters pertaining to the collection of internal revenue.

Office of the assistant commissioner (technical). The assistant commissioner (technical) is responsible for developing the basic principles and rules to ensure uniform application of the federal tax laws (except those relating to alcohol, tobacco, firearms and explosives).

Office of the assistant commissioner (compliance). The assistant commissioner (compliance) is responsible for compliance and appellate programs of the IRS and the supervision of such programs in the field. He or she is also responsible for overseeing the operations of the Appellate Division, the Audit Division, the Intelligence Division and the Office of International Operations.

Office of the assistant commissioner (employee plans and exempt organizations). The Employee Retirement Income Security Act of 1974 (ERISA) provided for the creation of this office, to be responsible for employee benefit plans.

Office of the assistant commissioner (accounts, collection and taxpayer service). This office performs functions in compiling information for audits in the processing of returns and in the internal administration of the IRS (When relief cannot be obtained through normal channels, this office's regional counterparts should be consulted.)

Office of the chief counsel. The chief counsel is the principal legal adviser to the commissioner. In addition to its counseling function, this office represents the IRS in all litigation in Tax Court and drafts all published IRS rulings and regulations.

The Field Organization

Regional service centers. The IRS maintains 10 regional service centers, whose names, addresses, states or areas and telephone numbers are as follows:

Service center:	Andover
States served:	Connecticut, Maine, Massachusetts, New Hampshire, New York (except New York City and Long Island), Rhode Island and Vermont
Address:	P.O. Box 311, Andover, MA 01810
Telephone:	(617) 681-5421
Service center:	Brookhaven
States served:	New Jersey and New York (New York City and Long Island only)
Address:	P.O. Box 777, Holtsville, NY 11742
Telephone:	(516) 654-6123

Service center: Philadelphia
Areas served: Delaware, Maryland, Pennsylvania, District of Columbia, U.S. territories and foreign countries
Address: P.O. Box 69, Bensalem, PA 19020
Telephone: (215) 969-2221

Service center: Memphis
States served: Indiana, Kentucky, North Carolina, Tennessee, Virginia and West Virginia
Address: P.O. Box 30309 AMF, Memphis, TN 38130
Telephone: (901) 365-5353

Service center: Atlanta
States served: Alabama, Florida, Georgia, Mississippi and South Carolina
Address: P.O. Box 48-481, Doraville, GA 30362
Telephone: (404) 455-2211

Service center: Cincinnati
States served: Michigan and Ohio
Address: P.O. Box 267, Covington, KY 41019
Telephone: (513) 684-1234

Service center: Kansas City
States served: Illinois, Iowa, Missouri and Wisconsin
Address: P.O. Box 24551, Kansas City, MO 64131
Telephone: (816) 926-5512

Service center: Austin
States served: Arkansas, Kansas, Louisiana, New Mexico, Oklahoma and Texas
Address: P.O. Box 934, Austin, TX 78767
Telephone: (512) 397-7501

Service center: Ogden
States served: Alaska, Arizona, Colorado, Idaho, Minnesota, Montana, Nebraska, Nevada, North Dakota, Oregon, South Dakota, Utah, Washington and Wyoming
Address: P.O. Box 9941, Ogden, UT 84409
Telephone: (801) 625-6365

Service center: Fresno
States served: California and Hawaii
Address: P.O. Box 12866, Fresno, CA 93779
Telephone: (209) 488-6001

District offices. IRS regions are further divided into 58 districts. The district office is the one closest to a taxpayer and is responsible for auditing returns, assessing deficiencies and reviewing protest letters. These offices also take delinquent returns, collect delinquent taxes, investigate civil and criminal violations of IRS laws (except those relating to alcohol, firearms, tobacco and explosives) and determine pension-plan qualifications.

For further information, contact any district office or the Internal Revenue Service headquarters, Department of the Treasury, 1111 Constitution Avenue, N.W., Washington, DC. 20224. Phone: (202) 566-5000.
33570 9:50

☆ VI ☆

GIVE ME YOUR TIRED, YOUR POOR, YOUR HUDDLED MASSES— BUT DON'T RUSH

Now that refuge of despair is shut, For other lives have twined themselves with mine.
                                    —JOHN DAVIDSON, *Lammas*

Kim Ourn didn't really want to come to America, but he had little choice. There was a time when being a Cambodian meant living in a charming land of lovely oriental villages, soft and delicate gardens and gracious manners. The small Asian country had somehow been spared the terrible price of the Indochinese War that ravaged Vietnam and Laos. But no longer. By 1977 and 1978, being a Cambodian meant danger and death. Millions of people were slaughtered in a horrible genocide, the bloody legacy of the Pol Pot regime's belief that only peasants were fit to live in a true and pure Communist society. In other words, business and professional people— which came to mean everyone who was literate, owned books or had ever taught in a school—would have to be exterminated. The country must undergo a superemergence of the peasant, at whatever the cost.

Kim Ourn knew the difficulties his country was facing, knew that the political struggle would escalate into wholesale war and that he would be a prime target. He was a high-ranking bank official who was personally acquainted with some of those in political and military power in Cambodia. He also realized that the country's political system as it stood was corrupt and that Pol Pot's militaristic guerrilla regime would eventually plunder its way to the major cities. So when he told his family that he was making a business trip to Thailand in early 1978, his wife and ten children all understood that it was also to make certain other arrangements. They would have to leave their homeland if they were to be saved. It was an agonizing decision but a necessary one. Thankfully, Kim Ourn had some contacts in the Catholic Church abroad, and he and his wife spoke a little English.

He would have to contact his eldest son, Quang, then studying in France, and tell him of the family's decision. But this would be delicate and very difficult. Spies were everywhere. Telegrams, cables, phone calls and letters of potential targets were being intercepted. There could be no indication that the family was planning to leave the country, for the new regime would utterly destroy anyone who might defame the new order.

Within three days of the time Kim Ourn managed to leave for his business trip to Thailand, the country was under the total control of the Khmer Rouge. The massacres had begun. Although he thought he could make arrangements while still in Southeast Asia, this soon became impossible. Time after time he tried to get news of his family, but there was nothing reliable. Years passed. He could not risk returning to the country, or all would surely be lost. His only option, it appeared, was to contact the United States embassy in Thailand and attempt to settle in the United States. And in the beginning of 1981, he found himself successfully relocated in Massachusetts—alone.

There was some news, finally, from France, about his eldest son. Quang was told by agencies in Cambodia, trying to track down other members of prominent families, that the entire Ourn clan had been captured and executed for crimes against the state. Hearing that, knowing there was nothing left for him to return to, the eldest son committed suicide. Kim, now in the United States, would not learn about it for many months. When he did, the shock was enormous. He had never thought that the family would actually die.

More time passed without any word, only some fleeting tales about the deaths of friends, or their escape, or their placement in refugee camps or their attempts to come to America. It was through a business friend who had also lost his family but had himself found his way to a refugee camp in Thailand that Kim learned one piece of wonderful news. His youngest son, Wan, had also managed to escape, with the help of neighbors. Nothing else could be learned about the other members of the family. It was five years since Kim had come to the United States. His was a tormented soul. Perhaps he could see his son. Perhaps he could save him.

Through friends Kim had made in Massachusetts, he was

told that contacting a United States senator might help. Kim did so. He said that the refugee camps were being raided, that death and disease were rampant and that young children had a low survival rate in them. Young Wan was only 11. There would have to be quick action. Senator Warren Rudman personally contacted the United States embassy in Thailand. The names and locations of family members and of other contacts were detailed. Five weeks later, Kim was informed that Wan was alive. More arrangements were made. And in January 1982, at Logan International Airport in Boston, Kim Ourn met the plane from which stepped, pale and thin, his 11-year-old son. Their embrace cannot be described in words.

The mid-1970s were equally tumultuous for the Republic of Lebanon. For 19 months Christian and Moslem factions clashed in a bloody civil war in which 60,000 people were killed, many more maimed and the nation's economy decimated. By the time it was over, a full 2 percent of Lebanon's population had met violent death; an equivalent catastrophe in the United States would take four million lives.

The trauma also affected Lebanese living elsewhere, who felt a mixture of fear and helplessness for their families trapped amid the strife. Karim Alhaan was fortunate that in 1976 his wife and children were with him in Houston, Texas. A portly, dark-skinned Lebanese, Alhaan had immigrated to the United States with his family in 1974. He used Arab-American contacts to get started in the retail clothing business. Though his English was poor, with a little outside guidance and a lot of hard work he saw the business make steady progress.

Back in 1974 Alhaan had tried in vain to persuade his brother Shanar to emigrate from Lebanon with him. Shanar earnestly believed it would be better to stay in Lebanon. America, he said, had its own problems. Shanar retained his optimism until 1976. Finally, with once-fashionable Beirut deteriorating swiftly, he and his wife and two children had had enough. They were ready to leave.

From his own experience, Alhaan knew that immigration to the United States was a long, slow process. Federal law restricts the number of visas that can be issued in any fiscal year to 290,000—and with few exceptions no more than 20,000 persons per year can immigrate to the United States from one foreign country. Alhaan was also familiar with the system of "preferences" by which the Immigration and Naturalization Service selects those who may enter the United States to settle.

The system is prescribed by statute and distinguishes among different categories of individuals. Members of professions, for example, such as architects (and who have lined up employment in the United States), are given higher priority than brothers and sisters of American citizens. The higher-preference individuals are the first to receive visas; each preference category is assigned a percentage of the 20,000-person limit; once that percentage is reached, such persons no longer have priority for that year.

Alhaan also knew that United States congressmen could assist in speeding up the immigration process. He placed a call to the office of his senator, whose staff explained that brothers and sisters of United States citizens fell within the so-called fifth preference for immigration visas. The first step, he was told, was for his brother to submit visa applications and supporting documents (for example, birth certificates, marriage certificates, photographs) to the U.S. embassy in Beirut. Shanar would then have to file what is called an immediate relative petition on behalf of his wife and two children. (Immediate relatives of United States citizens or persons admitted as permanent-resident aliens include the spouse and all children who are under 21 years of age.) While subject to the system of preferences, immediate relatives are exempt from the 290,000/20,000 yearly immigration quotas. In short, the combination of the fifth preference petition and immediate relative petition would, if approved by the immigration officials, qualify Shanar and his family for a visa number and for immigration to the United States.

The senator's staff monitored the application and attempted to speed it along by sending letters to the U.S. embassy in Beirut. Still, the process was lengthy and arduous. For four years the Alhaan family waited. It was not until the spring of 1980 that a break in the priority system allowed immigration visas to be granted. But there was a problem: While they were waiting, the eldest child, Dina, had turned twenty-one. The embassy refused to grant her a visa since she could no longer be considered an immediate relative.

For the Alhaans the choice was a terrible one: staying, or leaving Dina behind. They rationalized that they would not have to leave her behind for long; she could apply for immigration under a different category and eventually join them. She would have to take care of herself in Beirut until a new petition for her immigration was approved—this time under the second preference category, for unmarried daughters of aliens lawfully admitted for permanent residence. At least the worst of the civil war seemed to be over. Reluctantly, the Alhaans—with Dina's encouragement—decided to make their way to the United States and to leave her behind.

Their troubles had only just begun. Upon their arrival in the United States in 1980, a second preference petition was prepared on Dina's behalf. The senator's office called the Immigration and Naturalization Service numerous times to determine the petition's status but was told each time that there was no record of any such petition in INS files. Furthermore, the INS refused to accept a Beirut archbishop's baptismal certificate as a substitute for Dina's birth certificate. But the baptismal certificate was all the Alhaans had, since in Lebanon the archbishop was the governing authority for this type of record-keeping. To make matters worse, the INS informed the senator's office that Dina's mother's immigration file had never been received from the U.S. embassy in Beirut. Dina's petition, even when found, could not be considered, the INS said, until the mother's file had been located.

The senator's staff was befuddled. Paperwork was missing, and the Alhaans, whose command of English was poor, could not explain what had gone awry. As the length of separation from their daughter increased, Shanar became more distraught.

Finally, in February 1981, the senator's staff learned that the Alhaans had previously given all their paperwork—including the mother's file and the petition for Dina—to a Houston law firm. The lawyers had been hired for the family to help locate more persuasive evidence of Dina's birth date, but they had taken no action in the case. The missing documents having been found, they were delivered to the INS by the law firm at the senator's request.

In March 1981, the Houston office of the INS approved Dina's petition and forwarded it to the embassy. Still, the weeks passed without a final authorization. The embassy conducted its customary background investigation of Dina. She had to undergo a medical examination and appear for a personal interview. The interview did not take place until July 1981. More agonizing delay.

By the end of July, all was in order except one last matter: The embassy informed the senator and the Alhaans that it wanted proof of independence—that once Dina settled in the United States she would be able to survive financially without becoming independent on state or federal welfare programs. Karim Alhaan sent the embassy copies of his financial records,

IRS returns and bank statements, accompanied by a letter asserting that Dina would have steady employment in his clothing store. The senator wrote a letter attesting to the soundness of Karim Alhaan's business reputation. The embassy replied that it needed proof of Shanar's financial stability, not that of Dina's uncle. Letters flowed anew. Shanar was working with his brother in the clothing business, the senator wrote, and would be able to provide for Dina's financial needs if necessary. Finally, in August 1981, the embassy granted Dina an immigration visa.

The immigration process, drawn out in this case by communication problems, took five years. Without the senator's intercession, it no doubt would have taken even longer. And it could have failed altogether.

The matter of immigration or citizenship is often beyond the assistance of a senatorial office or governmental agency. It has to be taken up by Congress itself, and "private relief legislation" introduced. Numerous bills from all areas of the country and dealing with all types of matters, problems or requests are considered by congressional committees. Some of them get reported out and are passed.

In Korea, epidemics of diphtheria and smallpox can still be found, as can leprosy—with all the primitive fears associated with these diseases. Leprosy carries with it a taboo, and in Korea there are still colonies where victims are ostracized from their families and from society. In some areas of the country large leper camps are home to entire families, even though the children may not have the disease at all. Some private American agencies attempt to find couples in this country who wish to adopt the children of such circumstances.

San Kook Chung and Hwa Soon Chung are children of lepers in Korea. Because of their parents' disease, they were totally ostracized from society and were doomed to spend the rest of their lives in leper colonies. Through efforts of the Save the Children Foundation and the Red Cross, an American family in California was found who was willing to adopt them. But the proposed change of their nationality would not come about because the children were orphans, or had made a specific request on their own, or had any relatives or other connections in this country, so they were not covered by American immigration law. A private bill would have to be introduced on their behalf.

Beyond that, assurances had to be obtained from the United

States Public Health Services and from the Immigration and Naturalization Service that no threat of public health was involved, and assurances had to be given by the California family that they would be periodically checked for leprosy (which can be controlled and cured by modern medicine). After all of the necessary contacts were made and paperwork completed, a special bill was introduced in the Senate Judiciary Committee. Shortly thereafter, by virtue of H.R. 1396 (P.L. 96–42)—signed into law by the President of the United States of America—San Kook Chung and Hwa Soon Chung were put on a plane to San Diego.

Angelita Short was born on November 7, 1950, in the Philippines. Like many Philippine natives, she married an American serviceman—Angelita married Johnny Short in 1969. Three months after the marriage a daughter was born.

Two years later, in August 1971, Johnny was killed in an automobile accident in the Philippines. He was on duty at the time for the Navy, so there would be veteran's benefits coming. But that was little consolation to his wife and daughter. The two of them entered the United States as nonimmigrant visitors to accompany Short's remains for burial. But she failed to leave within the specified time, and when she was located, deportation proceedings began.

Angelita was living in Mount Prospect, Illinois, with her seven-year-old daughter, Talia. Angelita had completed five years of school in her native country and had attended three years of vocational high school in the United States. She had also received a diploma for nurses-aid training and had worked as a practical nurse. Her combined monthly income was approximately $1,200. She had real estate in Chicago valued at $16,000 with an outstanding mortgage of $17,000 and a home in the Philippines valued at $10,000. She had no other relatives residing in the United States.

And she was lucky.

Private-relief legislation was introduced on her behalf in the United States Senate, and Angelita and her daughter are now American citizens.

Similarly fortunate is a certain retarded man from Italy.

It was a gray day in Washington, D.C., and the weather in Boston, from where Patricia Soleno was calling, was no brighter. And it was not easy for congressional aide Karen Peterson to understand Soleno's thick Italian accent. Without the help of the congressman, Mrs. Soleno was saying, there was no way to resolve her problem. Karen listened intently as Mrs. Soleno struggled on. She was concerned about her brother, she said, because he was retarded and could not come to the United States. It was not his handicap itself, but the way in which it was regarded by United States law, which kept him in his native Italy: By the terms of Section 212(a)(i) of the Immigration and Nationality Act, an immigration visa cannot be granted to an alien who is mentally retarded.

Roberto Soleno, her brother, lived alone in a small town outside Milan. His parents were dead, his sister, Patricia, gone to the United States. She sent him $100 each month and, since his father had lived and worked in the United States, another $100 monthly in Social Security benefits. He was 29 and physically awkward. A psychiatrist who examined him described him as "oriented in time and space, cooperative, who answers simple questions posed to him and executes simple tasks and orders, revealing a limitation of general intellective ability." His I.Q. was measured at 50 to 60. Although he had never been able to hold a job, he was able to cook and clean and generally look after his own needs. In clinical jargon, Roberto was "mentally trainable." He could "perform simple jobs or work not requiring special skills or responsibilities."

Still, when Patricia Soleno filed a fifth preference petition for immigration on her brother's behalf in 1976, the U.S. embassy cited the psychiatrist's report and denied the petition on legal grounds. The statute was uncompromising; as long as Roberto was adjudged retarded, he could not be admitted into the United States.

Karen Peterson knew there was only one solution to the Solenos' dilemma: a private bill. Congress was unlikely to repeal Section 212(a)(i). And she knew that she'd have to establish a strong case for the congressman and his colleagues to be convinced that an exception to the statutory exclusion should be made on Roberto's behalf. During her investigation, she quizzed Patricia Soleno carefully about her financial situation, her ability to provide for Roberto in the event he could not find unskilled work or become more ill. Roberto could not become a ward of the state.

The congressman's staff drafted a bill that was assigned to the House Judiciary Committee's Subcommittee on Immigration, Citizenship and International Law, which had received reports from the Immigration and Naturalization Service, the State Department and the U.S. consulate at Naples. The INS report noted that Roberto's sister and her husband would assume full responsibility for the beneficiary if he were permitted to come to the United States and would be willing to post any required bond.

The subcommittee approved the bill in April 1978, and it was referred to the full Judiciary Committee, which in turn reported favorably to the House. The bill was passed into law later that year. For Patricia Soleno, it was the end of a long struggle. And she had had no particular connections, no political savvy. She had only picked up the phone.

What usually prevents the immigration process from working is simple bureaucratic inability or complacency. Delays in processing visa and job qualification certification requests are frequently not measured in weeks but in months and years.

In the fall of 1979, the Metropolitan Museum of Art in New York City decided that it could no longer do without a qualified research chemist for its art restoration projects and authentication service. It needed a person with extremely precise credentials: a background in pigment chemistry, a knowledge of art and art history and proven experience in the field of restoration. The position was advertised in the *New York Times*. Several dozen applicants responded, but none of them met the museum's particular requirements. So more advertisements were placed, in trade journals and elsewhere, and Metropolitan officials did a good deal of traveling to make personal contacts. Finally, in late January 1981, the museum thought it had found the right person—a well-known Dutch research chemist with a strong museum background. For his part, E. Rene de la Rie was ecstatic. He had wanted to work for a prestigious museum like the Metropolitan for some time and to live in the United States.

There was some delay in obtaining his visa and job classification certification through the United States Immigration and Naturalization Service, but the parties were assured that the process was going forward. So Mr. de la Rie disposed of his house in Amsterdam, left his previous employment with a national museum there, canceled his academic projects and withdrew from his teaching assignments. He traveled to the United States on a temporary visa to find an apartment and take up residence, although he knew he could not begin working at the Metropolitan Museum until a permanent visa had been approved.

But then the parties were, one might say, reinformed. It would be *eight months* before the visa would come through, because of a severe case backlog and an equally drastic reduction in force at the Immigration and Naturalization Service. De la Rie officially became a member of the museum staff in October 1981, but that was only on paper. As the Metropolitan noted in a letter to the certifying officer at the Department of Labor, "the new laboratories remain unused, the warrantees have expired on the delicate and costly instrumentation with which they are equipped, and the paintings' conversators and curators, who look after one of the world's greatest collections, are again forced to defer basic research projects and are entirely dependent on the good will of other institutions to help with only the most pressing problems which require scientific inquiry. Given the current economic situation, the museum can ill afford to fund a position which is not being filled as we are required to do in this instance because of the difficulties we have experienced over Mr. de la Rie's visa." In short, the museum wanted to know when things could be expedited.

In addition, museum officials asked friends, attorneys and well-connected patrons to write letters to their congressmen, informing them of the urgency of the matter and of the fact that the museum would not be able to wait for the Immigration and Naturalization Service backlog to dissipate. Whatever difficulties there were as to job classification requirements or the particular "preference status" of de la Rie's visa application, they would have to be ironed out soon or the entire laboratory facilities might have to be locked away. The museum would not withdraw an offer made to someone who had already quit his job, sold his house and moved out of his country—just because various United States agencies in Washington could not process a visa application in less than a year.

But bureaucratic backlogs are impersonal beasts, and they do not respond reflexively to complaints from either congressmen or their constituents. At INS the logjam was horrendous; whether the complete file of any particular case could even be found in time, or could be moved ahead in the standard procedure even if all the required papers could be located, was more or less academic. Only one examiner remained in the Immigration and Naturalization Service who dealt with this sort of case, and he was on vacation.

The museum persisted. It wrote letters to Senator Alan Simpson (chairman of the Foreign Relations Committee's Subcommittee on Immigration and Refugee Policy), to other members of Congress, to other officials in the Department of Labor, the Department of State and the Immigration and Naturalization Service. In this regard the prestigious Metropolitan was no different—no better or better off—than the average citizen or business enterprise.

The museum simply wanted its employee to start working for them—it did not seem to be such an unreasonable thing to ask.

But the bureaucratic process was intractable, it appeared. Phone calls to the various agencies involved yielded essentially the same results—messages that typing was backed up, files were out, paperwork had been transferred to another office, secretaries were out to lunch. By the end of November, nothing had changed. De la Rie left the United States for Holland, to visit friends and family for the holidays, without knowing his future at the museum.

More phone calls. It seemed that everybody in the government was either on vacation or out of the office or otherwise unreachable. It was not until January 1982 that anything positive would develop on Mr. de la Rie's visa. Then a caseworker for Senator Simpson was told that the application had been reviewed and favorable action was expected. A cable would be sent to de la Rie in Holland, to the Metropolitan Museum and to all others concerned. No less than three years had elapsed from the time the museum had begun its search, and a year after it had found the right person for the job.

That the would-be American comes from a friendly country has little bearing on how quickly his paperwork is processed.

Canada and United States share the longest common unfortified border in the world. There is no great wall between the two nations, no barbed wire, just a few relaxed check stations at points of entry. But what little physical difference exists between the United States and Canada is more than made up for in the difficulties presented by immigration.

George Delacroix first applied for a visa to the United States in February 1977. He wanted to come to the United States because of his interest and expertise in rare and antique books. In the rare-book business the opportunities were greater in the States than in Canada; it was as simple as that. But nothing was being done on his application. When he asked the U.S. consulate in Toronto what the problem was, he received a curious reply: If George Delacroix wished to invest, say, $40,000 in an American business, his visa application would be approved.

Now, that was strange. *The United States* asking ransom? There is nothing in the U.S. Code that requires a Canadian to invest $40,000 in an American business in order to obtain a visa. It was true that Delacroix had been contacted by an American firm on the possibility of his being an editor and manager, and he did have some Canadian friends who at one time wanted to start a rare-book business on their own and have George manage it. But George's forte was not business acumen or administrative skill. He just knew rare books, that's all. Ever since his high-school days, when he worked part-time as a stock boy in a publishing firm and eventually moved his way up to book editor in summers during college and finally as a full-time manuscript reviewer following graduation, he had been fascinated by rare books. Investment did not interest him.

Moreover, he did not have the money to invest in an American business so that he could obtain a visa. For months he considered borrowing the funds, and finally he did. The same rare-book business in Michigan that he had been considering for employment purposes, he now purchased. In June 1978 he sent papers to the consulate offices in Toronto, stating that he was an investor. But after more months of waiting for some sort of reply, there was still no word about a permanent visa approval.

George went in to talk to the Americans. It was an interview he'll long remember. He was told that some administrative changes had been made. His original priority date had been lost and, worse, the investor category that he was in had also been closed out. There was nothing to be done. No immediate action would be taken on his permanent visa application. He would have to remain in Canada, even though he had already purchased a business in the United States.

Meanwhile, the dealer from whom he had purchased the business would agree to continue operating it only for a certain period of time. After that, he would be taking up residence elsewhere. George tried to find another manager for the book business he purchased so that he could come to the United States, but to no avail. By the end of 1978, the business went into "dormancy." With some $40,000 owed, no visa and now no business, George had to try to sell off nearly 15,000 books to help pay for expenses.

He went back to the U.S. consulate in Toronto and discovered that if he could get special certification from the Department of Labor, a contingent visa could be granted and he could establish residency in the United States. But he was unable to persuade immigration authorities either in Toronto or in Washington about the urgency of his case. He hired an immigration lawyer (to whom he eventually paid more than $2,000). George's file was sent from one office to another. Finally, nearly a year later (in March 1981), a Labor Department certification was approved.

There were numerous other delays on the permanent visa application, and difficulties with his business. Eventually, having heard from another friend that writing to a senator's office might help, he contacted a caseworker for Senator Warren Rudman and asked for whatever help could be provided to a nonconstituent.

The senator's office initially met with the same noncomittal response that George had been getting for nearly five years. But the time came when a new priority date was assigned, and it appeared that Delacroix's visa application would be processed. Still, nobody could guarantee anything. By December 1981, the news was the same. No approval yet. As far as George was beginning to care, he should make plans for a permanent stay in Canada. The United States obviously did not want or need him. He was already bitter. Here was a country more prepared to take in people who cling to boats or who come from war-torn countries or who are otherwise so poor that churches stage fund drives and clothing bazaars for them, but would not consider that somebody who has invested $40,000 and waited five years would make a good American.

On February 18, 1982, though, Delacroix received the following letter from Senator Rudman:

> At long last! As of February 1, a visa number will be available to you. You should now contact the Consulate General in Toronto and tell them your priority date is within the cut-off date for February. As long as you have completed all the information in Packet Three and are documentary qualified, the Consulate will schedule an interview date for you.
>
> I know you must be very excited to have everything finally materialized after years of waiting. My very best wishes to you in your newly-adopted country.

George wasn't sure if he wanted to be an American anymore, but after so much effort he felt he had to give it a try. His first business venture had failed. But he would try.

And on February 2, 1982, George Delacroix became a permanent resident of the United States.

Pablo Garcia also wanted to come to America. But the United States' position on international communism runs the short gamut from contempt to xenophopia, and nowhere is this more clearly reflected than in its immigration policies. The Cold War never ends.

Moreover, the United States can no longer afford an open-door policy for the waves of immigrants who continue to knock, year after year. The image of thousands of dispossessed Europeans massed hopefully in the reception wards of New York during the late nineteenth and early twentieth centuries is a thing of the past. Now each case is much more strictly scrutinized, and even then the right to immigrate is granted grudgingly. Visas are denied if political associations are considered unsavory, or if there are complications about family matters, or if there are policy difficulties with the would-be immigrant's home nation. Many functionaries are involved, from consulates to the halls of the State Department to the desks of aides of senators and congressmen. And always, there is always the added human dimensions of desperation and hope that hover over each case.

Pablo Garcia's wish was hardly an idle one. Sometime previously, his wife and small child had gained refuge in the United States, emigrating from their native Uruguay and settling in New Hampshire. They had the help of a local nonprofit organization known as the Asociación Hispanos Activos. Maria Garcia and her child, Santos, had come to this country a year before, and they thought it would be simple for Pablo to follow them. For more than a year they tried to obtain a visa for him. Nothing. Finally, on April 10, 1980, word came from the State Department, through the U.S. embassy in Montevideo: Pablo Garcia is a Communist—a card-carrying Communist, as the saying goes. It seems that communism is rife in Uruguay, the small nation of three million situated at the southern tip of Brazil. There are several unions in the country, and in order to work at the manufacturing plant where Pablo works, one almost has to join a union. There is always widespread talk about people who refuse to join the labor movement—which is not specifically and openly Communist, but which nevertheless distributes Communist literature and spouts Communist slogans. Pablo had joined the union some time ago because he wanted to be able to work in peace and to be sure that he would have some job security. But even then he and his family talked about the better life in the United States. Finally, with the aid of the Mormon Church, to which they belonged, the Garcias visited the U.S. embassy. After checking on the possibilities of resettlement in New Hampshire, through local community efforts and through the Mormon Church, the embassy granted visas to the Garcia family—that is, to all of them except Pablo. He would have to satisfy the United States government that he was not a card-carrying Communist: Section 212(a)(28) of the Immigration and Naturalization Act prohibits the issuance of visas to persons who are or have been members of the Communist Party or affiliated organizations.

On May 25, 1979, although his family had begun to move out in the previous month, Pablo was informed that his visa application had been denied due to his affiliation with a union sympathetic to communism. It was a crushing blow. All he could do was undertake whatever efforts humanly possible to be re-united.

There was only one real possibility, it seemed, although it was slim. Pablo's case could be considered under the "defector" provision of the act—Section 212(a)(28)(i)(ii)—if he could show that he had ended his affiliation with the Communist Party of Uruguay and the Uruguayan revolutionary movement and if he had "actively opposed their doctrine" for a total of five years. In other words, if Pablo could not demonstrate that, for the past half decade, he had been out on the streets of Montevideo actively opposing the doctrine of international communism, he would have to wait another five years, during which time he'd have to become actively involved in anti-Communist activity. But to do that might cost him his job, or worse. It looked hopeless.

One of the people who was instrumental in bringing Pablo's wife and child to New Hampshire is his brother-in-law who lives there (having moved there many years before). And Rinaldo Angeles knew his way around the mailboxes of Congress. In the beginning of 1981, Angeles wrote to his congressman, Norman E. D'Amours, to see what could be done in Pablo's case. D'Amours' office contacted the Department of State and the U.S. embassy in Uruguay and submitted letters from Pablo's Church group and from friends stating that Pablo was not a Communist and had no Communist sympathies; on the contrary, he had become an elder in the Mormon Church of Uruguay. The State Department was not impressed.

Then, in January 1981, the Asociación Hispanos Activos took over. They wrote to Senator Warren Rudman, detailing the situation of Pablo Garcia, telling him that with the position of the State Department as to Garcia's Communist sympathies, "it will take your intervention to prove these accusations false, and clarify this matter." But the State Department said that Garcia could be considered for a visa only if he became an active non-Communist. Garcia said that he didn't have to show he was an active non-Communist because he always was one. The State Department didn't believe that, and it didn't seem to matter what his Mormon Church said. The impasse seemed unbreachable.

Work on the Garcia case began in the senator's office in February 1981. But because of administrative delays within the State Department and other agencies, nothing was really known about how the case would develop until sometime in April. That is when it became clear to Rudman's caseworkers that the State Department would not compromise on its position: Garcia was an active Communist and could not be considered for a visa in any other fashion but through the "defector" status.

There were more letters from the bishops and other officials of the Mormon Church both in New Hampshire and in Uruguay, disclaiming any involvement that Pablo supposedly had with the Communist Party and asserting that his position in the Church demonstrated his anti-Communist attitudes. The response was more diffidence by the State Department. All the while the family wondered if it would have to move back to Uruguay in order to be together again.

The senator's office eventually came to the conclusion that the embassy in Uruguay was perhaps the real cause of the problem. In early August the senator's office began to press other offices in the State Department in Washington. On September 21, 1981, William Chancey, a man with some authority at the State Department, was approached by a member of the senator's staff and asked about the Garcia situation—having been briefed earlier for five quick minutes in a hallway during a seminar.

It was almost a chance meeting, but that conversation would change Pablo's life. Chancey, having heard Rudman's staff member explain the problem, said that Garcia's activity was not one of such proportions that would pose a national threat. Chancey agreed that the embassy was making an unreasonable stand. He said he would investigate.

An answer came within three weeks. Chancey cited a waiver provision in the law allowing the State Department to waive the defector provision and grant the visa. The Immigration and Naturalization Service would now take the case.

Four months later, in February 1982, the actual visa came through. It took more weeks of communication to make sure that the waiver would stick, that the visa would eventually be granted. Finally, on February 25, 1982, notice came to the senator's office that the waiver and the visa had been honored and that Garcia could travel to the United States. He arrived in this country, nearly two years from the time that his family arrived, on March 16, 1982. The reunion was one of those glorious events in the lives of families who had been separated by circumstances—by war, international problems, strife—but not by choice. Garcia intends to begin working soon, but he is not so sure if he should join the local union.

GETTING THE MOST OUT OF THE IMMIGRATION AND NATURALIZATION SERVICE

What a Caseworker Needs to Know

The caseworker must have the applicant's full name (including maiden name if any and names from former marriages); the number of children and the age, date of birth and place of birth of each; the applicant's place of birth and parents' names; where citizenship is currently held; visa number and type (student, visitor, etc.); place and date of entry into the United States; and current address and telephone number.

State the reasons for wanting to immigrate (for example, to work in the United States, to marry an American, etc.) clearly and concisely. Note what office of the INS the applicant is working through and whether he or she is under a deportation order. If the prospective immigrant wants to work in the United States, he or she must have a labor certification (see page 161). If a serviceperson is attempting to bring a foreign spouse to the United States, was the marriage approved by the serviceperson's base?

When writing or calling on behalf of an applicant, supply all the information noted above and, if an initial application has been denied, explain why. In some instances an applicant will have to show the ability to support himself or herself in the United States, or have a sponsor. Those on visitors' visas must demonstrate some ties with their home country (family, business, property, etc.) that will ensure their eventually returning there.

And, an experienced caseworker points out, "once a person lies to the INS his chances of success are considerably lessened. If we are not provided the straight skinny, it makes it impossible for us to be helpful."

KEY FACTS

IMMIGRATION AND NATURALIZATION SERVICE
421 I Street, N.W.
Washington, DC 20536
Phone: (202) 633-4316, 4430 or 4354

Created by an act of Congress in March 1918, the Immigration and Naturalization Service (INS) is concerned primarily with administration of the laws relating to aliens—including their admission, exclusion, deportation and naturalization. Specifically the INS inspects aliens to determine their admissibility into the United States; guards against illegal entry into the country; investigates, apprehends and removes illegal aliens; adjudicates requests of aliens for benefits under the law; and examines alien applicants seeking to become United States citizens.

The Immigration and Naturalization Service also gives information and counsel to others around the world who seek U.S. citizenship. In cooperation with public schools, the INS provides intructional pamphlets and other materials to those wishing naturalization.

In addition to activities relating to citizenship, the INS's Border Patrol protects the national security of the United States and seeks to ensure the welfare of those residing here by stemming the flow of illegal immigration. The INS also assists other federal, state and local law-enforcement agencies to prevent the influx of illegal drugs.

For further information, contact the Office of Information, Immigration and Naturalization Service, Department of Justice, 425 I Street, N.W., Washington, DC 20536.

☆ VII ☆

GOLDEN NEMATODES AND PUERTO RICAN APPLE-PICKERS

Were we directed from Washington when to sow and when to reap,
we should soon want bread.

—THOMAS JEFFERSON, *Papers*

Russell Allen is proud of the seed potatoes he grows on his farm in Presque Isle in Aroostook County, the northernmost of Maine's 16 counties. Like his father before him, Allen works a tract of over 300 acres, part of which he leases from other landowners. He is a short, wiry man with close-cropped gray hair and a lot of farming wisdom. He talks slowly and clearly, especially when he explains about the production of seed potatoes: It costs more to grow them than other varieties because the quality of the tuber planted is higher, the fields must be sprayed more often to prevent infestation, the yield per acre is lower and perhaps most of all because seed potatoes must be handled during and after harvesting with greater care than other potatoes. As a result, they cost at least a dollar per hundredweight more than does common table stock.

Weather is also a problem. Presque Isle is farther north than Montreal (three hundred miles to the southwest) and just east of New Brunswick. There is frost in Presque Isle for more than eight months of the year. This factor, combined with the shallow topsoil in the area, severely limits what will grow on the small farms that are patched together like quiltwork to the north, south and west of Presque Isle. Yet nearly all the spuds grown in Maine come from Aroostook County, and for both quality and variety Maine continues to be a leader in the American potato industry.

The early return of cold weather each autumn inevitably means that a part of the crop—as much as 5,000 acres out of the little more than 100,000 acres planted—must be left unharvested every year, because the ground has frozen before the farmers can get the potatoes out of the earth. In a way, though, the inhospitable climate is a blessing, at least to the small number of Maine's growers who produce seed potatoes—that is, potatoes from which table stock is grown. A seed potato must be of high quality, free of any impurities or infestation, and plant pests that thrive easily in gentler environments find it virtually impossible to establish themselves in the cold weather of Aroostook County.

Potato farmers are particularly watchful for the roundworm parasite *Heterodera rostochiensis,* commonly known as the golden nematode. Although this pest is also dangerous to the roots of tomato and tobacco plants, there are special regulations applied to potatoes: Those grown in an area where golden nematodes have been found cannot be marketed as seed stock, even if the grower could prove that his crop is not infested. They may be sold only as table stock.

But golden nematodes have never been found in Maine—partly, no doubt, because it would be difficult for them to survive in the state's cold climate. Freedom from the golden nematode and similar pests has helped farmers in the area retain their position as prime suppliers of seed potatoes, even as other states and Canada have reduced Maine's share of the market for table stock. The cold climate, furthermore, allows potatoes to be stored inexpensively for long periods without loss of quality.

In 1972, Russell Allen's father, Edgar, leased a 100-acre tract of land adjacent to his own fields in Presque Isle. He planted the new acreage in seed potatoes, along with the 240 acres already under cultivation. But the Allens were unaware of a critical piece of the land's history: The farmer who had tilled it previously, a man named Dana Thompson, had in 1967 purchased seed potatoes from a grower in New York State and had replanted them on eight acres in Presque Isle. Later that same year, golden nematodes were found on the New York farm. As a result, the U.S. Department of Agriculture (USDA), in 1968, began testing Thompson's farm for the parasite.

The Department of Agriculture made no announcement of the fact that it was testing for golden nematodes on Thompson's property—perhaps in order to prevent the spread of rumors that would almost certainly have risen had word of the tests gotten around. In hindsight, the government's reluctance to feed the rumor mill was laudable: After all, eight annual investigations between 1968 and 1976 revealed no trace of golden nematodes (unaccountably, there was no testing in 1971).

The USDA's reticence was not without its costs, however—particularly to the Allens. Between 1972 and 1976 they had grown, harvested and sold four crops of seed potatoes. Then, in the winter of 1977, they were abruptly informed that they would not be permitted to sell their 1976 crop—even though it was already in storage and would have been used for planting that spring—because of the possibility that that crop of potatoes was infested.

The person who phoned the Allens with the bad news was Paul Eastman, director of the Division of Plant Industry in the Maine Department of Agriculture. Eastman unquestionably possessed the data that had been acquired over a decade's time, but it is not clear how long he had known of the connection between the infested property in New York and the farm in Presque Isle, nor why he waited so long to act on the information. He did tell the Allens, however, that the Canadian government was pressing the United States Department of Agriculture for assurances that seed potatoes exported to Canada from Maine contained no golden nematodes. Although the Americal officials were apparently satisfied that there was no danger of golden nematode infestation from the Allens' leased acreage, they had decided to act at the urging of the Canadians.

The call from Eastman informed the Allens for the first time of the tenuous connection between their potatoes and the golden nematode. Shortly thereafter they were approached by George Ledbetter, a USDA official, who asked them to sign an agreement to sell their potatoes as table stock only. To the Allens this meant money, pure and simple: They'd be signing away substantial hard-earned profits, with seed potatoes then fetching a dollar and more per hundredweight above the price of table stock and with their 1976 crop, lying in cold storage, amounting to 20,625 hundredweight. Edgar Allen understood that golden nematodes posed a serious problem to potato growers, but he also knew that there was no evidence of infestation on his farm. Indeed, now he could point to the eight annual USDA tests that had turned up negative. In addition, of the 100 acres that made up the Rutland farm, only 76 acres had been tested. Why hadn't the USDA been concerned about the remaining two dozen acres? The Allens didn't have to dig deep into their farming wisdom; for them the decision was simple. They turned down George Ledbetter's request.

But Ledbetter was not dissuaded. He returned several days

later, this time with a less deferential attitude and accompanied by two officials from the local federal-state inspection office. These gentlemen, he said, had been instructed not to issue the Allens any government tags for the shipment of seed potatoes. The USDA, like it or not, would simply embargo the 1976 Allen seed crop. Their potatoes could be sold as table stock or they could not be sold at all.

Faced with such a choice, the Allens were forced to sell their 1976 potatoes as table stock and, some $20,000 poorer, could only hope their 1977 crop would fare better. Their hopes were short-lived. Just before planting time, the government decided to intensify its effort to detect the presence of golden nematodes on the Rutland farm. Using a machine that took soil samples every two feet as it inched across the 76 acres previously tested, USDA officials again found no evidence of infestation. Yet the USDA was not ready to give the land a clean bill of health, and the sales restrictions were extended to cover the 1977 crop. Only the 24 acres of untested land was released for the cultivation and sale of seed potatoes.

Even had the entire tract been certified as pest-free, the harm already incurred by the Allens was more than momentary. As growers of seed potatoes, they had to guard their reputation as suppliers of high-quality, untainted merchandise or risk losing a business built up through years of hard work. As Russell Allen put it, "My reputation as a seed grower, as well as my ability to market my crop, was on the line. Once a rumor has started, it is difficult to stop and impossible to repair its damage. The correct information seldom surfaces." Their losses were clearly not confined to the columns of their ledger books.

The spring of 1977, harbinger as it was of that year's ill-fated harvest, also brought with it the death of Edgar Allen. The struggle with the federal bureaucracy was thus passed from father to son. Russell Allen's troubles were temporarily assuaged by advice from Paul Eastman that the Department of Agriculture might pay him for the losses resulting from the sales restrictions. Federal law authorizes the USDA to compensate growers ordered not to plant potatoes or tomatoes in infested areas, or for losses resulting from the destruction of those commodities by natural pests. Allen contacted Ledbetter, who in turn consulted his superiors in Washington. Their response struck Allen as still another bureaucratic gaffe. Apparently the government's reasons for restricting the sale of Allen's seed potatoes had been too flimsy, and now the USDA was in an embarrassing position. The federal statute did not expressly provide for compensation in the event of mere suspicion, without proof, of infestation. But bureaucratic embarrassment frequently turns to smugness. With Alice in Wonderland logic the USDA told Allen that, although the sales restrictions had been warranted even in the face of abundant evidence that the land was pest-free, compensation could not be granted because, of course, there was no proof of infestation.

Allen was flabbergasted. The U.S. Department of Agriculture wanted to have its seed potatoes and eat them too, and he wasn't going to stand for it. But where to turn? Almost in desperation he sought the aid of my office. After reviewing the situation, I proposed to broaden the scope of compensation provided by the statute to cover "increased costs, loss of sales, and a decrease in land value, with respect to such crop farming activity, as a result of [golden nematode] infestation, quarantine, or exposure." Such an amendment to the law would eliminate any need to show *actual* infestation in order to qualify for compensation.

The proposed legislation (H.R. 7956) was introduced in the fall of 1977, and it brought an immediate and critical response from the Department of Agriculture. A House agriculture subcommittee was told that, because Mr. Allen's case was one of only two "rather unique" compensation requests, it should be addressed by private rather than general legislation—that is, in a bill specially designed for Mr. Allen's relief alone.

The USDA's resistance to H.R. 7956 proved effective. On May 3, 1978, Allen's congressman introduced in its place a private bill entitled "An Act, for the relief of Russell Allen," which directed the secretary of agriculture to pay $52,703—based on Allen's accounting of lost profits—as compensation for "unjustified restrictions" placed on Allen's 1976 and 1977 crops. Once more, to Allen's amazement, the USDA objected. Although the House and Senate, in passing the bill, concluded that the restrictions on Allen's land were unwarranted, the USDA saw fit to engineer two amendments. The first left determination of the amount of damages to the secretary of agriculture, with $52,703 as a ceiling. The second, more poignant, change deleted the adjective "'unjustified" in describing the sales restrictions.

Allen took his money and went home. He was grateful for congressional assistance, but he also learned through the experience that those who make the laws do not always prevail completely over those whose responsibility is solely to administer them.

The Bryce family of St. Agatha, in Aroostook County, Maine, hasn't had much trouble growing potatoes. Its problems are more in picking them.

From the time he was a first-grader William Bryce helped with the potato harvest on his family's farm, also in Aroostook County. Like other farm children William was accustomed to helping with the chores on the family's 158-acre property, but the potato harvest is different. It begins in late August, when the public schools have already been in session for over a month and a half. But it is only then, with more than a hint of winter creeping through the cold evenings of northern Maine, that the potatoes are ready for harvesting. The picking season is short: A few weeks later the ground will be too hard for digging potatoes. This means that the laborious work has to be completed by the middle of October and to accomplish this the people of the potato-farming region of Aroostook County have adopted an unusual custom: They recess the schools for several weeks at this time, thus freeing thousands of schoolchildren for the potato harvest. Those who elect to join the force of pickers—and about two-thirds of the schoolchildren under twelve years of age customarily do—are paid according to the quantity of potatoes they pick. Current rates hover at about 50 cents a barrel. The children thus employed join the regular farmhands in the fields and are themselves often joined by their schoolteachers and mothers, who earn extra money in the harvest while keeping an eye on their pupils and offspring.

Objections to the traditional potato-picking recess in Aroostook County came from a variety of sources. Groups like the National Committee for the Education of Migrant Children suggested that the health and safety of the young pickers might be imperiled by dangerous pesticides and farm machinery. The federal government, of course, cited the provisions of the Fair Labor Standards Act.

To a visitor sitting in the rustic kitchen of the Bryce farmhouse with a view of some of the farm's brown and hilly fields through the window, William Bryce looks very much the part of the New England farmer. He's now fifty-one, a tall, tightly sinewed man with an erect posture that lends dignity to his appearance, even when his boots and hands are stained by the soil from which he earns his living. He is handsome in an austere sort of way, his features sharp and his eyes and hair nearly the same shade of steely gray. Unlike the New England stereotype, however, Bill Bryce is far from laconic. He enjoys talking—about his childhood, his Army experiences in World War II (the only time he's ever been away from northern Maine for longer than a week), about the people and countryside around St. Agatha and, more recently, about the federal government.

"When I started picking potatoes," he says, "all the harvesting was done by hand. There weren't any of those mechanical harvesters around here yet. 'Course, that was at the beginning of the Depression—around 1931 or '32—and we didn't get more than a few cents a barrel for what we picked, but that was money in those times. My brothers and I worked on the family farm alongside the other kids, and we got paid like everybody else. What we earned we'd put toward buying our winter clothes or Christmas presents for the family or putting aside money for college. Same as our kids do now. I was proud of the money I earned in the harvest, and the kids now are proud, too. There's no feeling like it for boys or girls of 10 or 12, or even younger, lining up at the end of the week for their own pay envelopes, right in line with the grown-ups. They feel that they've done something that matters, and they have. We couldn't get the potatoes out of the ground without them, not at what we can pay, and still make a profit. Perhaps regardless of what we paid. The harvest is too short, the size of the farms— most of them—too small and the wages we can pay too low to draw people from the labor market. The adults who join the harvest are mostly parents and others who can't really work full-time and who keep an eye on the children as they work. And with three, four or five from one family all working the harvest, the money adds up."

Bryce and other area farmers say that for most small farms mechanical harvesters are not satisfactory alternatives to manual picking. A 150-acre farm is too large for a single harvester, which can handle about 125 acres during the brief harvest season, but much too small to make two harvesters economically feasible. And since all the potatoes in northern Maine must be harvested during the same period, it is impossible to arrange for the farmers to share the expensive equipment. A fully outfitted mechanical harvester costs upward of $50,000.

Even many larger farms employ both methods, putting hand crews to work where the terrain would make mechanical harvesting difficult. Herschel Smith, whose 1,000-plus acres require six harvesters and two hand crews to gather in the annual crop, points out that on a farm the size of his "I couldn't find enough people willing to pick potatoes by hand if I combed the entire county." As it is, Smith employs over 200 young people each autumn during the potato harvest.

Although Smith and other large growers employ large numbers of students each year—some 2,000 pickers are hired every season, nearly two-thirds of them on school recess—few of the young people are affected by the child labor provisions of the Fair Labor Standards Act, which prohibits the employment of children under age 12 in most agricultural work. In a recent harvest, for example, Smith had only a dozen workers younger than 12.

It is the small farmers, though—those like William Bryce and Irene Bradford, a widow who farms 50 acres in tiny Patten, Maine—who do all of their picking by hand who depend on the younger children for the bulk of their labor force. And it's not only the economics of potato-picking that draw the people of the county to their children at harvest time; it's not only because they wish to preserve a custom that has existed for generations and to provide income to young people whom they know are as likely to spend what they earn on necessities—clothing or education—as on luxuries. Put simply, farm work builds character. They know it does. It's in their bones. The people of rural Maine, inured to the harsh climate of its northernmost county and accustomed to working hard for whatever they get from life, dismiss the objections of Washington legislators and bureaucrats who claim that the employment of children in the fields is exploitative and dangerous. Large growers and small agree that their own experience in the fields when they were children taught them to respect work, to be proud of the money they earned through labor, to be honest and responsible throughout their lives. It is hard to tell from listening to them talk what they are more proud of: their good labor practices and safety records, or the fact that virtually none of the youngsters who grow up in towns like Patten and St. Agatha ever turns delinquent or criminal in adolescence or adulthood.

Herschel Smith can barely recall the rare incidents clouding the good record of harvests past. "I haven't had a serious accident on my farm in all the time I've been farming—and that's more than 30 years now. Maybe a cut finger or hand once in a while, but we're careful to keep an eye on these children. After all, these kids are our own—relatives, neighbors, the children of friends, schoolmates. We expect them to work, of course, but we supervise them carefully. We pick the young children up each morning in the school bus and drive them home again in the evening, and when the weather's bad the bus stays out in the field all day so the kids can get in out of the rain in a hurry. While they're working the foremen are watching them, as are very often their older sisters and brothers, their mothers and sometimes their own teachers. As a result, the children learn that we value what they do and learn to respect work, to be responsible and to go by the rules.

"The way we keep track of how much a youngster has picked and how much he's earned is by a system of numbered tickets; every crew member has his own number. Every once in a while we catch one of the youngsters stuffing the ticket box—taking someone's tickets off and substituting his own. We usually get those kids straightened out and they stay straightened out for life. They learn honesty and cooperation, and they learn to respect the work that each person does and to value the money that's earned by labor."

The money the children do earn may not be much by current standards, but in northern Maine it may seem a small fortune to the child who has worked for it. A fifth-grader can make upward of several hundred dollars during the three-week harvest season. The chidlren who participate in the harvest know they are working, but they often enjoy the experience, just as they often spend part of their earnings on necessities like clothing and part on toys or gifts.

"Picking potatoes is kind of hard work," says nine-year-old Richalene Higgins, "but I like it better than going to school." Richalene is a straight-A student. Her quota was just under 10 barrels of potatoes a day, netting her about $100 for the harvest. Ten-year-old Todd Grass, in contrast, was an experienced picker, having worked in the harvests on the farms around Mars Hill since he was six. Now he can pick 35 barrels a day, which brings him nearly $300 for the harvest. Todd's mother and brother work alongside him, and together the family adds about $1,000 to their annual income—enough to outfit the boys for the year and permit them to save something as well.

An additional, unexpected feature of the potato harvest in Aroostook County is that it cuts across lines of class and income. Doctors, lawyers and their families are likely to be found in the fields picking alongside parents and children from working-class families. In recent years, in fact, relatively few of the adult pickers have been blue-collar types. On weekends, the harvest takes on the appearance of a social ritual—like barn-raisings in nineteenth-century rural America—bringing together members of a community while also producing tangible results.

Samuel Rideout, a physician, notes that what his children earn adds little to real family income, but he and his wife encourage their participation because, like the others in this countryside of self-reliance, they want their children to learn the lessons of industry and thrift.

The farmers responded to their labor dilemma with a combination of pragmatism—calling on their elected representatives to tell their story the way it was and, if need be, change the law—and homespun country wisdom. At the time, I was a congressman. I studied the situation and found the outsiders' objections without merit. Apparently the same unwarranted claims were hindering farmers elsewhere as well; they were people with local problems and local situations who had been getting along just fine, thank you, without federal intervention. The law may apply here, they said, but it doesn't apply very well; a little common sense would be in order. The result was an amendment to the Fair Labor Standards Act that would permit local children under the age of 12 to help in harvesting crops like potatoes and blueberries in Maine and strawberries in Washington—fruits and vegetables that must be picked within a short time if they are not to perish and thereby cause great financial losses (if not ruin) to their growers.

To the objections of those who believe that children who work in the potato harvest are as exploited as the children of migrant laborers and sweatshop tyrants, local residents countered with recollections of harvests in their own childhoods and with the enthusiastic testimony of their children. The educational process, they said, was not compromised—it was enhanced. They shared the concern about the early-fall recess and adopted a sensible rule calling for children in the lowest grades to attend regular classes. Aside from the lessons learned in the fields, they pointed out, the arguments against recessing the schools (which open in mid-August) for the harvest rest on prejudice rather than sound theory. Like most of his compatriots, Samuel Rideout said he is suspicious of idleness and is attracted to the idea of getting the students back to school after six weeks of summer vacation. About the recess, he observed, "Most of the teachers like it, and I don't think it hurts the children's schooling. Perhaps some of the schoolteachers find it disruptive, but you educate them too. We arrange it very well. It shortens up the vacation time."

The amendment pleased many Maine farmers, but as with many legislative solutions there were problems with its implementation. The Department of Labor completely subverted the intent of Congress by enacting a regulation that required that a farmer, in order to secure a waiver of the prohibition against employing 10- and 11-year-olds, must demonstrate that no workers above the age of 12 are available. Many of the farms that need to hire young children are small, however, and it is difficult for them to comply with the requirements of the law—to search for older workers and then document their un-availability by filling out a myriad of forms. "By the time I finished doing all that paperwork," says Irene Bradford, "my potatoes would have rotted on the vine or the ground would have frozen over. I don't know why those do-gooders in Washington want to keep our kids out of the fields. They ought to come up here to Patten and see how dangerous it is. It's not dangerous at all; picking potatoes puts a little iron in these children's souls."

Here was a classic case of Congress and constituents winning the battle, but losing the war to the bureaucracy.

Potatoes aren't the only crop whose picking season presents problems. Every autumn, in the northeastern apple-growing region that extends from central Maine all the way down to northern Virginia, signs begin to appear along the roadsides that run past the apple orchards: "Pick Your Own Apples." Many of them list the hours the orchards are open, the varieties of apples grown and the prices per bushel charged to those who pick their own and compared to already filled baskets. It is not unusual to see, on a Saturday or Sunday afternoon in New York's Ulster County, cars lining the highways near the apple orchards in such numbers that latecomers might have to hike nearly a quarter mile from their parking places to reach the entrances.

Various government agencies have attempted to boost interest in pick-your-own farms and orchards by publishing lists of crops, locations and dates of picking seasons. News-papers in the areas of the orchards frequently publish an-nouncements designed to entice families looking for pleasant, wholesome and economical ways of spending weekend hours with their children. Some city dwellers like to show their kids how things grow and are harvested. Others may be looking for a bargain: The price of a bushel of apples picked in the orchard is only a fraction of their packaged cost in the super-market or even loose at a roadside stand.

But orchardmen are not only fruit growers, they are busi-nessmen as well, and what has drawn them to invite school groups, parents with children and members of urban and suburban food-buying cooperatives to help with the apple harvest is, very simply, a labor problem: There are no longer enough apple pickers available to harvest the crop during the short fall period—approximately five weeks—when the apples must either be picked and put in cold storage or left to drop from the trees and rot on the ground. Pick-your-own customers are actually buying their apples wholesale from the grower, but to the orchardman that is not the important thing. The apple growers of the Northeast have been able to sell everything they can bring to market, which simply isn't enough. Each time a paying customer picks an apple, it's one less lost at the end of the harvest. Vincent Russo of the Mid-Hudson Valley Growers' Cooperative in New York state says it all: "It's wonderful: On the weekends people come in, have a good time picking apples and part of my crop is saved. I couldn't afford to hire them to do the same work."

Even where unemployment is higher than in New York's Hudson Valley—as in central Maine—growers still find too few domestic laborers available to harvest their apples. Other industries developed over the past 25 years in what were formerly exclusively agricultural regions, have absorbed most of the existing labor force. Picking apples, moreover, is hard work. Although an apple tree is not tall, virtually all the picking must be done from ladders in order to prevent damage to the fruit, which must be free of bruises in order to be salable as fresh eating or cooking apples. (The damaged crop is sold for less to the large companies that manufacture apple sauce and apple juice.) An apple picker spends long hours climbing ladders, picking and plucking fruit and carefully placing it in a large basket suspended on a strap worn around his or her neck. The picker descends when the basket is full, to begin the process again in another section. A full basket weighs about 40 pounds.

Small wonder, then, that growers find it almost impossible to recruit and retain a sufficient labor force throughout the apple harvest. In the northern states it is especially difficult to attract and keep pickers, because the weather is often already cool. Many migrants simply prefer jobs in warmer climates. For example, nearly 1,100 pickers were hired to work in a recent apple harvest in the six New England states. Only 900 actually reported to the fields when the picking was due to begin, and 150 of those left the orchards without picking a single apple. Of the remaining 750 recruits who commenced the harvest, only 262 of them were still at work when it ended five weeks later.

The New England Apple Council estimates the loss due to unharvested apples at over 84,000 bushel boxes per season.
According to Marvin Peck, a grower in Shelburne, Massachusetts, and for several years the president of the council, some
orchards have been bankrupted by work crews who fail to
report, or who leave without harvesting the crop. Labor is a
particularly sensitive issue for an apple grower because through
most of the year he needs little if any help to run an orchard.
"On a small place," says Peck, "one man can often do all the
work himself—spraying, pruning, everything—right up to
harvest time. But during those five weeks when the apples have
to be picked, he needs a crew that works quickly, with people
who are strong enough to put in a long day and keep coming
back to work until all the apples are in. The apples must not
only be picked but also stored by type and size. If the apples
aren't in cold storage (32 to 40 degrees) within 72 hours of
being picked, they'll start to decay."

The majority of the pickers available for the apple harvest
come from three groups: Jamaican, Puerto Rican or domestic,
recruited either locally or in other areas. The former two
groups are transported to the orchards either from their homes
or from other work sites (if they already are working in other
harvests farther to the south). According to the New England
Apple Council's reports, the least reliable group of the three is
the domestic group.

Peck, a ruddy man with a quick smile, remembers especially
the case of Westward Orchards in Harvard, Massachusetts. "Joe
Duffy, who owned Westward, agreed one year to hire 40 young
people from Boston, who were being trained in a special program for the unemployed. I guess this was in 1970 or '71. As
part of their training, most of them were brought out to the
orchard and shown around. They were taught how to use the
ladders and the buckets, how to select fruit for picking, things
like that. There wasn't really a lot to show them. Picking apples
is hard work, but it isn't hard to learn. Well, at harvest time,
only two of the pickers reported to work on the first day, and
neither of them lasted beyond the second day." By then it was
too late to recruit a second crew of pickers, and Duffy therefore
lost most of his year's crop.

The experience at Westward Orchards is not unique. Peck
recalls other cases of crews who failed to report, proved unable
or unwilling to perform the necessary work or disappeared
after obtaining some money or supplies from their employer.
For example, at Colonial Orchards in Sutton, Massachusetts, a

skeleton crew of five pickers arrived at the beginning of harvest, received money for groceries from the owner and left the orchard. They never returned.

Growers are required by law to reimburse their harvest workers for travel expenses from their homes or from the site of their last work. (In most cases they are able to delay making this payment until at least half the harvest is over, in order to ensure that workers remain on the job.) They must also pay—either in hourly wages or by piecework—at rates that match or exceed the federal minimum wage for each year. But it is doubtful that even very high wages would attract substantial numbers of domestic pickers: In a recent harvest, for example, the number of domestic workers applying for work as apple pickers was over 40 percent lower than the figure for the previous year.

In the past few years, to find enough pickers—and workers who are capable of performing consistently throughout the harvest season—apple growers have begun to look beyond the mainland, in particular to Puerto Rico and Jamaica. But in order to qualify for such workers the growers must satisfy a number of Department of Labor regulations. This applies especially in the case of pickers to be temporarily admitted from Jamaica, who can be hired only when employers have shown that no labor is domestically available. It is somewhat easier to hire Puerto Ricans, since they are American citizens—but to import them from Puerto Rico an employer must also demonstrate that he cannot obtain local labor.

The Department of Labor has staunchly resisted efforts by northeastern apple growers to procure adequate supplies of harvest labor from the Caribbean. Orchards are required to advertise each year for domestic workers, even when none are known to exist in an area; the Department of Labor has refused to consider requests for foreign workers until a local recruitment period of 60 days has passed. Only then, after the grower has waited and proven that insufficient local labor is available, may he apply to the Department of Labor for permission to import foreign workers. Often, however, there is no longer enough time for them to find and transport the workers they need.

Organizations such as the New England Apple Council ordinarily rely on the projections of their own members to predict how large a crop will be and how many people will be needed to harvest it. But the Labor Department has often disputed the figures offered by growers' associations, forcing them to resort to time-consuming and complicated appeals procedures that often drag on until long after the optimal time for hiring the workers needed.

After all, the apple growers insist, pickers should not be hired so close to when the harvest begins that they will be unable to arrive in time, nor so long beforehand that they are unlikely to show up on the appointed day. But that in fact is what often happens as a result of the efforts of the federal government to force the growers to comply with complicated regulations.

Jamaican pickers are the most sought-after in the apple harvest. Because those who are permitted by the Jamaican government to go to the United States to work in the apple- and sugar-cane harvests can earn as much in two or three months in the United States as they would in a year at home, it is the lucky laborer who is granted an exit visa to the United States. But the orchards are glad to pay the cost of their air fare—for one grower a few years back the transportation costs for foreign laborers alone exceeded $23,000 for a single harvest, but the costs were well justified. Despite the great differences in climate between their native country and New England, the Jamaicans have proven to be productive workers in the apple harvest.

The Jamaicans come to the orchards without their families. They are industrious and orderly. Although their customs and cuisine may be quaint in the eyes of their Eastern Seaboard hosts, their work habits are not. And they are good capitalists as well: Almost without exception, they prefer to work at piece rates rather than for an hourly wage, since they can make more money by being paid for each bushel of apples they pick.

But even with the help of hardworking pickers like the Jamaicans, it is a fortunate apple grower who is able to harvest all of his crop in a given season. Nor is it likely that Labor Department cooperation with the growers will result in very many of the pick-your-own signs disappearing from the roadsides of apple-growing areas.

Because the rules are made in Washington, and the bureaucrats who administer them insist on playing strictly by the book, the skirmishes seem to be perennial: Each year the growers complain to their elected representatives that the federal regulations on laborers threaten to put them out of business, and each year the congressional caseworkers are forced to hound the Labor Department to plead individual cases.

The battle is a continuing one, but there are lessons to be learned from the experiences of the past. Most of them are put to good use by professional caseworkers—still perhaps the constituents' best advocates in Washington.

If there is a common theme that runs through the three cases I have described, it is that even when congressional intent is clear, the law is often blunted and stultified by federal agencies that arrogate to themselves power of policymaking.

In response to what it sees as jurisdictional trespassing, Congress has passed a number of laws seeking to restrain improper agency activities. Until the constitutionality of such congressional restrictions is resolved by the U.S. Supreme Court, it is important for citizens to urge their representatives to persevere in their insistence that agency rules conform to congressional intent—rather than to the fiat of unelected administrative officials.

GETTING THE MOST OUT OF THE DEPARTMENT OF AGRICULTURE

What a Caseworker Needs to Know

The Department of Agriculture provides technical assistance to farmers about soil conservation and cost-sharing. A caseworker needs to know a farmer's crop, where his farm is located and its size.

Farm ownership loans up to $200,000 ($300,000 if guaranteed through another lender) are available to purchase real estate; operation loans are available up to $100,000 ($200,000 if guaranteed elsewhere). If a farmer can get a loan through non-government sources, he is seldom eligible for USDA support. A caseworker needs to know the farmer's financial status, type of industry, whether the business is new or established and if there are any delinquent loans outstanding (if so, with whom and the length of delinquency).

KEY FACTS

DEPARTMENT OF AGRICULTURE
Fourteenth Street and Independence Avenue, S.W.
Washington, DC 20250
Phone: (202) 655-4000

SCOPE

The Department of Agriculture is the federal government's third-largest agency, with 97,000 full-time employees. Created in 1862 by an act of Congress that was signed into law by President Lincoln, the USDA has an effect on every American every day. The eighth executive department to achieve Cabinet rank, the USDA is charged with improving from production, assuring consumers of an adequate food supply at reasonable prices and developing and expanding foreign markets for American agricultural products. The USDA also helps millions of Americans through food assistance programs. Its researchers are deeply involved in crop production, marketing, the use of agricultural products, food safety, animal diseases, pest control, nutrition and environmental quality. USDA programs in the fields of rural development, housing assistance and conservation are key elements of national growth policies.

RURAL DEVELOPMENT

Rural development is a cooperative process in which public agencies, private organizations and individual citizens work together to improve community facilities, services and economic opportunities for people living in the towns and farming communities outside metropolitan America.

Farmers Home Administration (FmHA)

The FmHA provides supervised credit for those in rural America unable to obtain credit from other sources at reasonable rates and terms. Loans for farming, home construction, conservation, public works and business and industrial development are available.

For further information, contact the Information Staff, Farmers Home Administration, Department of Agriculture, Washington, DC 20250. Phone: (202) 447-4323.

Rural Electrification Administration (REA)

The REA finances electric and telephone facilities in rural areas of the United States and its territories. Through self-liquidating loans and technical assistance, it is supposed to provide adequate and dependable electric and telephone service to rural people under rates and conditions that permit full and productive use.

For further information, contact the Office of Information and Public Affairs, Rural Electrification Administration, Department of Agriculture, Washington, DC 20250. Phone: (202) 447-5606.

MARKETING AND TRANSPORTATION SERVICES

Agricultural Marketing Service (AMS)

The AMS administers standardization, grading, voluntary and mandatory inspection, market news, marketing orders and regulatory and related programs.

For further information, contact Information Division, Agricultural Marketing Service, Department of Agriculture, Washington, DC 20250. Phone: (202) 447-6766.

Animal and Plant Health Inspection Service (APHIS)

The APHIS helps safeguard the health and quality of agricultural animals and plants and administers federal laws and regulations pertaining to the control and eradication of pests and diseases.

For further information, contact Information Division, Animal and Plant Health Inspection Service, Department of Agriculture, Washington, DC 20250. Phone: (202) 447-3977.

Federal Grain Inspection Service (FGIS)

The FGIS establishes official U.S. standards for grain and other assigned commodities and administers a nationwide system of official inspections to certify grades. All substantial exporters of U.S. grain are required to register with the FGIS and to provide agency officials with information about company ownership, management, control and locations.

For further information, contact Information Division, Agricultural Marketing Service, Department of Agriculture, Washington, DC 20250. Phone: (202) 447-6766.

Office of Transportation (OT)

The OT gives technical assistance, information and economic analysis to agricultural producers, shippers and carriers, and it administers research and programs designed to improve agricultural marketing.

For further information, contact Office of Transportation, Department of Agriculture, Washington, DC 20250. Phone: (202) 447-3963.

FOOD AND CONSUMER SERVICES

Food Safety and Quality Service (FSQS)

The FSQS was established by the secretary of agriculture in 1977 to assure that foods are safe, wholesome and nutritious; that they are informatively and honestly labeled; and that they are available in the marketing system through purchase of surplus food commodities and those needed in the national food assistance programs.

Food and Nutrition Service (FNS)

The FNS administers a number of federal-state programs, such as the food stamp program, providing food assistance to those in need.

For further information, contact Legislative Affairs and Information Officer, Food and Nutrition Service, Department of Agriculture, Washington, DC 20250. Phone: (202) 447-8138.

SCIENCE AND EDUCATION

Science and Education Administration (SEA)

The SEA coordinates the planning of agricultural research; conducts federal research programs in the food and agricultural sciences; ensures that the results of agricultural research are effectively communicated and demonstrated to farmers, processors, handlers, consumers and other users; and promotes the identification of high-priority national objectives in the food and agricultural sciences, initiating special projects to meet those objectives.

For further information, contact Information Staff, Science and Education Administration, Department of Agriculture, Washington, DC 20250. Phone: (202) 447-4111.

NATURAL RESOURCES AND ENVIRONMENT

Forest Service (FS)

FS programs are concerned with timber production, outdoor recreation, habitats for fish and wildlife, watershed protection and livestock grazing—as well as with wilderness management, forest engineering, land management planning, mining, land reclamation and reforestation, the marketing and utilization of forest products, resource surveys, urban forestry and pollution.

For further information, contact Information Office, Forest Service, Department of Agriculture, P.O. Box 2417, Washington, D.C. 20012. Phone: (202) 447-3760.

Soil Conservation Service (SCS)

The SCS has primary responsibility for developing and carrying out a national soil-and water-conservation program in cooperation with landowners and operators, community planning agencies and regional resource groups—as well as with other agencies of federal, state and local governments. The SCS also assists in agricultural pollution control, environmental improvement and rural community development.

For further information, contact Information Division, Soil Conservation Service, Department of Agriculture, Washington, DC 20250. Phone: (202) 447-4543.

ECONOMICS, POLICY ANALYSIS AND BUDGET

The World Food and Agricultural Outlook and Situation Board (WFAOSB)

The WFAOSB views all commodity and agricultural food data available in order to develop policy recommendations for the Department of Agriculture. The board also coordinates weather- and climate-monitoring activities within the USDA.

For further information, contact Chairman, World Food and Agricultural Outlook and Situation Board, Department of Agriculture, Washington, DC 20250. Phone: (202) 447-4230.

Economics, Statistics and Cooperatives Service (ESCS)

The ESCS collects and analyzes domestic and international agriculture-related information. Economic activities involve projecting supply, demand and use of crops and livestock; assessing the impact of foreign agricultural trade; analyzing the impact on food production of policies concerning the use, conservation and development of natural resources; and documenting and measuring the performance of the agricultural industry as an aid to creating food and fiber policies. Statistics are gathered and published about the nation's crops, livestock, poultry, dairy products, prices, labor and related agricultural subjects. The ESCS also compiles national statistics on farmer cooperatives.

For further information, contact Information Staff, Economics, Statistics and Cooperative Service, Department of Agriculture, Washington, DC 20250. Phone: (202) 447-4230.

INFORMATION

Each USDA agency provides information about its work to farmers, industry and consumers. The Office of Governmental and Public Affairs (GPA) plans, develops and executes departmental information programs and coordinates internal agency activities pertaining to the following: publications, both technical and popular; current information, which includes press, radio and television materials, and special reports; and visuals, including exhibits, photographs, graphics and motion pictures.

For further information, contact Office of Governmental and Public Affairs, Department of Agriculture, Washington, DC 20250. Phone: (202) 447-2791.

INTERNATIONAL AFFAIRS AND COMMODITY PROGRAMS

Agricultural Stabilization and Conservation Service (ASCS)

The ASCS is the agency of the Department of Agriculture which administers specified commodity and related land-use programs designed for voluntary production adjustment, resource protection, and price, market, and farm-income stabilization.

For further information, contact the Division of Information, ASCS, Department of Agriculture, Washington, D.C. 20250. Phone: (202) 447-4044.

Foreign Agricultural Service (FAS)

The FAS is the export and promotion agency for the Department of Agriculture. As such it is the promotional arm for the world's largest agricultural export business, through its network of counselors, negotiators, attachés, trade officers, marketing specialists, and analysts—many of them stationed overseas.

For further information, contact the Division of Information, FAS, Department of Agriculture, Washington, D.C. 20250. Phone: (202) 447-3448.

☆ VIII ☆

BREATHS OF LIFE FROM LABOR

Labor omnia vincit.

—VERGIL, *Georgics I*

Wyoming. The name alone conjures up vistas of vastness—big-sky country with enormous burnt-orange sunsets punctuated only by the dark silhouettes of cactus and a meandering cowboy or tumbleweed. The horizons are far away, speared by the sharp blue-and-white peaks of the Bighorn, Larami and Rocky Mountains. Flat plains are covered with thin grass and carved by scattered streams. Wildlife and the domesticated animals far outnumber the people. Most of it acquired as part of the Louisiana Purchase, Wyoming is the ninth largest state in area and the forty-ninth in population (estimated 1980 total: 470,000). There are only three cities in the state: Cheyenne (the capital), Casper and Laramie: none has over 52,000 inhabitants. Wyoming sends but one congressman to the House of Representatives, as it has since it became the 44th state in the Union in 1890.

It is a place of stark natural beauty and space-age contrasts. The incredible Devil's Tower, situated in Yellowstone National Park, rises some 865 feet above its 415-foot-wide base—a mute symbol, perhaps, of what lies beneath the flat grasslands and austere panorama: some of the most concentrated and sophisticated ICBM complexes in the continental United States. There are other things under the earth in Wyoming.

The area is fast becoming one of the nation's major mineral centers. In 1975, 48 percent of the state's assessed valuation rested in its deposits of uranium, coal and iron ore. The coal industry there began to boom when the low-sulphur deposits concentrated in the upper regions of the state came into great demand following enactment of strict air-pollution regulations in the early 1970s. Coal reserves are estimated at more than 36 billion tons, of which two-thirds is recoverable through strip mining or underground methods.

Still, most of the state's economy involves agriculture and beef and sheep raising, and Wyoming remains one of the nation's chief wool producers. Almost from the beginning of the white man's pioneering days, following trapper John Colter's explorations in the early nineteenth century, Wyoming has survived the forays of civilization: gold-rushers, railroads, coal-price wars, bloody disputes between cattle ranchers and sheep ranchers and rampant tourism. There have also been Indian raids, devastating winters and summer droughts. The conflicts involving the natural environment, exploration and exploitation, never far from view, work their way into the western-type difficulties pressing upon Wyoming's small population. There is no state income tax, but neither is there much income—an estimated $9,657 per family for 1980.

Wyoming sees its people on a different sort of plane from that elsewhere. It offers the kind of life that many find singularly worthwhile, providing isolation from big-city bustle and a splendid union with the earth of the type that can't be found back East or in the far western states. Down in the coal mines the miners' hardships are no different from those experienced in Kentucky, West Virginia and Pennsylvania, but Wyoming does not have the population base that can send a large congressional delegation to Washington. The state's strength is in its people—who reflect the countryside's rugged mountain atmosphere. They seldom ask for anything, and they put in their day's work as if they were the first pioneers.

Andrew Balleck was a kind of pioneer himself. In 1917, when World War I was finally coming to a close, having torn asunder most of Europe, Balleck came to this country from his native Czechoslovakia. He settled in the town of Sheridan, Wyoming, in Sheridan County, among the northernmost of the state's 23 counties. Although it offered little of the climate to be found in his native land and none of the history, there was substantial attraction in the pastoral plains and the stark natural wonders, the haunting, cool silences of the continental divide. Wyoming was a compelling place for Andy Balleck, then age 23. Its hardiness matched his. And, perhaps most importantly, there was work.

The Monarch, Kearney and Dietz mineworks were in need of pickers and shovelers. To meet the great demand for stove-burning coal in the still new twentieth century, Andy Balleck came to work in the mines of Sheridan. He picked coal for 45 cents per ton. It was backbreaking work, but Andy Balleck was able to stay with it, day after day. Balleck became attracted to the work, even to the hardship of it. In 1923, a timber fell on him and nearly crushed him to death; after five weeks in a hospital he went right back in the mines. He gave it all he had, even if he did not quite receive everything to which he may have been entitled.

When he was 28 Balleck met Mary Woolston at one of the square dances the company held, and within the year they were married. They moved into a tiny two-bedroom house and survived the Depression years, when the demand for coal was steady but money to pay for it was not. They had three children.

Mary was an adept gardener and her skills with vegetables provided a sideline income for the family—raising and selling the few crops that would grow in Wyoming's contrary soil and climate. With the end of the Depression came many changes, even as far away as Sheridan County: improvements in mining techniques, government interest in the welfare of the miners, compensation for injuries and other job-related physical difficulties, and working standards and regulations. Balleck became one of the senior miners for Monarch, Kearney and Dietz and continued to work steadily as the demand for coal—and nearly everything else—rose with the growing prosperity of the nation. For Andy, it also meant less dependence on the garden plots that Mary worked so diligently—and the possibility of putting some money away for the children and for his own future, for working the mines was not a job that could last forever. The dust, the dampness, the cramped quarters, the long days all began to take their toll.

In 1956, after 37 years working in the mines, Andy Balleck finally did retire. He was 62 years old. The company provided a small pension, but the Ballecks did not want for much. They were more than contented with the great spaces of their Wyoming countryside, the beautiful stillness and awesomeness of its winters. The cold and the unshattered silence reminded him of Slovakia. It was a time for settling into life of less physical exertion, and more time with his family. But within a couple of years after his retirement, Balleck noticed that the shortness of breath he felt climbing stairs or doing garden work, or even taking a brisk walk would not go away. He'd have difficulty doing most anything that required sustained exertion. And he would often feel a pain in his left side. And then, in 1969, when Andy was 75 years old, it happened: a sharp flash point of pain, the result of constricted blood flow and poor circulation of healthy oxygenated blood, all caused by another medical condition that he would have to battle like nothing else before: black lung.

One of the most feared and least treatable of miners' illnesses, black lung is more properly called coal workers' pneumoconiosis (CWP) and is caused by the accumulation of coal mine dust in the lungs. It exists in two forms. "Simple" CWP is a reaction to dust alone; it is classified as category 1, 2, or 3, according to the number of small spots visible in the patient's X rays. Category 3 represents the greatest accumulation of dust. Simple CWP, however, is not disabling, does not affect life expectancy and will not worsen in the absence of further exposure.

Unlike the simple form, "complicated" CWP may worsen even without further exposure to coal dust. It often leads to shortness of breath because of decreased lung function, and to premature death due to total failure of the lung system. The decreased lung function results from growth of fibrous masses in the lungs.

In the late 1970s, about 7 to 8 percent of working miners had simple CWP, and about .8 percent had the complicated form. Those figures are expected to decline with tighter regulation of working conditions, modern safety equipment and new methods of mining. Under the present standards, less than 3 percent of miners with 35 years' experience are expected to develop simple CWP; complicated, disabling CWP is expected to disappear altogether. But Andy Balleck did not start working in the coal mines 35 years ago. It was more like 60. He had complicated CWP.

Under the Coal Miners Compensation Act (or the Black Lung Compensation Act), the federal government established a program to provide for miners with these illnesses. The Department of Labor oversees black lung claims through a review panel and various subagencies. In 1978, the cost of compensation in the United States for miners classified as having black lung amounted to $1 billion annually, compared with $2.4 billion for all other industrial injury and sickness benefits. In other words, almost one-third of all industrial-compensation benefits were going to but 1/400th of the total working population. But the illness is almost totally disabling and incurable.

The black lung must be verified through a set of tests requiring both great exertion on the part of the patient and the certification of doctors who supervise the test. After a series of the required tests, the Ballecks filed the black lung benefit claim with the regional office and then with Washington, in 1970. For two years they heard nothing definite, despite many assurances from various officials in the Department of Labor. Finally, they were told—incredibly—that none of the medical reports nor the application had ever been received by the proper offices and that they could not be traced. After two years of waiting, the Ballecks would have to try again.

So in 1973, after a series of tests in which the now 79-year-old Balleck nearly passed out from the exertion, new papers were filed. The country's economic recession made it impossible for Andy to find any sort of work, even if he would be physically capable of putting in a full day's work at 79 years of age and with his growing disability. Mary continued with her gardening just as before, and the children helped out, but the money was growing short. The Ballecks could not live on either Andy's pension or the Social Security payments. They were unable to afford minor repairs on their home, such as replacing some worn-out pipes in the plumbing or fixing the stove.

Two and a half months after their second application, the Ballecks received word from the Department of Labor. The chest X rays taken of Andy were not plain enough—more tests would be required. They were done, the results forwarded. But then the Department of Labor decided that an administrative hearing would be necessary to determine the extent of the benefits to be awarded. Nevertheless, the Ballecks felt that finally, after an original diagnosis of black lung in 1969, something was happening. In 1974, the hearing was held before an insurance judge. It took two days and left the Ballecks hopeful that all would soon be well for them again, that he would now be fully compensated for all the years he had put into the mines.

The judge, however, ruled that Andy needed another medical opinion on the status of his black lung disease. So the family took him to a doctor for more tests. But before the doctor could send in the report, the Ballecks received a denial letter. Andy's claim was turned down by the Department of Labor for insufficient evidence. It was an amazing result. Andy had waited seven years to hear that his disease, his reminder of 37 years in the coal mines of Wyoming, would not be covered under the government program set up specifically for people like him. There had not been enough evidence to show the Department of Labor that Andy Balleck was slowly dying.

The family decided to try once more. In 1976, as the nation

celebrated 200 years of life, liberty and the pursuit of happiness, the Ballecks of Wyoming were to face the Department of Labor one more time. This time Andy passed out during one of the tests. His condition worsened. There were three letters from the Department of Labor telling them to be patient.

Andy Balleck did not have the money to hire a lawyer, and alone, unrepresented, he was no match for government attorneys and the mining company lawyers and the correspondence and hearings. He simply did not have the clout to press his claim in the right way with the right people.

On November 17, 1979, an article appeared in the *Sheridan Press* by reporter Ann Kennedy, detailing the Ballecks' fight for black-lung benefits. At the same time a determined young neighbor, Mrs. Margie Gustafson, joined in the struggle. Soon the story became big press in northern Wyoming. And Andy Balleck's situation became painfully more poignant. Now 85 years old, he fell and broke his hip. That injury, plus the increasing lung disability, made him a near-invalid; Mary had to care for him full-time. Their money had run so low that she could not afford to cook on their electric stove, so she switched to a coal oven. Whatever time she had left was spent picking coal, raising vegetables and continuing the struggle with the United States Department of Labor. "Sometimes I felt like going outside and screaming, it got so bad," she said. Mary said she was a nervous wreck, at 73.

The *Sheridan Press* story, which was followed up by additional publicity generated by Mrs. Gustafson and Richard Taberna, a Balleck family grandson, caught the attention of Senator Alan Simpson's office. Simpson was the junior senator from Wyoming, a Republican elected in 1978. It wasn't the Ballecks who brought the matter before him, but a constituent named Charley Popovich, who had read the story in the *Press* and who, as a coal miner himself, felt it important for Washington to lend some help. On December 7, 1979, Simpson responded by letter:

> How kind and considerate of you to forward the article from The Sheridan Press concerning Mary and Andy Balleck. [It] was touching and very human.

> My Field Representative in Rock Springs also saw the article and telephoned Mrs. Balleck. We have already made several inquiries on Andy's behalf and assure you of my willingness to be of every possible assistance in obtaining a decision on Andy's claim for black lung benefits.

Again, thank you for your thoughtfulness in communicating the Balleck article to me.

I was particularly interested in your comments on coal mining in that area of Wyoming. My grandfather, Peter Kooi, started the Kooi coal mine in that area and spent many delightful years of his life in Sheridan County.

With kindest of personal regards,

Sincerely,

Alan K. Simpson
United States Senator

Simpson's field assistants traced the trouble with Andy's benefit to the medical tests, which revealed more heart and vascular damage to his system than actual lung disease that would be fully compensable under a federal program. In Sheridan, Margie Gustafson said, "Can you imagine what it is like to go through this story for 10 years—again, and again and again? They've been through so much, they can't go through any more. At 70-some-years old, having to pick coal is ridiculous. Nobody can stand all that hardship. They've worked hard all their lives. Where's our country?" The senator's staff pressed on, with two caseworkers advocating the claim in Wyoming and one in Washington. Finally on December 21, 1979, Simpson's office was able to inform the Ballecks that Andy's black-lung benefits had been cleared and that the totally disabled, 85-year-old Sheridan resident would begin receiving compensation in January 1980—ten full years after the claim was first filed.

Now the Ballecks could look forward to some times that would be less heartrending than the past 10 of the 58 years they had spent together. Andy had become a kind of celebrity in Sheridan and elsewhere around Wyoming, and he received numerous phone calls and letters of praise and encouragement. Margie Gustafson brought over a bottle of champagne to help celebrate: This New Year would start differently.

All of the Balleck family came together by phone or mail to wish their father, their grandfather well at the time of his ultimate victory over the Department of Labor. Wrote Senator Simpson himself:

Just a note to let you know I am so very pleased to have been of assistance to you—and that we had such a great result. A very

Merry Christmas and a Happy New Year—and I am sure it will be!

With warmest of personal regards,

Sincerely,

Alan K. Simpson
United States Senator

On January 11, 1980, Mary Balleck wrote to Senator Simpson on behalf of her husband:

Please forgive me for taking this long to thank you for the Most (Beautiful) and Wonderful *gift*, you writing to us—no gift we received from friends and our familys, could replace your letter. You wish us a Happy Christmas. We did have a very Happy Christmas—thanks be to (God) for a Wonderful Friend you Mr. Senator Simpson. I thank (God) at Christmas Mass for you and ask to Bless you and yours for all you did for us—

Andy and I both cried when we read your letter, in all our 58 years we never got such Beautiful letter, how it comfort us and made us happy. I just can't put our feeling on this paper. I thank you with all my heart Andy thanks you with all his heart and all our friends they all call us and tell us how happy they are for us. I'm grateful to Charles Popovich and ask God to Bless him—I prayed and Beg God to Bless all that help us—Thanks thanks a million Senator Simpson.

God Bless you and yours

A few days later the senator replied in kind:

Just a note to thank you for your lovely letter of January 11, 1980. I really appreciated that. I do get enough of the other kind!

It was very thoughtful of you to take the time to do that, and I am most appreciative.

Again, my sincere thanks—your letter meant much to me.

With kind regards,

Sincerely,

Alan K. Simpson
United States Senator

All was well. The benefits began to flow in late January.

But not all stories have a happy ending. On February 2, 1980, Andy Balleck became one with the beautiful, silent grasslands of his beloved Wyoming. He died quietly in his sleep.

John Ritter, of Rock Springs, Wyoming, was also a career coal miner. Rock Springs is a town of about 19,000 on Bitter Creek in Sweetwater County, at the southwestern edge of the continental divide. Ritter spent most of his 80 years underground, picking and shoveling coal in the early days, literally pulling it out of the ground with his ax and bare hands and later with machines and modern elevators. Like Andy Balleck, Ritter didn't benefit from the new safety standards; he suffered from complicated coal workers' pneumoconiosis.

John Ritter has always been an unassuming man, dedicated to simple virtues such as a good day's work. There were times when he wondered aloud whether that was ever going to be valued again in this country, what with all the benefits offered to labor unions, and the strikes and the people who don't seem to be willing to do what is needed to make ends meet. His wife, Isabel, used to take in laundry during the Depression; they even tried their hand at raising sheep, but John just didn't have the talent for that. He knew the mines.

In 1943 he barely escaped death when he scrambled away from a minor cave-in. There have been worse accidents he's been able to avoid. But now he faces a painful, wheezing life in bed caused by the masses of fiber that have collected in his lungs over 50 years in the mines. He is so disabled that he requires a constant supply of oxygen—his lungs are simply incapable of taking in enough themselves to keep him alive.

Isabel must check on him constantly and also make sure there is no smoking in the bedroom or anywhere else in the house. A fire would be quick and merciless. John now needs periodic hospitalization and reexamination, complete physicals more than once per year so that the progress of his disease can be measured and new symptomatic treatments be made available. There is no cure for him, just the constant bedroom sounds of the oxygen apparatus and his labored breathing. Financially, of course, things are made more bearable by the disability benefits offered to miners like Ritter. But in 1980, the black lung compensation he'd been receiving inexplicably stopped. Isabel's frantic calls to the Department of Labor were fruitless, and the bills mounted: From January 1975 to July

1979, Ritter had been hospitalized eight times. Medical reports of his obstructive pulmonary disease described his condition as "chronic" and "advanced." Continuous oxygen therapy, with some antibiotics and cardiovascular medication, was the only recommended treatment. In short, went Isabel's plea, a man with acute respiratory failure cannot wait for a letter from a government agency, or abide one that says his claim is being processed or that more information is needed.

In February 1981, Isabel Ritter called the Wyoming office of Senator Simpson. She complained that the medical benefits for her husband's black lung disease had been slow or had not come at all and that there should be some action, quickly, or they would not be able to give John the oxygen treatment he absolutely must have.

The problem seemed small, but in the massive federal bureaucracy small problems have a way of enlarging. Apparently a transaction sheet with a breakdown of medical expenses had either not been sent or had not been received by the coal miners' compensation offices in Washington. The entire Ritter record was in danger of being placed in some sort of dead-letter file; it would take weeks to reestablish and reactivate. But John Ritter did not have weeks.

The Department of Labor initially responded that all was well: The entire list of medical expenses had been covered by the compensation plan, and there was no cause for alarm. But Isabel Ritter knew better: The canceled checks from her checkbook were testimony enough that thousands of dollars in oxygen therapy were not being reimbursed. She was running out of savings, and John literally was running out of breath.

But this was not enough. Even though Ritter had been hospitalized 27 times for black lung manifestations since his retirement from the mines in 1963, even though he spent months in chronic oxygen intensive-care units and had been receiving black lung benefits for years, the Department of Labor was demanding further assurance of the medical necessity of his treatment! So Dr. Howard P. Greaves of Rock Springs made a complete examination of Ritter and, in April 1981, submitted a detailed report on the 80-year-old former miner's condition. The last sentence said what had been amply documented before: "It is anticipated that he will continue to require continuous oxygen therapy at home interrupted only during periods of hospitalization or until he reaches the terminal stage of his Obstructive Pulmonary Disease."

More red tape. Finally, after further prodding from Simpson's office in Washington, the Department of Labor issued an authorization form that would allow reimbursement of benefits—provided that another transaction sheet, detailing the therapy involved, was submitted. That sheet was sent in June 1981—nearly six months from the time Isabel had first called the senator's office with her complaint about her inability to get anywhere with the Department of Labor.

The summer would come and go without any significant response. In September 1981, the Department of Labor again informed Mrs. Ritter that all was well. She need only submit her canceled checks with a list of the type of therapy for which the payments were made, and reimbursement would be forthcoming. All the canceled checks, receipts, and a list of expenses were duly submitted to the Department of Labor, and by mid-September Isabel had her check, for $6,129.22. It had taken almost a full year for the Department of Labor to recognize the fact that John Simpson was in the advanced stages of his disease and that constant, compensable oxygen therapy was required and fully reimbursable.

Every month, Isabel Ritter will send canceled checks to the Department of Labor to prove there is oxygen in her house, in tankfuls, at her husband's bedside. Considering what she has gone through already with John, she hopes never to have to face the Department of Labor again.

The black lung benefit office is not the only subagency within the Department of Labor to handle worker disabilities.

For 15 years Larry Dusablon was a post office employee in Woonsocket, Rhode Island, the seat of Providence County, with a population of nearly 46,000, making it one of the state's larger cities. The New England heritage is strong here; nobody asks for what is not theirs, but once something is due them they will go to the lengths necessary to obtain it. It is no different for Larry Dusablon. On August 7, 1978, as he was attempting to repair a sorting machine, a power surge severely injured him and nearly caused permanent blindness. Unable to continue at his post office job, he was forced to quit. But Dusablon had a family to support, so he applied for federal compensation benefits as part of his civil service. After all, he had put in long years as a postal employee—he thought there'd be little trouble.

Dusablon wanted to change his benefit coverage from the civil service plan to the programs available under the Federal Employee Compensation Act, under which periodic review would make larger benefits more likely and longer-running. Dusablon submitted the proper forms to the Department of

Labor to effectuate this change, thinking that the forms would be processed in due course. Perhaps he should have known better and realized that in a department the size of the Labor Department, forms and files can be lost—as well as interest. Perhaps he should have anticipated, as well, bureaucratic inertia.

In his case, phone calls were not returned, letters were not answered, the intercession of a lawyer friend met with no response and correspondence from his former boss was likewise to no avail. He was about to give up entirely.

On September 8, 1981, Dusablon visited the Woonsocket office of United States Senator John H. Chafee. Elected in 1976, Chafee had already made a name for himself through his criticism of American foreign policy. The Department of Labor is perhaps a more formidable opponent than foreign governments; the latter rarely fail to return phone calls and cablegrams.

A member of Chafee's staff, after meeting with Dusablon, found the office in the Labor Department responsible for overseeing the compensation program in question. (Easier said than done, because it was not located in Washington but in Boston.) After two days of phone calls, the caseworker was informed that in order for the postal worker to be covered by the Federal Employee Compensation Act he would have to fill out a "CALLO4 Form" and file it with appropriate attachments at the Boston office of the Civil Service Commission. The commission would then submit a copy to the Department of Labor office, certifying that Dusablon would no longer be on the retirement rolls of the Civil Service Commission (which ordinarily would have been the case had he not wished to alter his benefit status). Without the form, no benefits would be forthcoming.

Chafee's office was optimistic. On September 15, 1981, it wrote to Dusablon:

> According to the Civil Service Commission, a backlog in the Annuitant Service Division is responsible for the unfortunate delay which you have encountered. My office has been informed that the change in your status should be accomplished this week, and the Department of Labor will be notified that you have been dropped from the Civil Service annuity rolls. Once the Department of Labor receives this information, you will be contacted with regard to your level of compensation.

The letter asked Dusablon to contact the senator's office "if you do not receive any word from the Department of Labor within several weeks."

There was no word from the Civil Service Commission for the remainder of September. And none for October. Senator Chafee's office had made contact with the Civil Service Commission and with the congressional liaison office of the Civil Service Commission, trying to find somebody who could explain the reason for the delay. Finally, somebody was located who would say only that the Dusablon case would be "pulled ahead" of the large backlog and that if all went well the benefit-claim change could be made in three to four weeks.

In early November Dusablon again contacted Senator Chafee's office, which in turn initiated another whole series of contacts with both the Civil Service Commission and the Department of Labor. This time it appeared that a mixup at the Civil Service Commission was responsible for the delay. But the Civil Service Commission would not say what the "mixup" was, or when—or whether it would be corrected. More phone calls. Finally, the people at the Civil Service Commission apologized for the long delay (the original request having been made in April) and said that the form would be processed "this week."

Dusablon was dubious. It did not look as if he would see results by Thanksgiving or Christmas of 1981—just as he did not see any in 1980. The process was beginning to wear down on him and on his family. Without the benefits, he had been forced to take whatever light work would come around, but he was not able to stay at any job for long. His wife could do some part-time work, but she was busy taking care of their three-year-old. The family could not count on relatives to help them get by any longer. Nobody wanted handouts—just the benefits to which they were fully entitled. And it was one single form from a single office within the Civil Service Commission that had yet to come through, after all this time—one single form that could spell some peace of mind for Larry and his family.

Finally, on December 2, 1981, Dusablon received the following letter from Senator Chafee's office:

My office has been in touch with the U.S. Department of Labor with regard to the problem which you have encountered in obtaining disability benefits.

The Office of Personnel Management having submitted the proper forms to the Department of Labor, your name was added to the Department of Labor's periodic compensation role as of November 16, 1981. Your first regular check should be received by the end of this month. The Labor Department's Office of Workers Compensation Programs has indicated that you will also receive a supplemental check covering the period from November 16th through December 2nd. In addition, OWCP has informed my office that you will receive a check in the amount of approximately $19,000 early in 1982 as compensation for the Workers Compensation benefit level which you were entitled to receive while still on disability retirement.

I was pleased to look into this matter for you and regret the long delay which you have encountered.

With best wishes for the holiday season.

Sincerely,

John H. Chafee
United States Senator

There is no telling what the result would have been if Dusablon had waited for the Civil Service Commission to act. Certainly no one he himself had contacted there had moved the case along. It is not known how far behind his claim was before it was "pulled ahead" by the Civil Service Commission—after repeated overtures.

GETTING THE MOST OUT OF THE DEPARTMENT OF LABOR

What a Caseworker Needs to Know

A foreign national wanting to work in the United States needs a labor certification. In order to obtain this document, the national must show that he can do a job in the United States that no American can. There are guidelines for prospective employers as well, such as criteria for advertising in industry publications or certain newspapers to reach a particular audience, how long such advertising must continue, etc. The advertiser has to prove that there were no qualified Americans who applied. For certain occupations (such as medicine and nursing), examinations must be passed.

In a disagreement about wage rates on a building project, a caseworker needs to know the location of the work, if the building is under construction, the rates issue for the categories in question (electricians, carpenters, plumbers, etc.), the federal agency funding the project and the date the contract was signed.

For workmen's compensation claims, a caseworker must know the injured party's full name and Social Security number, the date of the injury, if and when the injured party returned to work, the name of the employer and whether any appeals have been made.

KEY FACTS

DEPARTMENT OF LABOR
200 Constitution Avenue, N.W.
Washington, DC 20210
Phone: (202) 523-8165

The Labor Department develops and executes administration policies regarding wage earners, their working conditions and their employment opportunities. The Department of Commerce and Labor was created by an act of Congress in 1903; the Department of Labor became a separate entity in 1913.

Central Structure

Office of the Secretary

The secretary's office consists of the secretary himself (a Cabinet member who advises the President), the Wage Appeals Board, the office of the inspector general, and a public-information service.

Office of the Under Secretary

The under secretary is the principal adviser to the secretary and is acting secretary in the secretary's absence. The under secretary oversees the Employees' Compensation Appeals Board, the Office of Administrative Law Judges, and the Benefits Review Board.

Women's Bureau

This division is responsible for promoting the welfare of wage-earning women. It has offices in 10 regions around the country.

The Solicitor of Labor

This is the legal arm of the Labor Department, responsible for administering and enforcing a broad range of statutes, including the Fair Labor Standards Act.

Administration and Management

The assistant secretary for administration and management has primary responsibility for coordinating the activities of the Labor Department's employees.

Policy, Evaluation and Research

The assistant secretary for policy, evaluation and research maintains liaison with other government agencies (federal, state and local) on policy and program planning and evaluation.

There are also deputy under secretaries of labor for legislation and intergovernmental relations and for international affairs.

Employment and Training Administration

The ETA encompasses a group of offices charged with implementing various federal employment affairs and programs, including the Comprehensive Employment and Training Act (CETA), the United States Employment Service (USES), the Office of Comprehensive Employment Development (OCED), the Office of National Programs (ONP), the National Apprenticeship Act and the Unemployment Insurance Service (UIS).

Labor-Management Service Administration

The assistant secretary for labor-management relations has responsibility for veterans' reemployment, pension and welfare plans, and relations between unions and management.

Employment Standards Administration

The assistant secretary for employment standards directs the Wage and Hour Division, the Office of Federal Contract Compliance Programs and the Office of Workers' Compensation Programs.

There are also assistant secretaries of labor for occupational health and safety and for mine safety and health.

Labor Statistics

The Bureau of Labor Statistics is the federal government's principal fact-finding agency in the field of labor economics, particularly with regard to collection and analysis of data on unemployment, wages, prices and productivity. It publishes the *Monthly Labor Review*, the *Consumer Price Index* and the *Occupational Outlook Quarterly*.

For further information, contact Office of Information, Publications and Reports, Department of Labor, Room 51032, 200 Constitution Avenue, N.W., Washington, DC 20210. Phone: (202) 523-7316.

☆ IX ☆

PRIVACY
AND INFORMATION

That wise Government, the general friend,
Might every where its eye and arm extend.

—ROBERT SOUTHEY,
The Poet's Pilgrimage to Waterloo

On the sensitive matter of obtaining personal information about you (or keeping it out of your hands), Big Brother—Orwell's futuristic demon of government—may already be here. Fortunately, though, Congress has sought to protect American citizens from unwarranted intrusion into their private affairs as well as from wrongful withholding of information that is rightfully theirs.

Whether you are a journalist or academician, a businessman or a blue-collar worker, a farmer or a scientist, a doctor or a lawyer, the pervasiveness of modern government makes it likely that at one time or another a federal agency will possess information about you that you had considered no concern of anyone else—or data that you want or need but that has not been made available to the public. Most agencies, however, have historically exhibited a natural inertia—if not downright refusal—when it comes to releasing records or opening files. Such secrecy sometimes is in the public interest and sometimes is against it. Who's to decide? Not, says Congress, the bureaucracy itself.

Under the Freedom of Information Act of 1966 and the Privacy Act of 1974, the parameters of federal information-gathering have been strictly defined. The two laws appear to be working well.

Through the Freedom of Information Act various interested individuals have gained access to material as diverse as Justice Department files (concerning corporate mergers), records of the Commodity Futures Trading Commission (pertaining to the Chicago Board of Trade's application to trade futures contracts in gold coins) and internal policy memoranda of the Social Security Administration (suggesting guidelines for deciding disability claims). Many others have been able to review personal data gathered about them by the Federal Bureau of Investigation or the Central Intelligence Agency. Between 1971 and 1980 there were 276 successful inquiries made by students and journalists, which developed into a number of newsmaking disclosures. Among them are the following:

- Memos from J. Edgar Hoover directing FBI agents to infiltrate and disrupt various left-wing organizations.
- Defense Department files containing the names of defense contractors and their respective profits.
- Environmental Protection Agency evidence that seven persons died from exposure to the pesticide Vacor Ratkiller.
- Justice Department memos indicating that Attorney General Robert Kennedy had authorized the wiretapping of Rev. Martin Luther King, Jr. on the grounds that an associate of the civil rights leader was suspected of being a Communist.
- Army documents concerning the My Lai massacre.
- FBI files on Julius and Ethel Rosenberg, Alger Hiss, Whittaker Chambers and Ezra Pound.
- Documents purportedly revealing CIA plots against the life of Fidel Castro.
- U.S. Forest Service records about that agency's efforts to evict gold miners from forest lands.
- Documents released by the Food and Drug Administration indicating that 10 nursing-home patients in Philadelphia had died as a result of experiments with the drugs Haldol and Nacton.
- CIA records of Army training programs in which police departments of 15 different cities were taught how to crack safes, commit burglaries and avoid detection when engaged in undercover and bugging operations.
- CIA arguments with several major American newspapers for keeping secret the agency's effort to salvage a sunken Soviet submarine.

In short, the Freedom of Information Act opened up a new and useful source of information: the federal government.

On the other hand, the Privacy Act has served to control the flow of information that agencies may have about citizens to agencies or persons not otherwise entitled to have access to it.

Because the government's store of information is so enormous and the right of access not absolute, acquiring government records is an exercise in the arts of communication, persuasion and—on occasion—compromise. Many of the sensitive disclosures related above succeeded only after the seekers had brought suit and obtained a court order. The purpose of this chapter is to outline the major provisions of the two acts and to guide the reader in requesting documents pursuant to the rights they create.

THE FREEDOM OF INFORMATION ACT

Basic Provisions

Though the Freedom of Information Act (FOIA) has been amended twice since its enactment in 1966, its basic structure has remained unchanged. (Amendments currently under consideration in Congress concern the act's exemptions from disclosure, and time limits for disclosure.) The full text of the present law is set out in Appendix B.

The Act applies to any federal agency, which means any executive or military department, government or government-controlled corporation, any establishment in the executive branch (including the executive office of the President) or any independent regulatory agency. It does *not* apply to Congress, to the judiciary or to state agencies.

Although the FOIA does not define "records," it is clear that the term encompasses at least documents—and court decisions have included at various times photographs, computer tapes and union authorization cards. Government records are divided into three categories of information. The first must automatically be published in the *Federal Register,* whether requested by a citizen or not: an agency's rules of procedure, its substantive regulations, information describing its organization and other matters basic to the public's understanding of how it functions. The second category need not be published but must be available for public inspection and copying: final opinions and orders rendered by the agency in adjudicating cases, policy statements and interpretations not published in the *Federal Register,* and certain agency staff manuals. It is not covered by the first two—which engenders the most litigation. Such information, if properly requested and *not statutorily exempt from disclosure,* must be made "promptly available" to the individual requesting it.

Nine kinds of records are exempt from disclosure (and only nine—the act permits no others). In addition, the agency need not withhold exempt records if it does not want to, *unless* some other statute requires that the information must not be released. The nine exemptions are for matters related to:

1. *National security.* Information deemed confidential—according to criteria established by an Executive Order drafted and signed by the President—"in the interest of national security or foreign policy."

2. *Agency personnel practices.* Information relating "solely to the internal personnel rules and practices of an agency."

3. *A special statute.* Information specifically exempted from disclosure by a statute (other than the Privacy Act), provided that the statute either requires the matters be withheld from the public in such a manner as to leave no discretion, or that it establishes particular criteria for withholding.

4. *Trade secrets.* This exemption is designed to protect free enterprise by shielding from disclosure information voluntarily submitted to the government by businesses if its release would harm their competitive position in the marketplace.

5. *Inter/intra agency memoranda.* This exemption is designed to permit agency personnel to exchange advice and ideas with one another without the stifling threat of publicity. The criteria that must be met to qualify for this exemption are not noted for their clarity.

6. *Personnel files.* Medical and similar files the disclosure of which would constitute a clearly unwarranted invasion of personal privacy.

7. *Law-enforcement and investigatory records.* Exempt if disclosure would interfere with law-enforcement proceedings, deprive an individual of a right to a fair trial or impartial adjudication, constitute an unwarranted invasion of personal privacy, disclose the identity of a confidential source, disclose investigative techniques and procedures or endanger the life or physical safety of law-enforcement personnel.

8. *Financial institution data.* Data "contained in or related to examination, operating, or condition reports prepared by, on behalf of, or for the use of an agency responsible for the regulation or supervision of financial institutions" (that is, about banks).

9. *Wells.* Geological and geophysical information, including maps, concerning wells.

Even a cursory review of these exemptions makes plain that their application to a particular FOIA request is not always clear; thus the litigation. The simplest advice is that since the exemptions are sometimes vague and never obligatory unless made so by some other statute, they should not deter you from making an FOIA request. The agency will let you know if it wishes to claim an exemption.

Making an FOIA Request

Preliminary concerns. Three statutory provisions must be kept in mind when requesting records under the Freedom of Information Act:

- The request must "reasonably describe" the records sought.
- The request must conform to the rules and procedures of the agency involved. (See *Appendix D.*)
- The agency may charge a fee to cover the cost of copying the records and for the time spent searching for them. However, if release of the records "can be considered as primarily benefiting the general public," the agency must release them free of charge. Under no circumstances may the agency charge for time spent reviewing documents for possible exemptions.

Finding out where the records are kept. An agency has no obligation to track down and release records over which it has no control. Therefore, before spending the time and money on a request, the seeker should be reasonably certain which agency has the records. If it is found that the records are not in the agency's possession, the seeker may be assessed a charge. Note that many agencies have more than one branch, and some requests will not be forwarded even within an agency. Moreover, if the request is forwarded, time has been lost.

The following methods are useful in tracking down appropriate agencies and branches in the event of uncertainty:

- Call the agencies you think are the likely custodians of the records in question. Most if not all of them have public-information (or FOIA) departments, which should be able to tell you if the types of records you seek are of the type usually kept, or if a branch office or another agency should have them.

• Consult the *United States Government Manual.* Revised yearly, this handbook lists all federal government agencies and describes their respective functions. It is available in libraries or from Superintendent of Documents, U.S. Government Printing Office, Washington, DC 20402 for about $15.00.

• Understand that regional offices usually maintain an agency's "working files"—those with facts pertaining to specific operations. If the information you seek is general or policy-making in nature, the national headquarters of the agency is more likely to have what you want.

• Determine the age of the information you seek. If the files are old (compiled and closed several years ago), they might be stored at the National Archives or at its regional records centers.

• Contact a regional Federal Information Center. Almost every state has one. (Appendix A lists locations and phone numbers of the Federal Information Centers. Consult the latest *United States Government Manual* for any changes in the list.)

Two strategic considerations. You may find that more than one agency possesses the records you want. In such a circumstance, further investigation would be to your advantage: Which agency has the better reputation for cooperation? Your elected representatives might well know the answer to that question. Is one of the agencies subject to an exemption—for example, a statute prohibiting it from releasing the records— while the other is not? A call to the agency should provide a quick answer. Another preliminary but important consideration is whether there is any possibility that the target agency will lose custody of the records in the near future. If your FOIA request was received after such a transfer has taken place, you're out of luck: The agency cannot honor it even if the records sought are not exempt from disclosure. But if the records were transferred *after* your request was received, your request is still legally enforceable.

Determining the agency's FOIA rules and procedures. By now you should know exactly what material you are looking for and which agency is likely to have it. But since the statute requires that you conform your request to the rules of that agency, you must consult those rules. Agency procedural rules are first published in the *Federal Register* (which appears daily); then they are compiled and updated in the *Code of Federal Regula-*

tions. Typically, the rules include a schedule of fees, a list of items that must be included in the request in order to locate the documents, notification if the request must be in writing and other pertinent procedural requirements. The *Code of Federal Regulations* is composed of 50 sections (called "titles"), many of which contain more than one volume. (If you plan to deal with an agency on a regular basis, you may wish to purchase the title pertaining to that agency from the Superintendent of Documents. They cost from $7 to $10 per volume. Appendix D lists the location in the *Code of Federal Regulations* of the FOIA rules and the Privacy Act rules for each agency. If you do not wish to buy a *Code of Federal Regulations* title, you can obtain the rules from the agency itself or consult the *Code* in a library that carries it.)

Drafting the request. Asking for information by letter ensures that there will be a written record in the event misunderstandings arise. Also, many people express themselves with more clarity on paper than vocally, and that is important if you want your request to be processed efficiently. In drafting the letter, make certain that you:

• Include a precise description of the records you seek. A description will be *legally* sufficient if it is clear enough to enable a professional employee of the agency, familiar with the subject area, to locate the records "with a reasonable amount of effort." As a practical matter, simple and precise requests get the quickest and least expensive agency response. Large-scale requests (for example, "all records concerning DDT") will obviously take up more of the agency's time—time for which you will pay unless the agency has agreed to waive fees. You might fare better to break down such large demands into a series of smaller, more specific requests. It is also a good idea to make direct, personal contact with agency personnel before sending the letter, to ascertain how it can best be worded in order to expedite the search.

• Have determined whether the materials you seek have been previously released under the FOIA. If so, the agency should have no difficulty finding the records so long as you can provide the name of the person (or organization) to whom they were disclosed and/or the date. Each release is given an identifying number; if you can supply it, so much the better. Note in your letter that a prior release should eliminate search fees.

• Have stated the reason you want to have the records. The FOIA does not require this, but explaining your need for the documents might persuade the agency to waive fees if there is a chance that disclosure could be considered "primarily benefiting the general public." An explanation of need might also avoid an exemption if it demonstrates that the benefit to the public resulting from disclosure outweighs the benefit advanced by strict application of the exemption. Finally, if your need for the material is immediate, an explanation of urgency might prompt a quicker response.

• Have decided how much you are willing to incur in fees. Generally, fees should be arranged in advance: You should have an idea of what it will cost, and the agency should have an idea of how much you are willing to pay. Some agencies, in fact, require a portion of the fees to be paid in advance. If you do not want to spend above a specific amount, indicate your limit in the request letter. If the agency estimates search and copying costs will exceed your ceiling, you might be able to narrow your request or reduce copying costs by asking to review the material once it is found. Some agencies maintain reading rooms in which you can conduct such a review.

• Have established your authority. Indicate in your request that it is pursuant to the Freedom of Information Act and that you are cognizant of your rights under that law, including the right to nonexempt portions of exempt files if such portions can be segregated from the rest of the files; the right to a response within the statutory time limits; and the right to appeal an adverse decision.

Your envelope should be addressed to the agency from which data is sought, with this notation: "Attention: Freedom of Information/Privacy Act Unit."

Rules by Which the Agency Must Abide

The statutory time limits: When must the agency respond? From the time it receives your request, the agency has 10 days (not counting weekends or legal holidays) to inform you whether it will comply with your request or claim an exemption. The agency can extend this period up to 10 more days if it can demonstrate "unusual circumstances." Such an extension, however, must likewise be claimed in a written notification to you.

If the time period has expired and the agency has not responded, you can appeal to the agency's chief officer, institute a legal action in federal court—or wait a bit longer. Displaying some patience will often be the best strategy. At such an early stage in the process you need not view the agency as an adversary. Keeping open lines of communication, by telephone or letter, will enable you to determine the cause of the delay, establish a tentative release date and clarify the request if a misunderstanding has occurred. The agency may tell you it has been forced to delay in order to satisfy the demands of another statute—especially when the information requested has been submitted to the government by a third party (such as a private corporation); some statutes require 30 days' notice to the third party before data are released. On the other hand, if it appears to you that an agency is stalling for no legitimate reason, it is important that you understand your full rights of appeal.

If the agency says the records are unavailable, destroyed or not in existence. Such responses need not end the inquiry. Call the agency or send another letter. If the records have been sent someplace else, ask where and when. If the agency claims the records don't exist, state any reasons you might have indicating the contrary. (It is always possible, given the size of the bureaucracy, that other agency personnel are more familiar with the type of material requested than the individual who processed your initial request.) Ask about the nature and scope of the search. Make the agency convince you that it made a genuine effort to locate the records sought. If you're told the files were destroyed, ask when; it is illegal to destroy records once they have been requested. In short, if you believe that the agency might be mistaken or evasive, don't give up. Remember that public servants are your employees. Treat them fairly, and expect good service.

When the agency responds by denying all or part of your request. If some or all of the requested materials are withheld, you still have the right to appeal to the head of the agency (or to whomever the head has appointed to handle FOIA appeals). The letter of denial from the agency is important: It should state that you have the right to appeal; indicate to whom the appeal should be addressed; and provide details as to which materials are being withheld, which exemptions are being claimed and the names and titles of the persons responsible for the decision to withhold the records. The letter should also state what fees you owe (and why they were not waived if so requested).

Your appeal should also be by letter. Make sure it is sent

within the time limit set by the agency's regulations (usually 30 days). You must make certain it is addressed to the correct official, states clearly the agency decision you'd like to challenge (including the dates of request and denial, the records sought and any other relevant information) and gives reasons you think the denial was wrongful.

Just as with the initial request letter, you should also establish your legal authority: that you are making an appeal pursuant to your rights under the Freedom of Information Act, that you expect a reply within the statutory time limit (20 working days from the date the appeal is received) and that you have a right to a definitive list of both documents retrieved and those withheld (under specified exemptions).

Even at the appellate stage, informal lines of communication should be maintained with the agency. Personal contact can move the process along to your greater satisfaction as well as promote a spirit of compromise. Remember that although agency personnel are supposed to be at your service, they should be treated as civilly as you would have them treat you.

If you feel you have been charged excessive fees, you can appeal the fee assessment using the same procedures as for an appeal of a denial.

If the appeal fails. If the agency refuses to change an initial adverse decision, or fails to respond within the 20-day time limit, you have the right to take the matter to court. Before rushing into litigation, however, consider two alternatives:

1. Lodge a complaint with the office of special counsel of the Merit Systems Protection Board if you feel the agency was "arbitrary or capricious" in denying your FOIA request. Although the special counsel has no power to order release of files, it can investigate wrongful withholding or records by agency officials. If the agency knows it has violated the law, such a complaint might prompt release of the records.

2. Ask your congressman or senator for assistance.

THE PRIVACY ACT

Basic Provisions

While the FOIA enables citizens to obtain federal agency records, the Privacy Act protects them from unwarranted disclosures about their private lives. The two laws overlap to a substantial degree, and their differences have never been fully explained by Congress or the courts. For example, the Privacy Act expressly provides that even though the FOIA might require personal records to be released to an individual who requests them, they are not barred from release if the same person objects. However, the FOIA exempts from disclosure records that if released would cause a clearly unwarranted invasion of privacy. The Privacy Act also expressly applies to federal "agencies" as that term is defined by the FOIA. The full text of the Privacy Act is set out in Appendix C.

In typically specific legislative language, the Privacy Act defines the records to which it applies as "any item, collection, or grouping of information about an individual that is maintained by an agency, including, but not limited to, his education, financial transactions, medical history, and criminal or employment history and that contains his name, or the identifying number, symbol, or other identifying particular assigned to the individual, such as a finger or voice print or a photograph." Put more simply, if the records in question pertain to you individually (for example, your tax file), you are protected by the Privacy Act. Such personal records maintained by the federal government cannot be released to anyone (or to any other agency) "except pursuant to a written request by, or with the prior written consent of, the individual to whom the record pertains."

Conversely, the Privacy Act provides that an agency must permit any individual, upon his request, to gain access to and copy any part of his personal records. Copying costs—but not search costs—can be charged to the individual making the request. Citizens also have the right to demand that their records be amended if they are not "accurate, timely, relevant, or complete."

As with the FOIA, Congress saw fit to provide for certain exceptions to the Privacy Act. For example, the Central Intelligence Agency (or any other agency whose principal function is criminal-law enforcement) can deny access to personal records— but cannot exempt itself from the requirement of prior written consent. In addition, any federal agency can exempt certain records from access: those already under the FIOA's national security exemption; investigative material compiled for civil or criminal-law-enforcement purposes; records maintained in connection with protective services accorded the President and other officials; records that are required by statute to be purely statistical in nature and use; material compiled solely for the purpose of determining suitability for federal civilian employment, promotion, military service, federal contracts or access to classified information (but only to the extent that disclosures would reveal the identity of a confidential source); and testing data used solely for appointment or promotion in the civil or armed services, the disclosure of which would impair objectivity or fairness.

Finally, federal agencies are not required to provide access to information compiled in reasonable anticipation of a civil action or proceeding.

Making a Privacy Act Request

There are numerous similarities between the data-request processes of the Privacy Act and the Freedom of Information Act. The request need not be in writing (unless the agency specifically requires it), but a written demand is best for expediting the process. The request must conform to the agency's regulations, which appear in the *Code of Federal Regulations* or can be obtained from the agency itself. You must lodge the request with the agency that has control over the records. Costs should be made clear in advance; fee schedules are listed in the agency's regulations. The more specific and clear the request, the faster the response.

The following additional factors should be kept in mind when invoking the Privacy Act:

- *Cite both the FOIA and the Privacy Act.* In asserting your right of access to the records, cite both laws as your legal authority: Many agencies will process a request under whichever statute provides greater access (if the records are exempt under the Privacy Act, they still might be available under the FOIA). If the agency you have approached does not subscribe to this policy—and some don't—it will let you know. You must limit your demands, at least initially, to what's available under the companion statute.
- *Identify yourself.* To protect your records from unauthorized release, you must identify yourself to the satisfaction of the agency. As a minimum, you should be prepared to offer your full name (including any other names used during the period when the records were compiled), your address and a notarized signature. If you want to inspect the documents in person, identification cards may be necessary.

• *Identify the records you seek.* The Privacy Act requires that each agency publish in the *Federal Register* a list of its records systems that contain information pertaining to individuals. These lists have been compiled in *Protecting Your Right to Privacy: Digest of Systems of Records,* available in libraries or from the Superintendent of Documents, U.S. Government Printing Office, Washington, DC 20402. Your request will be easier for the agency to process if it indicates to which particular records system you want access.

• *Time limits.* There is no statutory time limit within which the agency must respond under the Privacy Act. The Office of Management and Budget (OMB), which is authorized to create guidelines for the implementation of the Privacy Act, has provided that an agency "should" respond within 10 working days and provide access (if no exemption is asserted) within 30 working days. "OMB Guidelines" provide for further time to comply if the agency advises the requester that there is "good cause" for delay. ("OMB Guidelines" appear in the *Federal Register,* Volume 40, beginning at page 28,949, July 9, 1979.)

• *Administrative appeal.* The Privacy Act does not require that there be an administrative appeal in the event you are dissatisfied with the agency's response (or lack of one). Whether there is an intra-agency appeal process depends on the agency involved.

• *The right to request amendment of your personal records.* You have the right to request that your records be amended if you discover, upon reviewing them, that they are not accurate, timely, relevant or complete. The agency must acknowledge such a request within 10 working days and must determine its merits "promptly." If the request is denied, you have the right to appeal to the head of the agency or the appeals officer he has appointed. The agency's decision on appeal must be made within 30 working days, unless the agency has "good cause" for delay.

KEY FACTS

Various books are available on litigation under the federal Freedom of Information Act and the Privacy Act. Perhaps the most useful reference tool for laymen, however, is *Using The Freedom of Information Act: A Step by Step Guide.* It costs $1.50 and may be ordered from the Center for National Security Studies, Department R2, 122 Maryland Avenue, N.E., Washington, DC 20002.

APPENDIX A

FEDERAL INFORMATION CENTERS AND TELEPHONE TIELINES— GENERAL SERVICES ADMINISTRATION

State/City	Telephone[1]	Address	Toll-free Tieline To
ALABAMA:			
Birmingham........	322-8591	....	Atlanta, Ga.
Mobile..................	438-1421	....	New Orleans, La.
ALASKA:			
Anchorage...........	907-271-3650	Federal Bldg. & U.S. Courthouse, 701 C St., 99513.	
ARIZONA:			
Tucson.................	622-1511	....	Phoenix, Ariz.
Phoenix................	602-261-3313	Federal Bldg., 230 N. 1st Ave., 85025.	
ARKANSAS:			
Little Rock...........	378-6177	....	Memphis, Tenn.
CALIFORNIA:			
Los Angeles.........	213-688-3800	Federal Bldg., 300 N. Los Angeles St., 90012.	
Sacramento..........	916-440-3344	Federal Bldg.-U.S. Courthouse, 650 Capitol Mall, 95814.	
San Diego............	714-293-6030	Government Information Center, Federal Bldg., 880 Front St., 92188.	
San Francisco	415-556-6600	Federal Bldg.-U.S. Courthouse, 450 Golden Gate Ave., 94102.	
San Jose................	275-7422	....	San Francisco, Calif.
Santa Ana.............	836-2386	....	Los Angeles, Calif.

---

[1] The tieline numbers are toll-free only in the specified city.

FEDERAL INFORMATION CENTERS
AND TELEPHONE TIELINES—
GENERAL SERVICES ADMINISTRATION—CONTINUED

State/City	Telephone[1]	Address	Toll-free Tieline To
COLORADO:			
Colorado Springs..	471-9491	....	Denver, Colo.
Denver..................	303-837-3602	Federal Bldg., 1961 Stout St., 80294.	
Pueblo...................	544-9523	....	Denver, Colo.
CONNECTICUT:			
Hartford...............	527-2617	....	New York, N.Y.
New Haven...........	624-4720	....	New York, N.Y.
DISTRICT OF COLUMBIA.........	202-755-8660	7th and D Sts. SW., 20407.	
FLORIDA:			
Fort Lauderdale...	522-8531	....	Miami, Fla.
Jacksonville...........	354-4756	....	St. Petersburg, Fla.
Miami....................	305-350-4155	Federal Bldg., 51 SW. 1st Ave., 33130.	
Orlando	422-1800	....	St. Petersburg, Fla.
St. Petersburg.......	813-893-3495	Cramer Federal Bldg., 144 1st Ave. S., 33701.	
Tampa	229-7911	....	St. Petersburg, Fla.
West Palm Beach .	833-7566	....	Miami, Fla.
Other south Florida locations...	800-432-6668	....	Miami, Fla.
Other north Florida locations...	800-282-8556	....	St. Petersburg, Fla.
GEORGIA:			
Atlanta..................	404-221-6891	Russell Federal Bldg.- U.S. Courthouse, 75 Spring St. SW., 30303.	
HAWAII:			
Honolulu	808-546-8620	300 Ala Moana Blvd., 96850.	
ILLINOIS:			
Chicago.................	312-353-4242	Everett McKinley Dirksen Bldg., Room 250, 219 S. Dearborn St., 60604.	

[1] The tieline numbers are toll-free only in the specified city.

INDIANA:
Gary..................... 883-4110 .... Indianapolis,
Ind.
Indianapolis.......... 317-269-7373 Federal Bldg., 575 N.
Pennsylvania St.,
46204.
IOWA:
Des Moines........... 515-284-4448 Federal Bldg., 210
Walnut St., 50309.
Other Iowa
locations............. 800-532-1556 .... Des Moines,
Iowa.
KANSAS:
Topeka .... 913-295-2866 Federal Bldg.-U.S.
Courthouse, 444 SE.
Quincy, 66683.
Other Kansas
locations............. 800-432-2934 .... Kansas City,
Mo.
KENTUCKY:
Louisville .... 502-582-6261 Federal Bldg., 600 Fed-
eral Place, 40202.
LOUISIANA:
New Orleans......... 504-589-6696 U.S. Postal Service
Bldg., 701 Loyola
Ave., 70113.
MARYLAND:
Baltimore.............. 301-962-4980 Federal Bldg., 31 Hop-
kins Plaza, 21201.
MASSACHU-
SETTS: Boston .... 617-223-7121 John F. Kennedy Fed-
eral Bldg., Room E-
130, Cambridge St.,
02203.
MICHIGAN:
Detroit .... 313-226-7016 McNamara Federal
Bldg., 477 Michigan
Ave., 48226.
Grand Rapids....... 451-2628 .... Detroit, Mich.
MINNESOTA:
Minneapolis.......... 612-725-2073 Federal Bldg.-U.S.
Courthouse, 110 S.
4th St., 55401.
MISSOURI:
Kansas City........... 816-374-2466 Federal Bldg., 601 E.
12th St., 64106.
St. Louis................ 314-425-4106 Federal Bldg., 1520
Market St., 63103.
Other Missouri lo-
cations within
area code 314 ... 800-392-7711 .... St. Louis, Mo.

FEDERAL INFORMATION CENTERS
AND TELEPHONE TIELINES—
GENERAL SERVICES ADMINISTRATION—CONTINUED

State/City	Telephone[1]	Address	Toll-free Tieline To
Other Missouri locations within area codes 816 and 417	800-892-5808		Kansas City, Mo.
NEBRASKA:			
Omaha	402-221-3353	U.S. Post Office and Courthouse, 215 N. 17th St., 68102.	
Other Nebraska locations	800-642-8383		Omaha, Nebr.
NEW JERSEY:			
Newark	201-645-3600	Federal Bldg., 970 Broad St., 07102.	
Paterson/Passaic	523-0717		Newark, N.J.
Trenton	396-4400		Newark, N.J.
NEW MEXICO:			
Albuquerque	505-766-3091	Federal Bldg.-U.S. Courthouse, 500 Gold Ave. SW., 87102.	
Santa Fe	983-7743		Albuquerque, N. Mex.
NEW YORK:			
Albany	463-4421		New York, N.Y.
Buffalo	716-846-4010	Federal Bldg., 111 W. Huron St., 14202.	
New York	212-264-4464	Federal Office Bldg., 26 Federal Plaza, 10007.	
Rochester	546-5075		Buffalo, N.Y.
Syracuse	476-8545		Buffalo, N.Y.
NORTH CAROLINA: Charlotte	376-3600		Atlanta, Ga.
OHIO:			
Akron	375-5638		Cleveland, Ohio
Cincinnati	513-684-2801	Federal Bldg., 550 Main St., 45202.	
Cleveland	216-522-4040	Federal Bldg., 1240 E. 9th St., 44199.	
Columbus	221-1014		Cincinnati, Ohio
Dayton	223-7377		Cincinnati, Ohio
Toledo	241-3223		Cleveland, Ohio

[1] The tieline numbers are toll-free only in the specified city.

OKLAHOMA:
Oklahoma City ..... 405-231-4868 U.S. Post Office and
                                  Courthouse, 201 NW.
                                  3d St., 73102.
Tulsa ....   584-4193 .... Oklahoma City,
                                                                              Okla.
OREGON:
Portland .... 503-221-2222 Federal Bldg., Room
                                  109, 1220 SW. 3d
                                  Ave., 97204.
PENNSYLVANIA:
Philadelphia .... 215-597-7042 William J. Green, Jr.
                                  Federal Bldg., 600
                                  Arch St., 19106.
Allentown/Beth-
    lehem ....   821-7785 .... Philadelphia,
                                                                          Pa.
Pittsburgh .... 412-644-3456 Federal Bldg., 1000
                                  Liberty Ave., 15222
Scranton ....   346-7081 .... Philadelphia,
                                                                         Pa.
RHODE ISLAND:
Providence ....   331-5565 .... Boston, Mass.
TENNESSEE:
Chattanooga ....   265-8231 .... Memphis,
                                                                      Tenn.
Memphis .... 901-521-3285 Clifford Davis Federal
                                  Bldg., 167 N. Main
                                  St., 38103.
Nashville ....   242-5056 .... Memphis,
                                                                          Tenn.
TEXAS:
Austin ....   472-5494 .... Houston, Tex.
Dallas ....   767-8585 .... Fort Worth,
                                                                           Tex.
Forth Worth .... 817-334-3624 Fritz Garland Lanham
                                  Federal Bldg., 819
                                  Taylor St., 76102.
Houston .... 713-226-5711 Federal Bldg.-U.S.
                                  Courthouse, 515
                                  Rusk Ave., 77208.
San Antonio ....   224-4471 .... Houston, Tex.
UTAH:
Ogden ....   399-1347 .... Salt Lake City,
                                                                          Utah
Salt Lake City .... 801-524-5353 Federal Bldg., Room
                                  1205, 125 S. State St.,
                                  84138.
VIRGINIA:
Newport News ......   244-0480 .... Norfolk, Va.
Norfolk .... 804-441-3101 Federal Bldg., 200
                                  Granby Mall, Room
                                  120, 23510.

FEDERAL INFORMATION CENTERS
AND TELEPHONE TIELINES—
GENERAL SERVICES ADMINISTRATION—CONTINUED

State/City	Telephone[1]	Address	Toll-free Tieline To
Richmond	643-4928		Norfolk, Va.
Roanoke	982-8591		Norfolk, Va.
WASHINGTON:			
Seattle	206-442-0570	Federal Bldg., 915 2d Ave., 98174.	
Tacoma	383-5230		Seattle, Wash.
WISCONSIN:			
Milwaukee	271-2273		Chicago, Ill.

[1] The tieline numbers are toll-free only in the specified city.

APPENDIX B

"5 U.S.C. § 522"
THE FEDERAL FREEDOM OF INFORMATION ACT—TEXT

---

§ 552.   Public information; agency rules, opinions, orders, records, and proceedings.

(a)   Each agency shall make available to the public information as follows:

(1)   Each agency shall separately state and currently publish in the Federal Register for the guidance of the public—

(A)   descriptions of its central and field organization and the established places at which, the employees (and in the case of a uniformed service, the members) from whom, and the methods whereby, the public may obtain information, make submittals or requests, or obtain decisions;

(B)   statements of the general course and method by which its functions are channeled and determined, including the nature and requirements of all formal and informal procedures available;

(C)   rules of procedure, descriptions of forms available or the places at which forms may be obtained, and instructions as to the scope and contents of all papers, reports, or examinations;

(D)   substantive rules of general applicability adopted as authorized by law, and statements of general policy or interpretations of general applicability formulated and adopted by the agency; and

(E)   each amendment, revision, or repeal of the foregoing.

Except to the extent that a person has actual and timely notice of the terms thereof, a person may not in any manner be required to resort to, or be adversely affected by, a matter required to be published in the Federal Register and not so published. For the purpose of this paragraph, matter reasonably available to the class of persons affected thereby is deemed published in the Federal Register when incorporated by reference therein with the approval of the Director of the Federal Register.

(2)   Each agency, in accordance with published rules, shall make available for public inspection and copying—

(A)   final opinions, including concurring and dissenting opinions, as well as orders, made in the adjudication of cases;

(B)   those statements of policy and interpretations which have been adopted by the agency and are not published in the Federal Register; and

(C)   administrative staff manuals and instructions to staff that affect a member of the public;

unless the materials are promptly published and copies offered for sale. To

---

NOTE: The 1974 Amendments are in italics; the 1976 Amendment (b) (3) on page 189 is not.

the extent required to prevent a clearly unwarranted invasion of personal privacy, an agency may delete identifying details when it makes available or publishes an opinion, statement of policy, interpretation, or staff manual or instruction. However, in each case the justification for the deletion shall be explained fully in writing. *Each agency shall also maintain and make available for public inspection and copying current indexes providing identifying information for the public as to any matter issued, adopted, or promulgated after July 4, 1967, and required by this paragraph to be made available or published. Each agency shall promptly publish, quarterly or more frequently, and distribute (by sale or otherwise) copies of each index or supplements thereto unless it determines by order published in the Federal Register that the publication would be unnecessary and impracticable, in which case the agency shall nonetheless provide copies of such index on request at a cost not to exceed the direct cost of duplication.* A final order, opinion, statement of policy, interpretation, or staff manual or instruction that affects a member of the public may be relied on, used, or cited as precedent by an agency against a party other than an agency only if—

    (i)   it has been indexed and either made available or pub-

    (ii) lished as provided by this paragraph; or

           the party has actual and timely notice of the terms thereof.

    (3)   *Except with respect to the records made available under paragraphs (1) and (2) of this subsection, each agency, upon any request for records which (A) reasonably describes such records and (B) is made in accordance with published rules stating the time, place, fees (if any), and procedures to be followed, shall make the records promptly available to any person.*

    (4)   (A) *In order to carry out the provisions of this section, each agency shall promulgate regulations, pursuant to notice and receipt of public comment, specifying a uniform schedule of fees applicable to all constituent units of such agency. Such fees shall be limited to reasonable standard charges for documents search and duplication and provide for recovery of only the direct costs of such search and duplication. Documents shall be furnished without charge or at a reduced charge where the agency determines that waiver or reduction of the fee is in the public interest because furnishing the information can be considered as primarily benefiting the general public.*

           (B) *On complaint, the district court of the United States in the district in which the complainant resides, or has his principal place of business, or in which the agency records are situated, or in the District of Columbia, has jurisdiction to enjoin the agency from withholding agency records and to order the production of any agency records improperly withheld from the complainant. In such a case the court shall determine the matter de novo, and may examine the contents of such agency records in camera to determine whether such records or any part thereof shall be withheld under any of the exemptions set forth in subsection (b) of this section, and the burden is on the agency to sustain its actions.*

           (C) *Notwithstanding any other provision of law, the defendant shall serve an answer or otherwise plead to any complaint made under this subsection within thirty days after service upon the defendant of the pleading in which such complaint is made, unless the court otherwise directs for good cause shown.*

           (D) *Except as to cases the court considers of greater importance, proceedings before the district court, as authorized by this subsection, and appeals therefrom, take precedence on the docket over all cases and shall be assigned for hearing and trial or for argument at the earliest practicable date and expedited in every way.*

           (E) *The court may assess against the United States reasonable attorney fees and other litigation costs reasonably incurred in any case under this section in which the complainant has substantially prevailed.*

(F)   *Whenever the court orders the production of any agency records improperly withheld from the complainant and assesses against the United States reasonable attorney fees and other litigation costs, and the court additionally issues a written finding that the circumstances surrounding the withholding raise questions whether agency personnel acted arbitrarily or capriciously with respect to the withholding, the Civil Service Commission shall promptly initiate a proceeding to determine whether disciplinary action is warranted against the officer or employee who was primarily responsible for the withholding. The Commission, after investigation and consideration of the evidence submitted, shall submit its findings and recommendations to the administrative authority of the agency concerned and shall send copies of the findings and recommendations to the officer or employee or his representative. The administrative authority shall take the corrective action that the Commission recommends.*

(G)   *In the event of noncompliance with the order of the court, the district court may punish for contempt the responsible employee, and in the case of a uniformed service, the responsible member.*

(5)   Each agency having more than one member shall maintain and make available for public inspection a record of the final votes of each member in every agency proceeding.

(6)   (A)   *Each agency, upon any request for records made under paragraph (1), (2), or (3) of this subsection, shall—*

(i)   *determine within ten days (excepting Saturdays, Sundays, and legal public holidays) after the receipt of any such request whether to comply with such request and shall immediately notify the person making such request of such determination and the reasons therefor, and of the right of such person to appeal to the head of the agency any adverse determination; and*

(ii)   *make a determination with respect to any appeal within twenty days (excepting Saturdays, Sundays, and legal public holidays) after the receipt of such appeal. If on appeal the denial of the request for records is in the whole or in part upheld, the agency shall notify the person making such request of the provisions for judicial review of that determination under paragraph (4) of this subsection.*

(B)   *In unusual circumstances as specified in this subparagraph, the time limits prescribed in either clause (i) or clause (ii) of subparagraph (A) may be extended by written notice to the person making such request setting forth the reasons for such extension and the date on which a determination is expected to be dispatched. No such notice shall specify a date that would result in an extension for more than ten working days. As used in this subparagraph, 'unusual circumstances' means, but only to the extent reasonably necessary to the proper processing of the particular request—*

(i)   *the need to search for and collect the requested records from field facilities or other establishments that are separate from the office processing the request;*

(ii)   *the need to search for, collect, and appropriately examine a voluminous amount of separate and distinct records which are demanded in a single request, or*

(iii)   *the need for consultation, which shall be conducted with all practicable speed, with another agency having a substantial interest in the determination of the request or among two or more components of the agency having substantial subject-matter interest therein.*

(C)   *Any person making a request to any agency for records under para-graph (1), (2), or (3) of this subsection shall be deemed to have exhausted his administrative remedies with respect to such request if the agency fails to comply with the applicable time limit provisions of this paragraph. If the Government can show exceptional circumstances exist and that the agency is exercising due diligence in responding to the request, the court may retain jurisdiction and al-low the agency additional time to complete its review of the records. Upon any de-termination by an agency to comply with a request for records, the records shall be made promptly available to such person making such request. Any notification of denial of any requests for records under this subsection shall set forth the names and titles or positions of each person responsible for the denial of such request.*

(b)   This section does not apply to matters that are—

(1)   (A)   *specifically authorized under criteria established by an Execu-tive order to be kept secret in the interest of national defense or foreign policy and (B) are in fact properly classified pursuant to such Executive order;*

(2)   related solely to the internal personnel rules and practices of an agency;

(3)   specifically exempted from disclosure by statute (other than section 552b of this title), provided that such statute (A) requires that the matters be withheld from the public in such a manner as to leave no discretion on the issue, or (B) establishes particular criteria for withholding or refers to partic-ular types of matters to be withheld;

(4)   trade secrets and commercial or financial information obtained from a person and privileged or confidential;

(5)   inter-agency or intra-agency memorandums or letters which would not be available by law to a party other than an agency in litigation with the agency;

(6)   personnel and medical files and similar files the disclosure of which would constitute a clearly unwarranted invasion of personal privacy;

(7)   *investigatory records compiled for law enforcement purposes, but only to the extent that the production of such records would (A) interfere with enforcement pro-ceedings, (B) deprive a person of a right to a fair trial or an impartial adjudication, (C) constitute an unwarranted invasion of personal privacy, (D) disclose the identity of a confidential source and, in the case of a record compiled by a criminal law enforce-ment authority in the course of a criminal investigation, or by an agency conducting a lawful national security intelligence investigation, confidential information furnished only by the confidential source, (E) disclose investigative techniques and procedures, or (F) endanger the life or physical safety of law enforcement personnel;*

(8)   contained in or related to examination, operating, or condition re-ports prepared by, on behalf of, or for the use of an agency responsible for the regulation or supervision of financial institutions; or

(9)   geological and geophysical information and data, including maps, concerning wells.

Any reasonably segregable portion of a record shall be provided to any person request-ing such record after deletion of the portions which are exempt under this subsection.

(c)   *This section does not authorize withholding of information or limit the availability or records to the public, except as specifically stated in this section. This section is not authority to withhold information from Congress.*

NOTE: The 1974 Amendments are in italics; the 1976 Amendment (b) (3) is not.

(d)   On or before March 1 of each calendar year, each agency shall sub-mit a report covering the preceding calendar year to the Speaker of the House of Representatives and President of the Senate for referral to the appropriate com-mittee of the Congress. The report shall include—

(1)   the number of determinations made by such agency not to comply with requests for records made to such agency under subsection (a) and the reasons for each such determination;

(2)   the number of appeals made by persons under subsection (a)(6), the result of such appeals, and the reason for the action upon each appeal that results in a denial of information;

(3)   the names and titles or positions of each person responsible for the denial or records requested under this section, and the number of in-stances of participation for each;

(4)   the results of each proceeding conducted pursuant to subsection (a)(4)(F), including a report of the disciplinary action taken against the officer or employee who was responsible for improperly withholding records or an explanation of why disciplinary action was not taken;

(5)   a copy of every rule made by such agency regarding this section;

(6)   a copy of the fee schedule and the total amount of fees collected by the agency for making records available under this section; and

(7)   such other information as indicates efforts to administer fully this section.

The Attorney General shall submit an annual report on or before March 1 of each calendar year which shall include for the prior calendar year a listing of the number of cases arising under this section, the exemption involved in each case, the disposition of such case, and the cost, fees, and penalties assessed under subsection (A)(4)(E), (F), and (G). Such report shall also include a description of the efforts undertaken by the De-partment of Justice to encourage agency compliance with this section.

(e)   For purposes of this section, the term 'agency' as defined in section 551(1) of this title includes any executive department, military department, Government corporation, Government controlled corporation, or other establish-ment in the executive branch of the Government (including the Executive Office of the President), or any independent regulatory agency.

APPENDIX C

PRIVACY ACT—TEXT

Public Law 93-579
93rd Congress, S. 3418
December 31, 1974

AN ACT

To amend title 5, United States Code, by adding a section 552a to safeguard individual privacy from the misuse of Federal records, to provide that individuals be granted access to records concerning them which are maintained by Federal agencies, to establish a Privacy Protection Study Commission, and for other purposes.

Be it enacted by the Senate and House of Representatives of the United States of America in Congress assembled, That this Act may be cited as the "Privacy Act of 1974".

SEC.2.(a)   The Congress finds that—

(1)   the privacy of an individual is directly affected by the collection, maintenance, use and dissemination of personal information by Federal agencies:

(2)   the increasing use of computers and sophisticated information technology, while essential to the efficient operations of the Government, has greatly magnified the harm to individual privacy that can occur from any collection, maintenance, use, or dissemination of personal information:

(3)   the opportunities for an individual to secure employment, insurance, and credit, and his right to due process, and other legal protections are endangered by the misuse of certain information systems:

(4)   the right to privacy is a personal and fundamental right protected by the Constitution of the United States: and

(5)   in order to protect the privacy of individuals identified in information systems maintained by Federal agencies, it is necessary and proper for the Congress to regulate the collection, maintenance, use, and dissemination of information by such agencies.

See also, *Legislative History of the Privacy Act of 1974, S. 3418 (Public Law 93-579), Source Book on Privacy,* Committee on Government Operations, United States Senate and the Committee on Government Operations, House of Representatives, Subcommittee on Government Information and Individual Rights. 94th Cong., 2d Sess., September 1976. For sale by the Superintendent of Documents, U.S. Government Printing Office, Washington, D.C. 20402.

(b)   The purpose of this Act is to provide certain safeguards for an individual against an invasion of personal privacy by requiring Federal agencies, except as otherwise provided by law, to—

(1)   permit an individual to determine what records pertaining to him are collected, maintained, used, or disseminated by such agencies:

(2)   permit an individual to prevent records pertaining to him obtained by such agencies for a particular purpose from being used or made available for another purpose without his consent:

(3)   permit an individual to gain access to information pertaining to him in Federal agency records to have a copy made of all or any portion thereof and to correct or amend such records:

(4)   collect, maintain, use or disseminate any record of identifiable personal information in a manner that assures that such action is for a necessary and lawful purpose, that the information is current and accurate for its intended use, and that adequate safeguards are provided to prevent misuse of such information:

(5)   permit exemptions from the requirements with respect to records provided in this Act only in those cases where there is an important public policy need for such exemption as has been determined by specific statutory authority: and

(6)   be subject to civil suit for any damages which occur as a result of willful or intentional action which violates any individual's rights under this Act.

Sec. 3.   Title 5.   United States Code, is amended by adding after section 552 the following new section:

"§ 552a.   Records maintained on individuals

"(a)   DEFINITIONS—For purposes of this section—

"(1)   the term 'agency' means agency as defined in section 552(c) of this title:

"(2)   the term 'individual' means a citizen of the United States or an alien lawfully admitted for permanent residence:

"(3)   the term 'maintain' includes maintain, collect, use, or disseminate:

"(4)   the term 'record' means any item, collection, or grouping of information about an individual that is maintained by an agency, including, but not limited to his education, financial transactions, medical history, and criminal or employment history and that contains his name, or the identifying number, symbol, or other identifying particular assigned to the individual, such as a finger or voice print or a photograph:

"(5)   the term 'system of records' means a group of any records under the control of any agency from which information is retrieved by the name of the individual or by some identifying number, symbol, or other identifying particular assigned to the individual:

"(6)   the term 'statistical record' means a record in a system of records maintained for statistical research or reporting purposes only and not used in whole or in part in making any determination about an identifiable individual except as provided by section 8 of title 13: and

"(7)   the term 'routine use' means with respect to the disclosure of a record, the use of such record for a purpose which is compatible with the purpose for which it was collected.

(b)   CONDITIONS OF DISCLOSURE—No agency shall disclose any record which is contained in a system of records by any means of communication to any person, or to another agency, except pursuant to a written request by, or with the prior written consent of, the individual to whom the record pertains, unless disclosure of the record would be—

"(1)   to those officers and employees of the agency which maintains the record who have a need for the record in the performance of their duties:

"(2)   required under section 552 of this title:

"(3)   for a routine use as defined in subsection (a)(7) of this section and described under subsection (c)(4)(J) of this section:

"(4)   to the Bureau of the Census for purposes of planning or carrying out a census or survey or related activity pursuant to the provisions of title 13:

"(5)   to a recipient who has provided the agency with advance adequate written assurance that the record will be used solely as a statistical research or reporting record, and the record is to be transferred in a form that is not individually identifiable:

"(6)   to the National Archives of the United States as a record which has sufficient historical or other value to warrant its continued preservation by the United States Government or for evaluation by the Administrator of General Services or his designee to determine whether the record has such value:

"(7)   to another agency or to an instrumentality of any governmental jurisdiction within or under the control of the United States for a civil or criminal law enforcement activity if the activity is authorized by law, and if the head of the agency or instrumentality has made a written request to the agency which maintains the records specifying the particular portion desired and the law enforcement activity for which the record is sought:

"(8)   to a person pursuant to a showing of compelling circumstances affecting the health or safety of an individual if upon such disclosure notification is transmitted to the last known address of such individual:

"(9)   to either House of Congress, or, to the extent of matter within its jurisdiction, any committee or subcommittee thereof, any joint committee of Congress or subcommittee of any such joint committee:

"(10)   to the Comptroller General, or any of his authorized representatives in the course of the performance of the duties of the General Accounting Office: or

"(11)   pursuant to the order of a court of competent jurisdiction.

"(c)   ACCOUNTING OF CERTAIN DISCLOSURES—Each agency, with respect to each system of records under its control, shall—

"(1)   except for disclosures made under subsections (b)(1) or (b)(2) of this section, keep an accurate accounting of—

"(A)   the date, nature, and purpose of each disclosure of a record to any person or to another agency made under subsection (b) of this section: and

"(B)   the name and address of the person or agency to whom the disclosure is made:

"(2)   retain the accounting made under paragraph (1) of this subsection for at least five years or the life of the record, whichever is longer, after the disclosure for which the accounting is made:

"(3)   except for disclosures made under (b)(7) of this section, make the accounting made under paragraph (1) of this subsection available to the individual named in the record at his request: and

"(4)   inform any person or other agency about any correction or notation of dispute made by the agency in accordance with subsection (d) of this section of any record that has been disclosed to the person or agency if an accounting of the disclosure was made.

"(d)   ACCESS TO RECORDS—Each agency that maintains a system of records shall—

"(1)   upon request by an individual to gain access to his record or to any information pertaining to him which is contained in the system, permit him and upon his request, a person of his own choosing to accompany him, to review the record and have a copy made of all or any portion thereof in a form comprehensible to him, except that the agency may require the individual to furnish a written statement authorizing discussion of that individual's record in the accompanying person's presence:

"(2)   permit the individual to request amendment of a record pertaining to him and—

"(A)   not later than 10 days (excluding Saturdays, Sundays, and legal public holidays) after the date of receipt of such request, acknowledge in writing such receipt; and "(B) promptly, either—

"(i)   make any correction of any portion thereof which the individual believes is not accurate, relevant, timely, or complete; or

"(ii)   inform the individual of its refusal to amend the record in accordance with his request the reason for the refusal, the procedures established by the agency for the individual to respect a review of that refusal by the head of the agency or an officer designated by the head of the agency and the name and business address of that official;

"(3)   permit the individual who disagrees with the refusal of the agency to amend his record to request a review of such refusal, and not later than 30 days

"(4)   subject to the provisions of paragraph (11) of this subsection, publish in the Federal Register at least annually a notice of the existence and character of the system of records, which notice shall include—

"(A)   the name and location of the system;

"(B)   the categories of individuals on whom records are maintained in the system;

"(C)   the categories of records maintained in the system;

"(D)   each routine use of the records contained in the system, including the categories of users and the purpose of such use:

"(E)   the policies and practices of the agency regarding storage, retrievability, access controls, retention, and disposal of the records;

"(F)   the title and business address of the agency official who is responsible for the system of records;

"(G)   the agency procedures whereby an individual can be notified at his request if the system of records contains a record pertaining to him;

"(H)   the agency procedures whereby an individual can be notified at his request how he can gain access to any record pertaining to him contained in the system of records, and how he can contest its content; and

"(I)   the categories of sources of records in the system;

"(5)   maintain all records which are used by the agency in making any determination about any individual with such accuracy, relevance, timeliness, and completeness as is reasonably necessary to assure fairness to the individual in the determination;

"(6)   prior to disseminating any record about an individual to any person other than an agency, unless the dissemination is made pursuant to subsection (b)(2) of this section, make reasonable efforts to assure that such records are accurate, complete, timely, and relevant for agency purposes;

"(7)   maintain no record describing how any individual exercises rights guaranteed by the First Amendment unless expressly authorized by statute or by the individual about whom the record is maintained or unless pertinent to and within the scope of an authorized law enforcement activity;

"(8)   make reasonable efforts to serve notice on an individual when any record on such individual is made available to any person under compulsory legal process when such process becomes a matter of public record;

"(9)   establish rules of conduct for persons involved in the design, development, operation, or maintenance of any system of records, or in maintaining any record, and instruct each such person with respect to such rules and the requirements of this section, including any other rules and procedures adopted pursuant to this section and the penalties for noncompliance;

"(10)   establish appropriate administrative, technical, and physical safeguards to insure the security and confidentiality of records and to protect against any anticipated threats or hazards to their security or integrity which could result in substantial harm, embarrassment, inconvenience, or unfairness to any individual on whom information is maintained; and

"(11)   at least 30 days prior to publication of information under paragraph (4) (I) of this subsection, publish in the Federal Register notice of any new use or intended use of the information in the system, and provide an opportunity for interested persons to submit written data, views, or arguments to the agency.

"(f)   AGENCY RULES—In order to carry out the provisions of this section, each agency that maintains a system of records shall promulgate rules, in accordance with the requirements (including general notice) of section 553 of this title, which shall—

"(1)   establish procedures whereby an individual can be notified in response to his request if any system of records named by the individual contains a record pertaining to him;

"(2)   define reasonable times, places, and requirements for identifying an individual who requests his record or information pertaining to him before the agency shall make the record or information available to the individual;

"(3)   establish procedures for the disclosure to an individual upon his request of his record or information pertaining to him, including special procedure, if deemed necessary, for the disclosure to an individual of medical records, including psychological records, pertaining to him;

"(4)   establish procedures for reviewing a request from an individual concerning the amendment of any record or information pertaining to the individual, for making a determination on the request, for an appeal within the agency of an initial adverse agency determination, and for whatever additional means may be necessary for each individual to be able to exercise fully his rights under this section; and

"(5)   establish fees to be charged, if any, to any individual for making copies of his record, excluding the cost of any search for and review of the record.

The Office of the Federal Register shall annually compile and publish the rules promulgated under this subsection and agency notices published under subsection (e)(4) of this section in a form available to the public at low cost.

"(g)(1)CIVIL REMEDIES.—Whenever any agency

"(A)   makes a determination under subsection (d)(3) of this section not to amend an individual's record in accordance with his request, or fails to make such review in conformity with that subsection; (excluding Saturdays, Sundays, and legal public holidays) from the date on which the individual requests such review, complete such review and make a final determination unless for good cause shown, the head of the agency extends such 30-day period; and if, after his review, the reviewing official also refuses to amend the record in accordance with the request, permit the individual to file with the agency a concise statement setting forth the reasons for his disagreement with the refusal of the agency, and notify the individual of the provisions for judicial review of the reviewing official's determination under subsection (g)(1)(A) of this section;

"(4)   in any disclosure, containing information about which the individual has filed a statement of disagreement, occurring after the filing of the statement under paragraph (3) of this subsection, clearly note any portion of the record which is disputed and provide copies of the statement and, if the agency deems it appropriate, copies of a concise statement of the reasons of the agency for not making the amendments requested, to persons or other agencies to whom the disputed record has been disclosed: and

"(5)   nothing in this section shall allow an individual access to any information compiled in reasonable anticipation of a civil action or proceeding:

"(e)   AGENCY REQUIREMENTS—Each agency that maintains a system of records shall—

"(1)   maintain in its records only such information about an individual as is relevant and necessary to accomplish a purpose of the agency required to be accomplished by statute or by executive order of the President;

"(2)   collect information to the greatest extent practicable directly from the subject individual when the information may result in adverse determinations about an individual's rights, benefits and privileges under Federal programs;

"(3)   inform each individual whom it asks to supply information, on the form which it uses to collect the information or on a separate form that can be retained by the individual-

"(A)   the authority (whether granted by statute, or by executive order of the President) which authorizes the solicitation of the information and whether disclosure of such information is mandatory or voluntary:

"(B)   the principal purpose or purposes for which the information is intended to be used;

"(C)   the routine uses which may be made of the information as published pursuant to paragraph (4)(I) of this subsection; and

"(D)   the effects on him, if any, of not providing all or any part of the requested information;

"(B)   refuses to comply with an individual request under subsection (d)(1) of this section;

"(C)   fails to maintain any record concerning any individual with such accuracy, relevance, timeliness, and completeness as is necessary to assure fairness in any determination relating to the qualifications, character, rights, or opportunities of, or benefits to the individual that may be made on the basis of such record, and consequently a determination is made which is adverse to the individual; or

"(D)   fails to comply with any other provision of this section, or any rule promulgated thereunder, in such a way as to have an adverse effect on an individual,

the individual may bring a civil action against the agency, and the district courts of the United States shall have jurisdiction in the matters under the provisions of this subsection.

"(2)   (A)   In any suit brought under the provisions of subsection (g)(1)(A) of this section, the court may order the agency to amend the individual's record in accordance with his request or in such other way as the court may direct. In such a case the court shall determine the matter de novo.

"(B)   The court may assess against the United States reasonable attorney fees and other litigation costs reasonably incurred in any case under this paragraph in which the complainant has substantially prevailed.

"(3)   (A)   In any suit brought under the provisions of subsection (g)(1)(B) of this section, the court may enjoin the agency from withholding the records and order the production to the complainant of any agency records improperly withheld from him. In such a case the court shall determine the matter de novo, and may examine the contents of any agency records in camera to determine whether the records of any portion thereof may be withheld under any of the exemptions set forth in subsection (k) of this section, and the burden is on the agency to sustain its action.

"(B) The court may assess against the United States reasonable attorney fees and other litigation costs reasonably incurred in any case under this paragraph in which the complainant has substantially prevailed.

"(4)   In any suit brought under the provisions of subsection (g)(1) (C) or (D) of this section in which the court determines that the agency acted in a manner which was intentional or willful, the United States shall be liable to the individual in an amount equal to the sum of—

"(A)   actual damages sustained by the individual as a result of the refusal or failure, but in no case shall a person entitled to recovery receive less than the sum of $1,000; and

"(B)   the costs of the action together with reasonable attorney fees as determined by the court.

"(5)   An action to enforce any liability created under this section may be brought in the district court of the United States in the district in which the complainant resides, or has his principal place of business, or in which the agency records are situated, or in the District of Columbia, without regard to the amount in controversy within two years from the date on which the cause of action arises, except that where an agency has materially and willfully misrepresented any information required under this section to be disclosed to an individual and the information so misrepresented is material to establishment of the liability of the agency to the individual under this section, the action may be brought at any time within two years after discovery by the individual of the misrepresentation. Nothing in this section shall be construed to authorize any civil action by reason of any injury sustained as the result of a disclosure of a record prior to the effective date of this section.

"(h)   RIGHTS OF LEGAL GUARDIANS.—For the purpose of this section, the parent of any minor, or the legal guardian of any individual who has been declared to be incompetent due to physical or mental incapacity or age by a court of competent jurisdiction, may act on behalf of the individual.

"(i) (1)   CRIMINAL PENALTIES.—Any officer or employee of an agency, who by virtue of his employment or official position, has possession of, or access to, agency records which contain individually identifiable information the disclosure of which is prohibited by this section or by rules or regulations established thereunder, and who knowing that disclosure of the specific material is so prohibited, willfully discloses the material in any manner to any person or agency not entitled to receive it, shall be guilty of a misdemeanor and fined not more than $5,000.

"(2)   Any officer or employee of any agency who willfully maintains a system of records without meeting the notice requirements of subsection (e)(4) of this section shall be guilty of a misdemeanor and fined not more than $5,000.

"(3)   Any person who knowingly and willfully requests or obtains any record concerning an individual from an agency under false pretenses shall be guilty of a misdemeanor and fined not more than $5,000.

"(j)   GENERAL EXEMPTIONS.—The head of any agency may promulgate rules, in accordance with the requirements (including general notice) of sections 553 (b)(1), (2), and (3), (c), and (e) of this title, to exempt any system of records within the agency from any part of this section except subsections (b), (c)(1) and (2), (e)(4)(A) through (F), (e)(6), (7), (9), (10), and (11), and (i) if the system of records is—

"(1)   maintained by the Central Intelligence Agency; or

"(2)   maintained by an agency or component thereof which performs as its principal function any activity pertaining to the enforcement of criminal laws, including police efforts to prevent, control, or reduce crime or to apprehend criminals, and the activities of prosecutors, courts, correctional, probation, pardon, or parole authorities, and which consists of (A) information compiled for the purpose of a criminal investigation, including reders and alleged offenders and consisting only of identifying data and notations of arrests, the nature and disposition of criminal charges, sentencing, confinement, release, and parole and probation status; (B) information compiled for the purposes of a criminal investigation, including reports of informants and investigators, and associated with an identifiable individual; or (C) reports identifiable to an individual compiled at any stage of the process of enforcement of the criminal laws from arrest or indictment through release from supervision.

At the time rules are adopted under this subsection, the agency shall include in the statement required under section 553(c) of this title, the reasons why the system of records is to be exempted from a provision of this section.

"(k)   SPECIFIC EXEMPTIONS.—The head of any agency may promulgate rules in accordance with the requirements (including general notice) of sections 553(b)(1), (2), and (3), (c), and (e) of this title, to exempt any system of records within the agency from subsections (c)(3), (d), (e) (1) (e) (4) (G), (H), and (I) and (f) of this section if the system of records is—

"(1)   subject to the provisions of section 552(b) (1) of this title;

"(2)   investigatory material compiled for law enforcement purposes, other than material within the scope of subsection (j)(2) of this section: *Provided, however,* that if any individual is denied any right, privilege, or benefit that he would otherwise be entitled by Federal law, or for which he would otherwise be eligible, as a result of the maintenance of such material, such material shall be provided to such individual, except to the extent that the disclosure of such material would reveal the identify of a source who furnished information to the Government under an express promise that the identity of the source would be held in confidence, or, prior to the effective date of this section, under an implied promise that the identify of the source would be held in confidence:

"(3)   maintained in connection with providing protective services to the President of the United States or other individuals pursuant to section 3056 of title 18:

"(4)   required by statute to be maintained and used solely as statistical records;

"(5)   investigatory material compiled solely for the purpose of determining suitability, eligibility, or qualifications for Federal civilian employment, military service, Federal contracts, or access to classified information, but only to the extent that the disclosure of such material would reveal the identity of the source who furnished information to the Government under an express promise that the identity of the source will be held in confidence, or, prior to the effective date of this section, under an implied promise that the identity of the source would be held in confidence;

"(6)　testing or examination material used solely to determine individual qualifications for appointment or promotion in the Federal service the disclosure of which would compromise the objectivity or fairness of the testing or examination process; or

"(7)　evaluation material used to determine potential for promotion in the armed services but only to the extent that the disclosure of such material would reveal the identity of a source who furnished information to the Government under an express promise that the identity of the source would be held in confidence, or, prior to the effective date of this section, under an implied promise that the identity of the source would be held in confidence. At the time rules are adopted under this subsection, the agency shall include in the statement required under section 553(c) of this title, the reasons why the system of records is to be exempted from a provision of this section.

"(1)　(1)　ARCHIVAL RECORDS.—Each agency record which is accepted by the Administrator of General Services for storage, processing, and servicing in accordance with section 3103 of title 44 shall, for the purposes of this section, be considered to be maintained by the agency which deposited the record and shall be subject to the provisions of this section. The Administrator of General Services shall not disclose the record except to the agency which maintains the record, or under rules established by that agency which are not inconsistent with the provisions of this section.

"(2)　Each agency record pertaining to an identifiable individual which was transferred to the National Archives of the United States as a record which has sufficient historical or other value to warrant its continued preservation by the United States Government, prior to the effective date of this section, shall, for the purposes of this section, be considered to be maintained by the National Archives and shall not be subject to the provisions of this section, except that a statement generally describing such records (modeled after the requirements relating to records subject to subsections (e)(4)(A) through (G) of this section) shall be published in the Federal Register.

"(3)　Each agency record pertaining to an identifiable individual which is transferred to the National Archives of the United States as a record which has sufficient historical or other value to warrant its continued preservation by the United States Government, on or after the effective date of this section, shall, for the purposes of this section, be considered to be maintained by the National Archives and shall be exempt from the requirements of this section except subsections (e) (4) (A) through (G) and (e) (9) of this section.

"(m)　GOVERNMENT CONTRACTORS.—When an agency provides by a contract for the operation by or on behalf of the agency of a system of records to accomplish an agency function, the agency shall, consistent with its authority, cause the requirements of this section to be applied to such system. For purposes of subsection (i) of this section any such contractor and any employee of such contractor, if such contract is agreed to on or after the effective date of this section, shall be considered to be an employee of an agency.

"(n)   MAILING LISTS.—An individual's name and address may not be sold or rented by an agency unless such action is specifically authorized by law. This provision shall not be construed to require the withholding of names and addresses otherwise permitted to be made public.

"(o)   REPORT ON NEW SYSTEMS.—Each agency shall provide adequate advance notice to Congress and the Office of Management and Budget of any proposal to establish or alter any system of records in order to permit an evaluation of the probable or potential effect of such proposal on the privacy and other personal or property rights of individuals or the disclosure of information relating to such individuals and its effect on the preservation of the constitutional principles of federalism and separation of powers.

"(p)   ANNUAL REPORT.—The President shall submit to the Speaker of the House and the President of the Senate, by June 30 of each calendar year, a consolidated report, separately listing for each Federal agency the number of records contained in any system of records which were exempted from the application of this section under the provisions of subjections (j) and (k) of this section during the preceding calendar year, and the reasons for the exemptions, and such other information as indicates efforts to administer fully this section.

"(q)   EFFECT OF OTHER LAWS.—No agency shall rely on any exemption contained in section 552 of this title to withhold from an individual any record which is otherwise accessible to such individual under the provisions of this section."

Sec. 4   The chapter analysis of chapter 5 of title 5, United States Code, is amended by inserting: "552a. Records about individuals." immediately below: "552. Public information; agency rules, opinions, orders, and proceedings."

Section 5.   (a)(1)   There is established a Privacy Protection Study Commission (hereinafter referred to as the "Commission") which shall be composed of seven members as follows:

(A)   three appointed by the president of the United States,

(B)   two appointed by the President of the Senate, and

(C)   two appointed by the Speaker of the House of Representatives.

Members of the Commission shall be chosen from among persons who, by reason of their knowledge and expertise in any of the following areas-civil rights and liberties, law, social sciences, computer technology, business, records management, and State and local government-are well qualified for service on the Commission.

(2)   The members of the Commission shall elect a Chairman from among themselves.

(3)   Any vacancy in the membership of the Commission, as long as there are four members in office, shall not impair the power of the Commission but shall be filled in the same manner in which the original appointment was made.

(4)   A quorum of the Commission shall consist of a majority of the members, except that the Commission may establish a lower number as a quorum for the purpose of taking testimony. The Commission is authorized to establish such committees and delegate such authority to them as may be necessary to carry out its functions. Each member of the Commission, including the Chairman, shall have equal responsibility and authority in all decisions and actions of the Commission, shall have full access to all information necessary to the performance of their functions, and shall have one vote. Action of the Commission shall be determined by a majority vote of the members present. The Chairman (or a member designated by the Chairman to be acting Chairman) shall be the official spokesman of the Commission in its relations with the Congress, Government agencies, other persons, and the public, and, on behalf of the Commission, shall see to the faithful execution of the administrative policies and decisions of the Commission, and shall report thereon to the Commission from time to time or as the Commission may direct.

(5)   (A)   Whenever the Commission submits any budget estimate or request to the President or the Office of Management and budget, it shall concurrently transmit a copy of that request to Congress.

(B)   Whenever the Commission submits any legislative recommendations, or testimony, or comments on legislation to the President or Office of Management and Budget, it shall concurrently transmit a copy thereof to the Congress. No officer or agency of the United States shall have any authority to require the Commission to submit its legislative recommendations, or testimony, or comments on legislation to any officer or agency of the United States for approval, comments, or review, prior to the submission of such recommendations, testimony, or comments to the Congress.

(b)   The commission shall:

(1)   make a study of the data banks, automated data processing programs, and information systems of governmental, regional, and private organizations in order to determine the standards and procedures in force for the protection of personal information; and

(2)   recommend to the President and the Congress the extent, if any, to which the requirements and principles of section 552a of title 5, United States Code, should be applied to the information practices of those organizations by legislation, administrative actions, or voluntary adoption of such requirements and principles, and report on such other legislative recommendations as it may determine to be necessary to protect the privacy of individuals while meeting the legitimate needs of government and society for information.

(c)   (1)   In the course of conducting the study required under subsection (b) (1) of this section, and in its reports thereon, the Commission may research, examine, and analyze—

(A)   interstate transfer of information about individuals that is undertaken through manual files or by computer or other electronic or telecommunications means;

(B)   data banks and information programs and systems the operation of which significantly or substantially affect the enjoyment of the privacy and other personal rights of individuals;

(C)   the use of social security numbers, license plate numbers, universal identifiers, and other symbols to identify individuals in data banks and to gain access to, integrate, or centralize information systems and files; and

(D) the matching and analysis of statistical data, such as Federal census data, with other sources of personal data, such as automobile registries and telephone directories, in order to reconstruct individual responses to statistical questionnaires for commercial or other purposes, in a way which results in a violation of the implied or explicitly recognized confidentiality of such information.

(2) (A) The Commission may include in its examination personal information activities in the following areas: medical; insurance; education; employment and personnel; credit, banking and financial institutions; credit bureaus; the commercial reporting industry; cable television and other telecommunications media; travel, hotel and entertainment reservations; and electronic check processing.

(B) The Commission shall include in its examination a study of—

(i) whether a person engaged in interstate commerce who maintains a mailing list should be required to remove an individual's name and address from such list upon request of that individual;

(ii) whether the Internal Revenue Service should be prohibited from transfering individually identifiable data to other agencies and to agencies of State government;

(iii) whether the Federal Government should be liable for general damages incurred by an individual as the result of a willful or intentional violation of the provisions of sections 552a (g) (1) (C) or (D) of title 5, United States Code; and

(iv) whether and how the standards for security and confidentiality of records required under section 552a (c) (10) of such title should be applied when a record is disclosed to a person other than an agency.

(C) The Commission may study such other personal information activities necessary to carry out the congressional policy embodied in this Act, except that the Commission shall not investigate information systems maintained by religious organizations.

(3) In conducting such study, the Commission shall

(A) determine what laws, Executive orders, regulations, directives, and judicial decisions govern the activities under study and the extent to which they are consistent with the rights of privacy, due process of law, and other guarantees in the Constitution:

(B) determine to what extent governmental and private information systems affect Federal-State relations or the principle of separation of powers:

(C) examine the standards and criteria governing programs, policies, and practices relating to the collection, soliciting, processing, use, access, integration, dissemination, and transmission of personal information; and

(D) to the maximum extent practicable, collect and utilize findings, reports, studies, hearing transcripts, and recommendations of governmental, legislative and private bodies, institutions, organizations, and individuals which pertain to the problems under study by the Commission. (d) In addition to its other functions the Commission may—

(1)   request assistance of the heads of appropriate departments, agencies, and instrumentalities of the Federal Government, of State and local governments and other persons in carrying out its functions under this Act:

(2)   upon request, assist Federal agencies in complying with the requirements of section 552a of title 5, United States Code;

(3)   determine what specific categories of information, the collection of which would violate an individual's right of privacy should be prohibited by statute from collection by Federal agencies; and

(4)   upon request, prepare model legislation for use by State and local governments in establishing procedures for handling, maintaining, and disseminating personal information at the State and local level and provide such technical assistance to State and local governments as they may require in the preparation and implementation of such legislation.

(e)   (1)   The Commission may, in carrying out its functions under this section, conduct such inspections, sit and act at such times and places, hold such hearings, take such testimony, require by subpoena the attendance of such witnesses and the production of such books, records, papers, correspondence, and documents, administer such oaths, have such printing and binding done, and make such expenditures as the Commission deems advisable. A subpoena shall be issued only upon an affirmative vote of a majority of all members of the Commission. Subpoenas shall be issued under the signature of the Chairman of any member of the Commission designated by the Chairman or any such member. Any member of the Commission may administer oaths or affirmations to witnesses appearing before the Commission.

(2)   (A)   Each department, agency, and instrumentality of the executive branch of the Government is authorized to furnish to the Commission, upon request made by the Chairman, such information, data, reports and such other assistance as the Commission deems necessary to carry out its functions under this section. Whenever the head of any such department, agency, or instrumentality submits a report pursuant to section 552a (o) of title 5, United States Code, a copy of such report shall be transmitted to the Commission.

(B)   In carrying out its functions and exercising its powers under this section, the Commission may accept from any such department, agency, independent instrumentality, or other person any individually identifiable data if such data is necessary to carry out such powers and functions. In any case in which the Commission accepts any such information, it shall assure that the information is used only for the purpose for which it is provided, and upon completion of that purpose such information shall be destroyed or returned to such department, agency, independent instrumentality, or person from which it is obtained, as appropriate.

(3)   The Commission shall have the power to—

(A)   appoint and fix the compensation of an executive director, and such additional staff personnel as may be necessary, without regard to the provisions of title 5, United States Code, governing appointments in the competitive service, and without regard to chapter 51 and subchapter III of Chapter 53 of such title relating to classification and General Schedule pay rates, but at rates not in excess of the maximum rate for GS-18 of the General Schedule under section 5332 of such title; and

(B) procure temporary and intermittent services to the same extent as is authorized by section 3109 of title 5, United States Code.

The Commission may delegate any of its functions to such personnel of the Commission as the Commission may designate and may authorize such successive redelegations of such functions as it may deem desirable.

(4) The Commission is authorized—

(A) to adopt, amend, and repeal rules and regulations governing the manner of its operations, organization, and personnel;

(B) to enter into contracts or other arrangements or modifications thereof, with any government, any department, agency, or independent instrumentality of the United States, or with any person, firm, association, or corporation, and such contracts or other arrangements, or modifications thereof, may be entered into without legal consideration, without performance or other bonds, and without regard to section 3709 of the Revised Statutes, as amended (41 U.S.C. 5);

(C) to make advance progress and other payments which the Commission deems necessary under this Act without regard to the provisions of section 3648 of the Revised Statutes, as amended (31 U.S.C. 529); and

(D) to take such other action as may be necessary to carry out its functions under this section.

(f) (1) Each [the] member of the Commission who is an officer or employee of the United States shall serve without additional compensation, but shall continue to receive the salary of his regular position when engaged in the performance of the duties vested in the Commission.

(2) A member of the Commission other than one to whom paragraph (1) applies shall receive per diem at the maximum daily rate for GS-18 of the General Schedule when engaged in the actual performance of the duties vested in the Commission.

(3) All members of the Commission shall be reimbursed for travel, subsistence, and other necessary expenses incurred by them in the performance of the duties vested in the Commission.

(g) The Commission shall, from time to time, and in an annual report, report to the President and the Congress on its activities in carrying out the provisions of this section. The Commission shall make a final report to the President and the Congress on its findings pursuant to the study required to be made under subsection (b) (1) of this section not later than two years from the date on which all of the members of the Commission are appointed. The Commission shall cease to exist thirty days after the date on which its final report is submitted to the President and the Congress.

(h) (1) Any member, officer, or employee of the Commission, who by virtue of his employment or official position, has possession of, or access to, agency records which contain individually identifiable information the disclosure of which is prohibited by this section, and who knowing that disclosure of the specific material is so prohibited, willfully discloses the material in any manner to any person or agency not entitled to receive it, shall be guilty of a misdemeanor and fined not more than $5,000.

(2)   Any person who knowingly and willfully requests or obtains any record concerning an individual from the commission under false pretenses shall be guilty of a misdemeanor and fined not more than $5,000.

Sec. 6.   The Office of Management and Budget shall—

(1)   develop guidelines and regulations for the use of agencies in implementing the provisions of section 552a of title 5, United States Code, as added by section 3 of this Act; and

(2)   provide continuing assistance to and oversight of the implementation of the provisions of such section by agencies.

Sec. 7.   (a)   (1)   It shall be unlawful for any Federal, State or local government agency to deny to any individual any right, benefit, or privilege provided by law because of such individual's refusal to disclose his social security account number.

(2)   the provisions of paragraph (1) of this subsection shall not apply with respect to—

(A)   any disclosure which is required by Federal statute, or

(B)   the disclosure of a social security number to any Federal, State, or local agency maintaining a system of records in existence and operating before January 1, 1975, if such disclosure was required under statute or regulation adopted prior to such date to verify the identify of an individual.

(b)   Any Federal, State, or local government agency which requests an individual to disclose his social security account number shall inform that individual whether that disclosure is mandatory or voluntary, by what statutory or other authority such number is solicited, and what uses will be made of it.

Sec. 8.   The provisions of this Act shall be effective on and after the date of enactment, except that the amendments made by sections 3 and 4 shall become effective 270 days following the day on which this Act is enacted.

Sec. 9.   There is authorized to be appropriated to carry out the provisions of section 5 of this Act for fiscal years 1975, 1976, and 1977 the sum of $1,500,000, except that not more than $750,000 may be expended during any such fiscal year.

Approved December 31, 1974.

APPENDIX D

Freedom of Information Act

Action, 45 CFR 1215
Actuaries, Joint Board for the
    Enrollment of, 20 CFR 902
Administrative Conference of the
    United States, 1 CFR 304
Agency for International
    Development, 22 CFR 212
Agricultural Marketing Service, 7
    CFR 900
Agricultural Research Service, 7
    CFR 510
Agricultural Stabilization and
    Conservation Service, 7 CFR
    798
Agriculture Department, 7 CFR 1
    Foreign Economic Development
        Service, 7 CFR 2101
    Office of General Sales Manager,
        7 CFR 2507
    Office of Inspector General, 7
        CFR 2620
    Office of Operations and
        Finance, 7 CFR 3010
Air Force Department, 32 CFR 806
Air Force Department, schedule of
    fees for copying, certifying and
    searching records and other
    documentary material, 32 CFR
    813
Alaska Natural Gas Transportation
    System, Office of Federal
    Inspector, 10 CFR 1504
Alcohol, Tobacco and Firearms
    Bureau, 27 CFR 71
American Battle Monuments
    Commission, 36 CFR 404

American Battle Monuments
    Commission, 36 CFR 405
Animal and Plant Health
    Inspection Service, 7 CFR 370
Animal and Plant Health
    Inspection Service, 9 CFR 165
Architectural and Transportation
    Barriers Compliance Board, 36
    CFR 1120
Arms Control and Disarmament
    Agency, 22 CFR 602
Army Department, 32 CFR 518
Arts and Humanities, National
    Foundation, 45 CFR 1100
Blind and Other Severely
    Handicapped, Committee for
    Purchase From, 41 CFR 51-7
Census Bureau, 15 CFR 60
Central Intelligence Agency, 32
    CFR 1900
Chrysler Corporation Loan
    Guarantee Board, 13 CFR 400
Civil Aeronautics Board, 14 CFR
    310
Civil Aeronautics Board, 14 CFR
    384
Civil Rights Commission, 45 CFR
    704
Coast Guard, 33 CFR 1
Commerce Department, 15 CFR 4
Commodity Credit Corporation, 7
    CFR 798
Commodity Futures Trading
    Commission, 17 CFR 145
Comptroller of the Currency, 12
    CFR 4
Consumer Product Safety
    Commission, 16 CFR 1015
Consumer Product Safety

Privacy Act

INDEX